The Timber-Frame Home

Design · Construction · Finishing

Tedd Benson

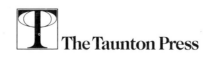
The Taunton Press

Cover photo: Brian E. Gulick

All photos by the author unless otherwise noted.
Illustrations by Joel McCarty, using a computer-aided system from AutoDesk, Inc.,
Sausalito, California. Gratitude is due them, in general, and to Patricia Harris, in
particular, for technical support and encouragement.

First printing: March 1988
Second printing: February 1989
Third printing: March 1990

International Standard Book Number: 0-918804-81-7
International Standard Book Number: 0-942391-60-8 pbk.

Library of Congress Catalog Card Number: 87-72009

Printed in the United States of America

A FINE HOMEBUILDING Book

FINE HOMEBUILDING® is a trademark of The Taunton Press, Inc.,
registered in the U.S. Patent and Trademark Office.

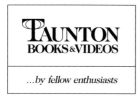

The Taunton Press, Inc.
63 South Main Street
Box 5506
Newtown, Connecticut 06470-5506

To the ladies who make me rich in love:
Christine, my wife, and Corona and Emily, my daughters.

Acknowledgments

Many, many people—family, friends, colleagues, clients and strangers—have contributed to this project, most willingly, some unwillingly, some unwittingly, but all, I trust, to good effect. So, I have many thanks to give.

. . . to my mom and dad, Mr. T.M. and Mrs. Mary Lou Benson, who taught me all I know about high standards. Through their lives they showed me that there is no other kind of quality until there is quality in life. They set a standard of living that remains for me a clear, but elusive, goal.

. . . to the nameless ancient masters of timber-frame craft and architecture, for making the task of attempting to describe techniques and standards for modern timber-frame buildings daunting, but worthwhile.

. . . to the members of the Timber Framer's Guild of North America for their vitality, skill and commitment, and for making the timber-frame revival a reality.

. . . to the men and women of Benson Woodworking Company for doing without me at my best and for putting up with me at my worst. It is to their credit, and theirs alone, that our company has thrived during the creation of this book. They are remarkable human beings, generous and forgiving, every one.

. . . to clients past and present who have welcomed me into their homes for discussion and photography. In my quest for clear illustrations for this book, I have rearranged their furniture, interrupted their lives and irritated their pets. Only they will know whether it has been worth it.

. . . to Brian Smeltz for his help with photo editing.

. . . to the good Doctor Robert L. (Ben) Brungraber, for boundless energy, enthusiasm and insight. His review of and advice on the engineering and joinery sections were invaluable.

. . . to Kathy Nerrie for minding the company in my absence and in my presence.

. . . to Joel McCarty, who did much more than make the drawings for this book. He was always there. He gave me encouragement, counsel and even words in my times of need.

. . . to Laura Tringali, my genial but demanding editor, who was with this book from the whisper of an idea to its conclusion five years later. She scrutinized every line on every page, asking hard questions, reformulating ideas and discovering order and light where I saw only chaos and mist. Throughout, she was steady and consistent when I was foundering and mercurial. Laura is much more than an editor; she is a friend.

I am deeply indebted to all of the above and many more.

Contents

Introduction

This book is about a modern timber-frame homebuilding system. It developed because our company decided it wanted to build homes, not just frames. As one of our staff designers wrote in a letter to a client, "No amount of breathtaking timber framing will compensate for a building that is difficult to move around in, hard to heat or cool, expensive to maintain or displeasing to the eye."

Knowledge of this building system did not come easily. I began timber framing in 1974, seeing it as an opportunity to bring more craftsmanship into homebuilding. Through the first years I was fully absorbed in attempting to master sharp framing chisels and tight joints, trying to tame timbers. But eventually, when I looked up from my blissful work, I began to notice that a fine timber frame alone did not a happy client make. Although our clients certainly appreciated our work, they also had other concerns. Would there be enough bedrooms and storage? Would the frame make sense with the floor plan? What about insulation? Would the electrician know how to run the wires? Should there be a solarium? What about plumbing? What would all this cost? It was disturbing to my clients and myself to find that we could consistently offer neither specific answers to these important questions nor proven construction strategies. We were winging it far too often. I soon realized that it was time to shift my emphasis from the timber frame to the timber-frame house.

So I began to spend less time working wood and more time at the drawing board—through the years, I've been fortunate to have had a group of dedicated associates whose fine timber-framing skills have made it easier for me to put my tools aside. I embarked on marathon strategy sessions with clients, contractors and manufacturers of products we wanted to use. It soon became clear that every design and construction precept needed to be reconsidered, for most conventional construction methods and details are inappropriate or inadequate for timber-frame buildings. In time I came to understand we would have to invent many new solutions for our houses rather than adapt existing ones. I came to understand that modern timber-frame house design needed a revival to parallel the revival of timber joinery.

I undertook my first book about timber framing, *Building the Timber Frame House,* because I feared the craft I had grown to love might fail to find a secure place in modern homebuilding. I was afraid timber framing would not capture the imagination of others as it had mine, that my framing chisels and slicks would lie unused in a drawer, that I would become a dancer without a beat. I feared these things might happen if the traditional values, standards and techniques used to create some of the finest buildings of the world fell prey to modern impatience and misguided technology. That first book was my rallying cry, but I didn't know if anyone was listening.

I could have spared myself the anxiety. Not only were people listening, but I was not, as I had thought, a voice crying in the wilderness. The unique merits of timber-frame structures needed no herald. In our company's first few years, I knew of only one other enterprise that shared our goals and enthusiasm. That company was run by my good friend and colleague Ed Levin, who is still a partner in the company, now called Paradigm. Now there are well over 200 companies specializing in timber framing in all parts of the country, and the number of timber-frame homes built each year is in the thousands.

My fear now is that in the joy of reviving the craft of timber framing in its purest form, it would be all too easy to lose sight of the perspective that the frame is, after all, just one component of a building. I am concerned that potential timber-frame homeowners, drawn to the inherent beauty and durability of the frame, will be so intimidated by the prospect of finishing it off that they settle for a lesser type of housing. And that clients who do persevere will wind up with a white elephant that fails to fulfill its true design potential. I worry that the standards of workmanship of the frame will not be carried throughout the rest of the house, due to the inexperience of tradespeople with this type of building system. If these things happen with enough frequency, there is a good chance that timber framing will inadvertently be lumped together with dome-making as just another interesting but out-of-the-mainstream building form.

A properly designed and built timber-frame home is an intriguing, exciting mix of ancient building method and modern technology. It's a model of energy efficiency and comfort that is sensible as well as beautiful. To help ease the transition between the requirements of housing today and the craft as it was in the days when it reigned as the predominant building method, I have written this book. It is my attempt to integrate timber framing with the best attitudes, ideas and technology of modern times, to make timber-frame housing a viable and accessible alternative in the 20th century. The book describes the procedures created by my staff and me (with much help from many colleagues and professionals in other fields) to design, enclose and make livable the frames we build. But in addition to presenting a compilation of typical design and construction solutions for timber-frame homes, I have also given the principles inherent in each solution. There are hundreds of factors to be considered in building a house, and no two houses are ever exactly alike. Local climate and geology influence foundation design. The budget might demand a choice between a dream kitchen and a dream roof. As homebuilders and homeowners, our only hope is in a solid knowledge of existing choices and in the ability to plan for hard and careful compromises. So, as well as being about how to do, this book is about how to think, how to plan and how to balance the scales.

Inevitably, you will find chunks of personal prejudice and opinion between these pages, for to sail through the many decisions required for good homebuilding, it's necessary to be propelled by the strong winds of committed values and firm beliefs. Why such philosophical talk about something as worldly as homebuilding? Because what is worldly about homebuilding is that it happens on this earth, it uses natural and man-made materials and it requires money. The rest of homebuilding has to do with beliefs, feelings, spirit and passion. Certainly shelters can be made without these, but they probably will not be the kind of structures that speak positively and warmly to future generations of occupants. For most people, homebuilding is full of the most sensitive emotions. It separates them from their life's earnings, either to a good or ill end. It can bring families together or tear them apart, for homebuilding can be a dark and dangerous sea full of shoals and turbulent currents. I believe a well-designed and well-constructed timber-frame house is worth the voyage, and I offer this book to help chart the course.

Tedd Benson

Tedd Benson
Alstead Center, N.H.
January, 1988

I. Timber-Frame Home Development

A properly designed and built timber-frame house is an intriguing mix of an ancient building system with modern technology. Simple, classic architecture yields exciting living spaces.

There are two important challenges for those who build timber-frame homes today. Both concern all those associated with the project, for the timber-frame housebuilding process is more like a chorus line than a solo dance, requiring all parties to play an active role. The first challenge is to cherish and nurture the values and standards set centuries ago, to understand in both spirit and substance the legacy of durable, classic timber-frame building that we have inherited from our forefathers. What is it that makes a structure so fine that it survives numerous centuries? Is it the construction, the architecture or both? What makes people love a building enough to repair and restore it? To give direction to our modern efforts, it's necessary to first thoroughly investigate the historical precedents. To know where we should go, we need to know where the craft has been.

The second challenge is to bring the timber-frame house into the 20th century. This requires a careful analysis of the limitations and opportunities inherent in the building system. Then we need to take a fresh look at modern homebuilding requirements, picking carefully from current standards and materials, and casting off conventions when necessary to create the highest quality work.

In this chapter, we'll look at both challenges, beginning with an exploration of the development of the timber-frame house through history and the attributes that give it timelessness. You won't find a chronicle of each event in the evolutionary path here, just some of the high points. I wish only to capture a sense of the fine thread that united timber buildings through so many centuries and in so many parts of the world, for it is just this thread we should weave into the fabric of our contemporary houses. Then we'll conclude the chapter with a discussion of the goals, problems and opportunities in timber framing today.

The legacy

What is apparent through even a cursory look at the history of building is that dwellings always clearly reflect the relationship of people to their world. Instead of following a single course, timber-frame buildings therefore evolved simultaneously along with rising and falling civilizations on several continents. They responded to technological advances, the availability of resources and to social prejudices (always a mirror of the people who built them). Despite this, out of the history of timber framing emerges a continuity of architectural patterns and styles, and a consistency in human values. There are, for instance, many more similarities than differences between an oriental structure like the Kondo Temple in Japan and a European structure like Westminster Hall in England. Both buildings were constructed as a monument to a religious ideal, and the timbers in each were both structure and decoration. Each building demonstrates mastery of a complex craft in a simple rectilinear form with a steeply pitched roof. The focal point in each building is the cantilevering of forces from the roof to the walls; the finely crafted roof timbers not only draw the eye upward to the heavens, they create a sense of balance and mystery, reflecting the forces of God and the universe. One more thing they both have in common: Though many centuries old, they both still stand.

The first timber-frame buildings appeared at about the time of the birth of Christ. They probably evolved from skeletons of tied-together poles around which skins or mattings were wrapped. Such dwellings were usually the homes of nomadic peoples. When permanent settlements became desirable, pole skeletons slowly gave way to more stable and durable timber structures. If we define a timber frame as a self-supporting network fastened with wooden joinery, then there are two significant events in its evolution. The first was the creation of the mortise-and-tenon joint between 500 B.C. and 200 B.C., which meant the tools and technological sophistication existed to work the wood. The second occurred sometime in the 10th century, when a framework was developed that was rigid enough to support itself on top of the ground. Prior to this, the posts of a house were stuck directly in holes and stabilized by compacted earth, a technique that allowed a minimum of interconnection between timbers, but also caused the posts to rot. Seemingly a small achievement, building a self-supporting structure was actually quite revolutionary, as it required that timbers be organized so posts would remain rigid while supporting the beams. Joinery had to become more sophisticated to serve both binding and supporting functions. Constructed in this way, buildings became more durable and expressive, and demanded greater skill to create.

Westminster Hall, built in England around 1395, is a simple but finely crafted form. The focal point is the cantilevering of roof forces. (Illustration by Marianne Markey.)

The network of posts and beams in a timber-frame house forms a structure that is rigid and self-supporting. (Design Associates, Inc., Architects.)

The development of timber-frame buildings differed from region to region, depending on many factors, such as the availability of material. In Egypt, Persia and Greece, where timber was limited, early temples were built with wooden columns and lintels; their forms were the basis for later stone temples. The scholar Vitruvius, writing at the end of the first century B.C., apparently saw the last of the wooden temples. He described the Temple of Ceres as a timber building with brick and terra-cotta infilling and decoration. Because of the scarcity of material and fear of fire, later temples and public buildings were built of masonry when possible, but timber framing had evolved into an accepted building method and was used for dwellings and less significant public buildings. According to Hansen, editor of *Architecture in Wood*, Vitruvius described the construction, calling it *opus craticiom,* or "timber framing."

Vitruvius also wrote that the best building timbers in his day were oak, elm, poplar, cypress and fir—surprisingly similar to our contemporary opinion. Some of these were occasionally imported from Africa, Syria and Crete, but importation of lumber was expensive and reserved for only the most important buildings. In addition, knowledge of new woods tended to make local builders less satisfied with what they had at hand. Palm trunks did not make good timbers after all, and other readily available woods were worse, as Martin Briggs describes in his book, *A Short*

History of the Building Crafts (see bibliography, p. 229): "Sycamore is neither very strong nor supple; and of acacia and tamarisk it can only be said that they are the least unsuitable of native trees for building purposes" (p. 116). Not surprisingly, since a growing understanding was combined with a growing scarcity of wood, timbers began to be replaced by masonry in the Middle East.

By contrast, in parts of northern Europe that were heavily wooded, a building style emerged around the ninth century in which the timber framework was vertically infilled with thick wooden planks or more timbers, making a veritable fortress of wood. Also in heavily wooded areas, timber framing was occasionally used along with log building—for example, some Swiss chalets have horizontal logs laid between the joined timbers. Where log construction was dominant, timber framing was still used for the roof system.

The skills and tools required for log building were certainly similar to those for timber framing, but in other ways the differences were vast. Early log building was rudimentary, using simple corner joints and the natural length of the logs to determine building dimensions. Stacking logs is a much more basic means of creating a structure than joining vertical and horizontal timbers into a rigid skeleton, and the aesthetics and feel are significantly different. Log walls look massive and earthbound; as the weight of the wood and gravity keep the structure together, so the

As in ancient times, modern buildings sometimes combine timbers and logs, as does this Japanese-style house designed and built by Len Brackett.

heavy horizontal lines seem to hold it snugly to the ground. The feeling of early log buildings, usually built over pits and with few penetrations in the walls, was probably somewhat like a cave of wood, a decided disadvantage in the minds of people who were working their way out of the pits and caves and into the light. By contrast, timber framing allowed early builders to use fewer pieces of wood, and required the use of structural engineering to keep buildings erect. Timber frames also have a much lighter appearance than log buildings, and rise out of the ground with a more vertical statement. Demanding the use of some complex joinery and geometry, timber framing forced the mind of man to expand.

In the less forested areas of Europe and for buildings of grand purpose, timber framing dominated log building by the Middle Ages. The ancient use of skins to cover the frame gave way to infilling with wattle-and-daub (a mud and plaster system) or later, with brick. In both cases, the structure was visible to both the interior and exterior, instead of just to the inside. The architects and inhabitants of these buildings obviously found the structure fascinating and, in an effort to keep up with the Joneses, made the frames ever fancier and denser with timbers. Through the centuries wood became scarcer (especially in the British Isles), but still frames displayed more and more timbers, not as a requirement of the structure, but to trumpet the wealth of the occupant. Over the years frames have become more conservative in their use of timbers, but only because vanity has found other forms of indulgence.

It is easy to understand why, at any time previous to modern time, local resources had significant impact on construction techniques. People simply did not settle where there weren't sufficient building materials, and when they built they presumably used the handiest material. Structures thus naturally reflected the landscape—bricks were used to a greater degree when there was clay in the soil, stone when the shape and quantity of rocks allowed, and timbers when there were sufficient trees. In the limestone areas of Great Britain, timber framing was never fully practiced because there just wasn't enough wood to make it practical. Here, as in many other parts of the world, masonry and timbers were used together, the massive stone walls supporting soaring timber-frame roofs. Stone protected the timbers from the deteriorating effects of the ground, and timbers made the great spans. Most of the great halls and cathedrals were a mix of the two materials.

An open roof system

PARALLEL RAFTERS

KING POST

COLLAR TIE

PLASTERED MASONRY VAULT

STONE OR BRICK WALLS

By the Middle Ages, the craft of timber framing was fully developed and, by the standards of the time, timber-frame homes required the least amount of labor. Timber was therefore preferred even when it was relatively scarce, and the condition and variety of available trees often determined the shape and style of the frame. According to Martin Briggs, "The feature of Lycian carpentry was the short lengths of timber employed, for the trees that grow on the steep Lycian slopes have gnarled boles and twisted trunks." William the Conquerer's Domesday Book of 1086, an inventory prepared for taxes, indicates that England, although once almost completely forested, was by then only 15% forested. (Three centuries later, the figure was closer to 10%.) Medieval buildings often displayed crooked, twist-ed timbers, which are now practically a definition of that period's architectural style. But it wasn't a fad propagated by some early rendition of *House Beautiful*—it was all they had.

During this period, English carpenters developed ingenious systems for spanning great widths without long timbers, and created an almost astonishing array of scarf joints (p. 47) to splice timbers longitudinally. Scarce resources sparked creativity and, partly because of this, some of the greatest carpentry of all time is evident in the timber-frame roofs of the Middle Ages. Still it should be noted that the open-trussed roofs would be stronger with a timber locking the walls together; a scarf joint is not as strong as a timber that doesn't need one.

The gnarled and twisted timbers common in medieval buildings indicate the quality of resources, not the architectural fashion. (Photo by Rob Tarule.)

In France, long timbers were unavailable by the second half of the 14th century, and so multi-storied, jettied building became common. Here successive stories were stacked upon short posts rather than being joined to posts that passed through all the floor levels. (While horizontal beams can be scarfed, this is a problem in vertical posts because of the extreme compression loads they bear.) To keep the structure rigid, these buildings required bracketing as well as bracing to secure posts to beams. For joinery considerations, horizontal beams would project beyond vertical posts at the outer walls; a timber bracket (much like a shelf bracket) was used in the corner between the post and the projecting beam to reinforce the connection. In a later outgrowth of this type of construction, the jetties were cantilevered. Especially popular in the cities, this architectural style accentuated the building's lines and created more space in the floors above the narrow street. But because it resulted in unsanitary conditions in the darkened streets below, jettied construction was ultimately outlawed.

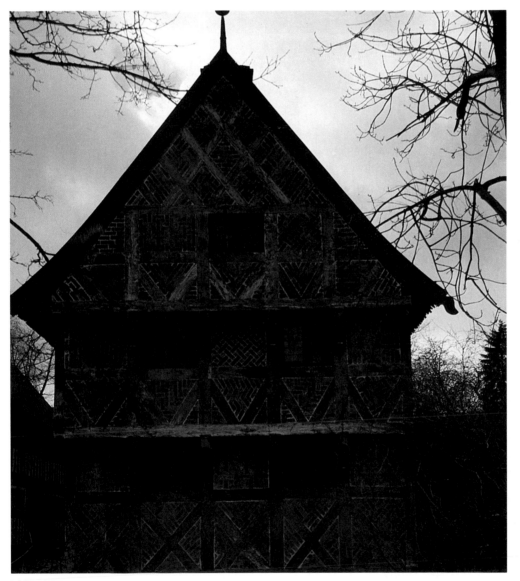

When timbers became scarce in Europe, tall buildings were constructed by stacking successive stories using short posts and overhanging beams. The timber brackets in this 15th-century German building, which resemble shelf brackets, reinforce the structure. (Photo by Chris Madigan.)

As surely as timber limitations influenced building design, so did timber abundances. When the colonists came to this country, Europe had been denuded of timber resources. The settlers suddenly found themselves in the midst of virgin forests with trees long enough to run the length of almost any building. Although they did not immediately devise new techniques to take advantage of this wealth, colonial Americans eventually developed a unique building style that featured long timbers for posts, plates, rafters and tie beams. These buildings were strong, simpler to construct than their old-world counterparts and, ironically, used fewer timbers.

The kind of building that evolved on the free soil of this country represents one of the most important developments in timber-frame housing. Even though framing techniques were refined over several thousand years and in all

Old English-style frame

LARGE, NATURALLY
CURVED BRACES

CLOSE STUDDING

Early American-style frame

LONG, CONTINUOUS PLATE

SIMPLE BRACING

(FLOOR SYSTEMS REMOVED FOR CLARITY.)

parts of the world, it appears to be here, in America, that a high-quality timber-frame house style developed specifically to accommodate the common man. In societies with a clearly defined class hierarchy, the finest efforts were invested in the religious institutions and copied at the next level down; similarities between cathedrals and castles are not coincidental, nor between castles and manor houses. How many and how fast building improvements filtered down depended on the distribution of wealth and the organization of the society, but timber-frame house construction of any consequence did not generally make it to the common levels. This is not to say that some form of timber framing was not practiced at these levels, only that since so few structures survived, clearly they were greatly inferior. The Swiss chalets (some of which are completely timber-framed) and the 15th-century timber-frame townhouses common to Belgium, Germany and the Netherlands, probably come closest to being true residential styles.

The sad fact is that many of the wonderfully picturesque manor houses in Europe were surrounded by the hovels of the peasantry. Decent housing was to be enjoyed only by the wealthy, and only because others suffered for it. The feudal society in Japan was even more divisive. Commoners might have wanted to build houses like those built for nobility or the warrior class, but were forbidden to. The restriction was class, not money, although if a commoner had enough money it was sometimes possible through bribery to obtain a desired architectural element, such as a decorative gate or sliding panels. Feudal building restrictions were not removed until 1867, and a consistent residential Japanese building style has been developed only in the last 120 years. Although Japanese timber-frame houses are quite different from Western styles, they evolved along a similar path, including the eventual casting off of the oppressive notions that brought the craft of timber framing (but not timber-frame housing) to its highest moments. It is coincidental that the barriers over which the common people of two completely different societies peered in envy and misery were overcome within a short time of each other. When the colonists stepped onto the shores of America,

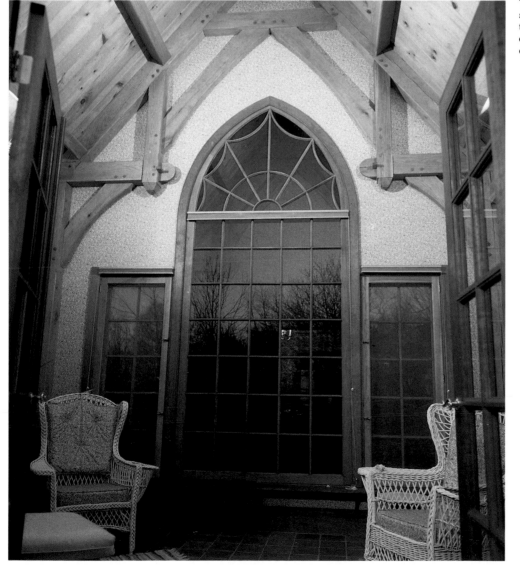

The contemporary-American style of timber-frame housing tends toward open spaces and, even in small rooms, a feeling of spaciousness.

and when the Tokugawa shogunate collapsed in Japan in 1867, it became possible for the common people of these countries to attempt to live in dignity and comfort.

This newfound freedom did not immediately lead to a revolution in architecture or frame construction, for there was no real dissatisfaction with the buildings, just with their occupants. So the first timber-frame buildings in America looked an awful lot like the ones left behind in England, and the homes the free Japanese built greatly resembled the Minka buildings they had been forbidden to own. Indulging in forbidden fruit was probably one reason for this, but it's also natural to embrace familiar archetypes. It took a long time for more independent styles to develop.

In America, the colonists learned the hard way about the effects of the climate on foundation and enclosure systems. Extreme changes in temperature heaved the soil, and it was soon obvious that an exterior cladding was necessary to protect the building from the weather. The first timber frames were oak, which was the wood used in England, but later frames used a great variety of species. Eventually, not only were frames redesigned to take advantage of the abundance of virgin trees, they were also redesigned to accommodate new raising techniques. In England, small groups of professionals made the frames for most houses, using joinery and assembly methods that would allow individual pieces to be placed into a frame. But in America, a great spirit of cooperation and neighborliness brought whole communities together for raisings, and timber frames were designed in large units that could be preassembled, then raised in a single day.

Frames also became more utilitarian. Being on free soil meant that class distinctions were dissolving; even the leaders and the wealthy would have been reluctant to act like the oppressive nobility of the old country. So in spite of the rich supply of timber, builders used their knowledge to make strong frames without wasting material or labor on embellishments and showy styles. Simplicity was the hallmark of the Early American timber frame.

Early American timber-frame houses also shared a similar design, derived from generally accepted notions about function that had evolved through many centuries. In his book *Home,* Witold Rybczynski points out that these notions were vastly different from our own current requirements (see bibliography, p. 229). The issues of comfort and privacy, for example, barely existed at certain times in history, and played little part in house design. Subsistence was usually much more to the point, and the first homes often housed animals as well as people because they were critical to survival. The plan of St. Gall, on the facing page, reveals the way homes looked around 850 A.D. The basic ingredient was a central living area, or hall, in which all activities took place. At its center was a firepit—no chimney, just a hole above the pit for smoke to escape. On the outside of the living area were rooms for sleeping and for animals. That's it. None of the house plans show a second-floor living area, probably because it would have been too smokey for habitation. These early plans are rather ingenious, for the central room is insulated by the animal and bedroom areas. The outer wing is terrific insulation and probably the first air-lock entry. Since structural requirements were given priority, it was also a nicely integrated plan. The living area is really the entire main timber structure and the outer wing simply leans against it as a shed-like substructure. Every room is defined by posts and beams. Still, this was not a home that was warm or comfortable in the way we think of those concepts today: It was a place for cooking and working and sleeping—in short, surviving.

Eventually, the development of the chimney made the living space more tolerable and allowed a second floor to become common. But the central hall stayed and simply became grander as architecture began to be used to demonstrate social position. The hall of the late Middle Ages was a soaring and much more highly embellished version of the smoke-filled hall that preceded it. The technology of the chimney and the improving craftsmanship of the carpenters refined the hall, but there was still no attempt to organize for privacy or for specific activities. When other rooms were added for living, there wasn't a hallway for passage between; you had to go through one room to get to the other. In the castles and manors, workrooms were separated from living areas, but this was done more to segregate servant from master than for convenience.

The first American homes also began as a hall and a parlor. Between them was a chimney with a fireplace facing each room. The second floor was a copy of the first with bedrooms on either side of the chimney. Framing was simple. The house was narrow and tall, usually four posts long and two posts wide. Because people had to have shelter quickly, and usually had only minimum means, the home was designed to expand as needs grew and finances allowed. The frame was easy to make and raise, and provided all the living space that was immediately necessary. Later, a lean-to was added to the eave side, which often became the kitchen. This house shape is now referred to as the saltbox, and it was similar in concept to the bedrooms and animal areas in the St. Gall plans. Later houses commonly included the kitchen as a part of the original construction. The house either maintained the saltbox shape or had more room on the second floor, in which case it became a colonial style. This basic plan is so common that any other is considered an exception.

The pattern of the Early American house was still based on survival—the family gathered around the chimney for warmth and to cook; upstairs was for sleeping. Most houses used this plan because it was an easy way to fit the necessary living spaces into the frame. It was also entirely funtional. Instead of grand expanses, there were low ceilings on two floors, allowing as many spaces as possible to fit within the frame and keeping those spaces warmer. It was a style that reflected the distinctly different idea of life in the new country.

Until the mid-1800s and the advent of stud framing, the timber-frame house continued to evolve and reflect the changing lifestyles of many different kinds of people from New England to the South and out to Ohio. Soon the houses had many different kinds of living areas with hallways between major rooms for privacy. There were timber-frame farmhouses and timber-frame townhouses. There were elegant homes and simple homes, and many styles flourished in the variety and abundance of the expanding new world.

A building from the plan of St. Gall

SMOKE ESCAPE

STALLS

STALLS

CENTRAL LIVING AREA

FIREPIT

SLEEP AREAS

SLEEP AREAS

Timber-frame houses adapt well to modern times. The building method can be used to produce graceful homes that are as energy-efficient as they are beautiful. (Photo by Brian E. Gulick.)

The modern timber-frame house

As with most things, the modern timber-frame building system and the home it supports has had to respond to our place and time. If timber framing had not lain fallow these past 150 years, it would probably have been altered radically by the great social and scientific forces of the 20th century. It is just as well, perhaps, that it was put aside before being compromised by the age of machines. What we're left with is an opportunity to bring timber framing back in its very purest form. But the revival of interest in the joiner's craft has not been enough to make the timber-frame house thrive. For modern appeal, the whole concept of the house had to be considered. And the timber-frame house has done well, adapting nicely to the paraphernalia of our era while still providing security, pleasure and comfort—ingredients too often lacking in the modern home.

In this section, we'll look at some of the goals in building a modern timber-frame house. As well as including practical construction objectives, such as good energy performance, these goals include the elusive ideals that allow a house to provide an extraordinary living experience, to enhance our physical, intellectual and emotional lives. This is where we'll begin. While these intangibles are rarely on the list of requirements for a new house, they should be, for when a dwelling exudes them, it becomes a place of growth and comfort, and it becomes a home.

Homes today contain a host of modern conveniences and have become veritable cocoons of controlled weather systems. There was a time when winter was a life-threatening experience and getting clean was too hard a task to undertake more than once a month. Today's home has freed us from worry about mere survival, and a vast majority of the population has more time than ever before to explore other aspects of life. Unfortunately, designers and builders spend so much time making sure a house contains all the right stuff that they expend practically no energy on its soul. Too often, houses that liberate people from harsh weather and the chores of daily living do little else. They do nothing for the senses, nothing for the spirit and nothing to enhance or ennoble the time and energy set free.

Even something as basic as comfort is rarely considered by modern architecture, points out Witold Rybczynski in *Home.* "During the six years of my architectural education, the subject of comfort was mentioned only once. It was by a mechanical engineer whose job it was to initiate my classmates and me into the mysteries of air conditioning and heating. He described something called the 'comfort zone,' which, as far as I can remember, was a kidney-shaped, crosshatched area on a graph that showed the relationship between temperature and humidity. Comfort was inside the kidney, discomfort was everywhere else. This, apparently, was all that we needed to know about the subject. It was a curious omission from an otherwise rigorous curriculum; one would have thought that comfort was a crucial issue in preparing for the architectural profession, like justice in law, or health in medicine" (p. vii).

Creating a comfortable space requires more than a soft chair, and making comfortable houses is not automatic to any form of construction. Comfort comes from qualities in the building that offer a sense of security, balance and order. Perhaps today more than ever there is a need for

houses to offer these amenities, because although our lives have changed in many ways, under the surface not much is different. The anxieties today come from different sources, but they create the same needs. Our forefathers fought off freezing winters and wild animals; the future, however uncertain, was clearly in their hands. In today's wilderness, the adversaries are not so well defined. We struggle for security, but we are almost always at the mercy of others, and this causes instability as surely as a beast howling at the door. Much about life is disconcertingly temporal, and there is comfort in buildings that transcend the ephemeral qualitites of life and conventional measures of strength.

This the timber-frame building system does quite naturally. As John Burroughs, the naturalist, writes in his essay "Roof-tree": "If the eye could see more fully the necessities of the case,—how the thing stands up and is held together, that it is not pasteboard, that it does not need to be anchored against the wind,—it would be a relief. Hence, the lively pleasure in what are called 'timber houses', and in every architectural device by which the anatomy, the real framework, of the structure, inside or out, is allowed to show, or made to serve as ornament. The eye craves lines of strength, evidence of weight and stability" (*The Writings of John Burroughs.* Vol. 7, *Signs and Seasons* [Boston and New York: Houghton Mifflin Co., Riverside Press, 1886], p. 271).

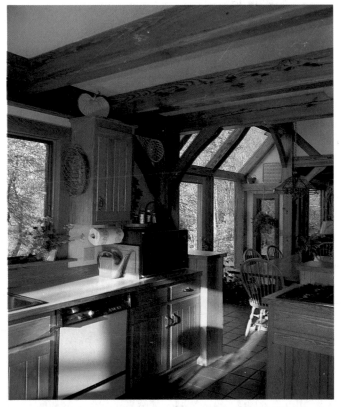

Exposing the framework of the timber structure to the interior lends a feeling of security and balance. The timber-frame structure also becomes the mounting surface for the solarium glass in this house.

As Burroughs suggests, the beauty and art of architecture often lie in the form and function of the structure itself. Viewers are captivated not by the road that a bridge supports but by the splendor of the interaction of cables, trusses, beams and ties. The wholeness of the parts performs the magic. Architects have long understood that a pleasing sense of structure can be an important ingredient in design. If the framework itself is not attractive, the architect might try to imitate structural features with finish details, for instance, by building up the exterior corner boards so they look like supporting columns or decorating the building with imitation timbers. Designers who specialize in restaurant decor have the latter trick down to a science. By my own estimation, probably 75% of the restaurants in this country feature exposed fake timbers. Adding nonsupporting frame members after a building is complete is ridiculous, and some of the results are nothing short of ludicrous. Why would anyone feel that a plastic 4-in. by 8-in. "beam" spanning 80 ft. would lend a feeling of stability to the atmosphere? Such design error is simply not possible in a timber-frame building because the sturdiness and beauty of the structure are integral to the system.

Our forefathers reinforced this inherent strength by building, even overbuilding, structures that would have a life beyond their own generation. Relying on hand tools and hard labor, they did things right the first time so that work would not have to be repeated. There is a vigorous sense of integrity in these unyielding buildings, which survive despite their age, and to me overbuilding seems to pose only one threat: the product might last too long. Small sin, for as a consequence the world is blessed with enduring pyramids, temples, cathedrals, bridges, houses and barns.

As our forefathers built for the future, so must we today. But beyond it being ecologically important that today's houses serve later generations, it is also psychologically uplifting to know that in the worst of times a house will stand and that it will have value and purpose beyond our lifetimes. It's a very uncertain feeling to have the building you live in shake in every wind. I lived in a house that seemed to visibly deteriorate with each passing day, and I can categorically say that it caused insecurity and frustration. I began to wonder if it wasn't I who was leaning and decomposing. On the other hand, I grew up in a house that had been built at the turn of the century by a man who had made his wealth mining gold; he used the highest standards of the time, lovely woodwork and detail. When the house passed eventually to my parents, who made their wealth in children (or was it their poverty?; there were eleven of us), it was given some tough tests. But when the snows and winds came, we always felt safe. When there were low spirits and little money, the house itself offered encouragement of better days to come. My feelings about good homebuilding were born in that great old house and nothing less has been satisfactory since.

In design, there are many goals we may strive for to enhance and refine the essential strength and durability offered by the timber frame. Our ancestors, in building for the future, also designed for the future, and here, too, we can follow their lead. As we have seen in the first section of this chapter, floor plans were not so much personally appropriate as they were reflections of typical living patterns and commonly held views about how houses should be arranged—houses were not designed on the basis of architectural whim or passing fancy, as are many today. The shape of buildings also followed principles that were felt to have universal appeal. For their classic, enduring architecture, colonial Americans used simple, graceful lines that were historically familiar to them and that promised to hold strong into the future.

Old timber-frame structures were built for the future, not to satisfy an architectural whim or passing fancy. They were based on design principles felt to have universal and enduring appeal.

Modern timber-frame builders should also strive for classic lines, respecting the role the medium plays in design. Without a doubt, connecting large timbers with mortise-and-tenon joinery imposes limitations on the form and style of a building. You will not soon see a timber-frame dome, and if you do, stay out of it, for structurally it would be like a fish out of water. In timber-frame buildings, the walls generally should not be much higher than the posts (whose height depends on the available length of timbers). The joints are best as orthogonal intersections. The frame is rectilinear, and when it is assembled the timbers form a cohesive alliance, gaining strength through balance and symmetry. Timber frames are disinclined to perform feats for the purpose of architectural curiosity, but this is not to suggest that building with timbers means limited design opportunity. A study of Japanese architecture or a look at any of Cecil Hewett's books on English building construction (see bibliography, p. 229) will demonstrate that, within the constraints imposed by the timbers, there is chal-

lenge enough to design graceful and beautiful houses that are the essence of domestic architecture.

Using structure as an aesthetic consideration presents some interesting design opportunities, as we will explore in later chapters. Posts and beams can be used to define areas. Frame members can be deliberately placed to create a desired feeling. For instance, a large summer beam might be located over the center of a living room to create a feeling of unity, symmetry, strength and stability. This would be a formal place in which people would group together. Another space might be left open to the roof to create a sense of expansiveness and drama. Here timbers could be arranged for a lighter, more playful effect. This might be a place for fun and informal entertaining. When these and other techniques are used effectively, when the frame and the floor plan intertwine, then each area of the house is naturally well decorated and feels complete, even during construction, when the house is still just a frame silhouetted against the sky.

In a timber-frame building, structure is also an aesthetic consideration. The summer beam in this living room lends an air of strength, as well as providing visual interest in the ceiling.

Timber-frame houses are being enthusiastically accepted because they come with good credentials from the past. The task now is to design and build modern homes that are simple but flexible, classic but not out of touch. Perhaps it is obvious by now that I think we should take our cue from the American tradition, adapting and inventing a new style while still respecting the archetypal forms. For example, to be affordable for the average person, Early American houses were arranged simply, usually containing four bents and three bays. Our timber-frame houses tend to follow the same pattern, yet within this basic form we have created hundreds of different floor plans. We still rely

on a central chimney, attaching a small wood stove or furnace to it to heat almost entirely any of our well-insulated houses. And we still often build with the saltbox shape (or variations of it), orienting the low wall to the wind and the high wall to the sun for good energy performance.

Although we don't have the great virgin forests colonial American builders had, our techniques and framing styles are also similar. We use the same kinds of wood, albeit in smaller and shorter pieces. Frames through history changed to suit available materials, and modern builders should be ready to adapt. For instance, a frame designed for oak timbers under 16 ft. in length should not be the

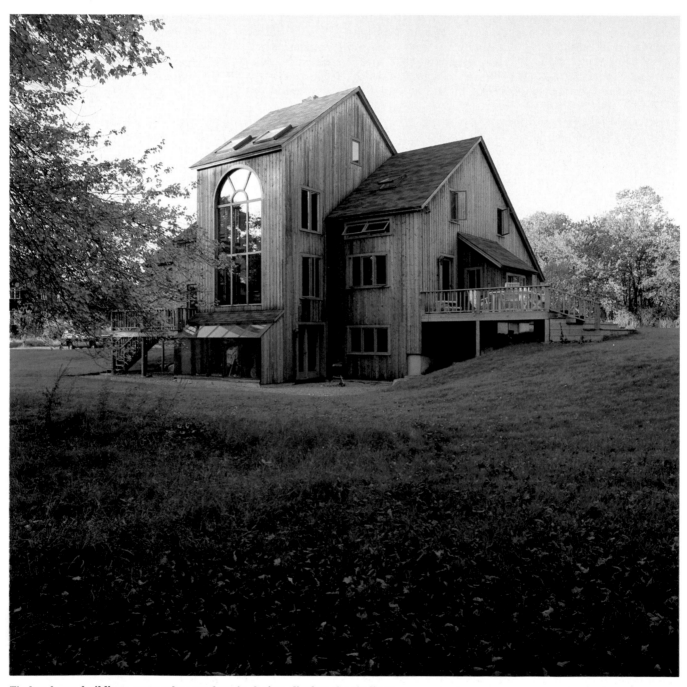

Timber-frame buildings, even when modern in design, display classic lines.

same as for one using fir timbers available in 40-ft. lengths. Since we have cranes available to lift timbers, assembly and raising techniques can be similar to those used in colonial America even though we can't (or for safety don't choose to) muster a community of people for a raising. The use of a crane can and should affect the engineering and layout of a frame in the same way that the helping hands of neighbors altered frame design for the colonists. With the crane, we have the opportunity to make frames stronger by assembling more pieces together in a single unit.

There are some situations, however, for which there is no historical precedent, and modern builders must invent viable 20th-century construction alternatives. A realistic route must be provided for each plumbing pipe and electrical wire. Allowance must be made for bathroom fixtures, kitchen appliances and a heating system. It is necessary to consider the requirements of smoke and burglar alarms, stereo systems and telephones. Rooms must accommodate king-size beds, microwave ovens, hot tubs and computers. Some of our clients have the security system of Fort Knox; others don't even bother to lock their doors. One house has an exercise room up on the roof, another has a bomb shelter down in the basement.

Fortunately, the timber-frame building system solves more problems than it creates. Timber framing is naturally compatible with passive solar heating, for example, and with its goal of keeping areas open to one another so that heat can move through the house without fans and ducts. Since the loads of the building are directed to a few large posts instead of to many small framing members, timber-frame houses lend themselves to open floor plans. The necessary expanses of south-facing glass can be installed between posts without difficulty. Glass and timbers complement each other, and from the very beginning we have tried to capitalize on this relationship in our houses. There is no prototype in history for making timber solariums, so we have invented this technology using new ideas but attempting to adhere to old standards.

The most important asset of the timber frame to modern building technology is the basis it provides for an extremely effective insulating system. With the frame bearing all the building loads, the insulation can be a completely separate system. This has the benefit of minimizing thermal breaks and simplifying construction. After some experimentation, we discovered a product called a stress-skin panel, which is a sandwich of interior and exterior sheathing with a core of rigid foam insulation. Using this bit of high technology, we are now able to wrap the timbers in unbroken insulation, achieving the same energy performance as a super-insulated platform-framed house, but without going to nearly the same extremes. In fact, many people express an interest in our homes because of the buildings' remarkable energy efficiency, not because of a primary attraction to the timber frame itself. To us, developing this insulating system felt like a major breakthrough, vastly different from what we knew of European or traditional American enclosure techniques. But ironically, it was not really a new concept at all, as it resembles the primitive method of enclosing a frame with animal skins.

As mechanical and design innovations for the modern timber-frame house have evolved, it has become apparent that in many areas the procedures that are used in standard construction are not necessarily transferable. To keep construction efficient while maintaining traditional standards, it has been necessary to adapt materials and invent new methods. Some of these developments take timber-frame house builders outside the information available in architecture and construction guides, and there are risks involved when going against the grain of conventional practice.

National and local building codes often pose problems for the construction of timber-frame homes because they were written to govern other building techniques. When the building official is presented with an unusual situation, the tendency is to lean on the letter of the law instead of the spirit. The result is that innovative ideas face a rocky

The stress-skin panel is basically a sandwich of interior and exterior sheathing on either side of a core of rigid foam insulation. The panels are installed outside the frame, wrapping it in an unbroken layer of insulation.

road even though they may be better than code requirements. For example, some building codes demand that all structural members be stamped by a lumber grader to indicate that they meet the stress grade. This is well and good until you want to use oak for the frame. To date, the only grading rules for oak are for appearance—allowable stress grades have not been developed. Therefore, although you might reasonably demonstrate that the timber frame you intend to build exceeds the code requirements by a factor of three, a building inspector has the right to prevent you from building it. Wiring is another example. Code requires wires to be in the center of the insulation cavity to prevent them from being punctured by nails entering from either side. This seems like a right-minded rule, but not for every circumstance. We have a situation where the safest and easiest place to put the wire is on the inside of the stress-skin panel surface and the outside of the timber. Yet the strictest interpretation of the code suggests that we have to put the wire in a more difficult and vulnerable position. In such cases, most reasonable building inspectors will use their own judgment or require an engineer's stamp on the building plans.

A similar kind of problem is often caused by people in the building trades who fear the unknown. To compensate for their insecurity, they raise their prices, even though the task may not be any more difficult or complicated— just different. To prevent this sort of costly ignorance, consumers must be thoroughly educated about construction procedure specific to timber-frame houses. They need to be prepared to educate potential contractors and subcontractors, and know when the price does not accurately reflect the difficulty of the job.

Dealing with codes and construction trades can make building a timber-frame house more vexing than it need be. But as this type of construction becomes more and more popular, the problems will begin to disappear. Codes will adapt regulations to govern these new situations and tradespeople will become familiar with the new materials and techniques. In the meantime, it is necessary for those who wish to construct a timber-frame house to become familiar with building details and the standard solutions to various situations that may arise. In part, that is the very reason for this book.

In my experience, building a timber-frame house takes more time than building a conventional house. First of all, the plans need to be more detailed because nothing can be taken for granted. Building inspectors have a tendency to want to see more on paper so that they can satisfy themselves that code is being met. Tradespeople will need to have more explained by way of drawings so they can understand procedure and the interface of materials. Owners who are overseeing their own projects usually keep the job under control by limiting the number of subcontractors on the site at any one time, and so time is traded for quality control.

Another factor that inhibits a quick pace is that owners tend to choose labor-intensive details. Once people see the craftsmanship of a fine timber frame, they usually prefer finish work more in keeping with the quality of the frame. High-quality materials are harder to get than cheap materials (even if they are not more expensive) and good work takes more time (and is definitely more expensive) than bad work. The moral of the story is that nothing good comes easily. A timber-frame home is built to unusually high standards and costs more time and usually more money, too.

Since I'm ending this chapter with a dose of realism, I'll mention another downside fact. A timber frame is made of wood, and wood—especially in timber dimensions— cracks, shrinks and twists. Any timber above 4 in. thick cannot be reliably or economically dried in kilns because it takes too long. Air-drying is also impractical for the same reason. Even when it is possible to make the frame of dry timbers, seasonal shrinking and swelling results in dimensional change or surface checking. We have made frames of timbers that were dried in a kiln and a few from timbers that were resawn from larger timbers over 100 years old. In both cases, there certainly was not as much movement as in frames built from green wood, but there was definitely visible change as the frame acclimated to its new environment. It is just the nature of wood. If you want a door that will never warp or shrink, get one of the new metal or fiberglass doors. Although a shirt made of polyester can be made never to wrinkle, there is something about cotton that is unlike any man-made fiber; if you like the feel and texture and the individual character of natural materials, it is difficult to accept substitutes. Buying quality sometimes means accepting the wrinkles, and the timbers in a frame definitely "wrinkle." This can be seen as a drawback, but it is also proof that they are the real thing.

The shrinking and checking in timbers are like wrinkles in cotton—evidence of the unique character of a natural material.

II. The Structure

Uncompromising standards of workmanship and engineering allow timber-frame buildings to stand for centuries. This connection consists of a post, two summer beams (to the right and left of the post) and a bent girt (at top).

Sound timber framing requires standards of workmanship and engineering that are uncompromising. Weak examples of the craft have either not survived at all or survive marginally, ravaged by forces they were not equipped to withstand. But properly designed and well-constructed timber-frame buildings stand sturdily, almost defiantly, despite centuries of use. Better than words, far better than textbooks, these many thousands of surviving timber-frame buildings silently instruct.

Critical to building timber-frame structures to the highest standards is a broad understanding of theory and good practice; next come some creativity and flexibility. For each frame starts out as not much more than a blank canvas, made up of the hopes and dreams of the future occupants (brought down to earth by budget limitations and site requirements). During design, there is nothing about the shape or flavor of the building that dictates more than the most general arrangement of timbers. When the timbers are arranged, the wood species still has to be selected and the timbers individually sized. Information about the arrangement, species and size of the timbers does not automatically lead to an understanding of the joints that will be used. And when the joinery is determined, decisions still must be made about embellishments and finishes. Of course, all of these considerations must be juggled along with the architectural concerns of the building. Compare this decision-making process with the methodology of conventional stud framing, where once you have decided where the walls go, you put them all together in the usual way—16 in. on center, nailed to top and bottom plates.

To me, timber framing has more in common with the design and making of wooden furniture than it does with conventional building procedure. In the same way that a handcrafted chair is more than a place to sit, a timber frame is more than its structure. In both cases it is virtually impossible to separate design from construction, and there are few pat answers to any given question. Be it chairmaking or timber framing, to make successful decisions about woods, finish, style, function and construction, you must first understand the structural requirements of the craft. To achieve the necessary overview, we'll look here at engineering and the physical characteristics of the timber frame. In the next chapter we'll experiment with frame design, and in Chapter IV we'll explore home design. Although we'll be discussing frame design separately from house design, it is important to realize that both must evolve together when plans are being drawn (see p. 67).

The anatomy of a timber frame
A typical timber frame can be divided into four major systems: walls, floor, roof and cross sections called bents. Walls are the linear compositions of timbers that run parallel to the ridgepole and bents are the major structural elements perpendicular to the walls. A simple frame might

**Typical parts in a timber frame
(showing two roof systems)**

RIDGEPOLE

STRAINING BEAM

PLATE

PRINCIPAL
RAFTER
CONNECTS
TO PLATE.

ROOF PURLIN

STRUT

QUEEN POST

COLLAR TIE

CONNECTING
GIRT

BENT GIRT

STUD

KNEE BRACE

FLOOR JOIST

WALL PURLIN

DIAGONAL STRUT

SUMMER BEAM

PRINCIPAL POST

PRINCIPAL
RAFTER
CONNECTS TO
PRINCIPAL POST.

JOIST

TIMBER SILL

GIRDER

contain three or four bents, two walls, a floor system on one or two levels, and a roof system inclined toward the center equally from each wall. It could be this simple, but there is also no limit to how complex each system might be. The systems can be further subdivided into the vertical, horizontal or inclined timbers that make up each unit.

Historically and geographically there is some inconsistency in nomenclature, but basically the vertical members are posts, struts and studs. Struts can also be inclined, and are used in the roof system as a secondary support for rafters. Studs are secondary posts, primarily used as nailers or for decoration. The horizontal members, or beams, are girts, sills, plates, girders, joists, collar ties, tie beams, ridgepoles and purlins. Girts are the horizontal members in bents or walls that span between major posts. Sills support the post bottoms at ground level, while plates support rafters; girders are major beams that run between sills. Inclined members are generally either rafters or braces. The identification of most pieces in the frame is further refined by function and location. Therefore there are bent girts and connecting girts, roof purlins and wall purlins, principal rafters and common rafters. A few other timbers have interesting names: queen posts, king posts, prick posts, crown posts and even samson posts, as well as summer beams, hammer beams, anchor beams and dragon beams.

The timbers within the walls, floor, roof and bents interact to form a self-supporting structural unit. This unit is often a complex web consisting of many hundreds of pieces, each absorbing and transferring a share of the building load. The accumulating loads are collected and passed on through the frame from the minor members (which tend to fall in the center of the building) to ever larger timbers, until eventually they are received by the principal posts. From here, the loads are passed to the foundation and ultimately distributed to the earth below. To design a frame properly, each timber must be positioned to respond to specific loads and sized to resist the forces that will act upon it. Loads must be directed to the posts without putting undue stress on any timber. Every joint must be planned to transfer the load effectively from one timber to another, and to keep the entire frame rigid enough to stand erect.

When function comes together with form in a well-designed timber-frame building, the frame itself can become a work of art. It takes on the natural balance, symmetry and beauty that are the essence of timber framing. The intelligent placement and careful connection of each timber component coupled with the athletic way loads are relayed through a frame result in a mighty combination of muscle and intellect that is bound to impress.

Some unusual timber members

SAMSON POST IS BRACED TO TIMBER IN FOUR DIRECTIONS.

BRACE

SAMSON POST

UPPER-LEVEL POST

ANCHOR BEAM

INTERNAL WALL

JOIST

DRAGON BEAM

ANCHOR BEAM IS UNUSUALLY LARGE BEAM THAT TIES TWO POSTS TOGETHER WITHIN THE BENT. THEY ARE USUALLY FOUND IN BARNS, AND EMPLOY THROUGH-TENONS.

DRAGON BEAM IS MAJOR TIMBER THAT RUNS DIAGONALLY, CANTILEVERING OVER CORNER OF BUILDING.

The forces

Reading this chapter will not turn you into a structural engineer, but if designing timber frames required the full knowledge of one, I would not be writing this now. On the other hand, it is essential that timber-frame designers have a good understanding of the forces that will bear on a frame and their effects. It's also important to know how to calculate loads and to size timbers. These calculations require the use of lengthy formulas or tables, which, although admittedly complicated, are not beyond the reach of the determined person. They are beyond the scope of this book, however, and so I refer interested readers to my first book, listed in the bibliography (p. 229), for that information. I also must stress that it is critical to recognize that point at which the services of a licensed engineer are required. Any frame worth cutting, joining and assembling is worth an investment in proper engineering.

Still, don't let science override common sense. I learned this lesson the hard way, after designing and building an office for my parents' mail-order business. It was not a timber-frame building, but we used timbers for internal posts and carrying beams. Wanting to impress my parents with my knowledge, I carefully calculated each timber size and demonstrated to them that though the beams would have to be very large to support the supplies on the second floor, the posts to support the beams could be quite slender. We could save money on the posts, I boasted. My mother told me several times that the posts looked too small. When I started to argue the math, she stopped me and said, "Those posts are just too small." She didn't need formulas to tell her that. The skinny posts stayed (because my mother has the patience of a saint), and the building was completed and piled high with the paper of their business.

One day, when my mother happened to be away from her usual place in the office, the elderly lady across the alley backed out of her garage, had an anxiety attack with her foot on the gas pedal, and crashed into the side of the office. The car came far enough through the wall to start quite a nice domino effect with the shelves of papers and boxes. The slender posts broke like matchsticks, and the forces that saved my mother (and the driver) had nothing to do with my timber sizing. While I could not have anticipated a car coming through the wall, I have learned to pay attention to gut-level intuition.

Now we'll look at the four primary types of forces acting upon the frame members: compression, tension, shear and bending moment. Although just about any exception is possible, each of these forces tends to be associated with particular timbers or framing circumstances, as you will see in the following discussion.

Compression Loads bearing on posts are resisted by an equal reaction on the opposite end, resulting in a compression force in the timber. Posts that support a girt, plate or rafter end receive the load from the top, but the load could be received from a horizontal beam at any point along the length of the post. Although heavy loads are often directed into the posts, seldom is there a compression problem. Wood is strongest along the grain, and posts are usually relatively large because they must accommodate the joinery of intersecting members. When there is a failure in compression, it usually comes in the form of buckling—lean on a wooden yardstick with the weight of your body and it will buckle sideways and break. So even though compressive failure of a timber post is unlikely, avoid using long, slender timbers or long unsupported posts.

Where many members intersect and wood has been removed for the joints, a post could buckle under an extreme compression load. The calculation for the maximum load in compression should be done using the smallest timber section left after the joints are cut. Most formulas assume that the post is acting alone, but the beams that join to the post can add structural value back to the post by serving as buttresses, helping to prevent buckling even of slender posts.

Tension A force pulling a timber from either end causes tensile stress, which amounts to two forces playing tug-of-war with a timber. It's usually not the timber that fails in this circumstance, but the joint. Joints always include the end of at least one timber, where it is difficult to generate substantial resistance to withdrawal. (Tensile strength is achieved through the use of pegs or a locking geometry, as discussed on p. 42.) Therefore, if a timber is subjected only to tension, the cross-sectional area needed for the joint would determine the width or depth of the timber. But there is usually more than this one force at work, which will affect the choice of joinery and timber size.

Forces acting on timbers

HORIZONTAL SHEAR

VERTICAL SHEAR

BENDING MOMENT

COMPRESSION

TENSION

A king post is a good example of a timber under tensile stress from the weight of the girt at its base, while also receiving a load from the rafters through the king-post braces, as shown below. (Collar ties between rafters must also resist the potential for opposing rafters to spread at their bases.) Knee braces, which play a major role in keeping the frame rigid, are often subjected to significant tensile stress. Though not always the case, the loads on the braces usually come from a force pushing against the side of the building; this puts the first brace to encounter the load in tension and the opposite brace in compression. Failure in brace connections under tension is fairly common, and frames can be made a great deal stronger if they are designed with a compression member (instead of a tension member) to react to the load. (See p. 37 for more discussion about braces.)

Timber members under stress

RAFTER

KING POST

BRACE

BENT
GIRT

FORCE

KING POST IS IN TENSION BECAUSE ITS TOP IS
HELD BY RAFTERS, WHILE ITS BOTTOM IS PULLED
DOWNWARD BY GIRT LOAD AND BRACE LOADS.

BRACE
IN TENSION

BRACE IN
COMPRESSION

SECOND KNEE BRACE TO
ENCOUNTER LOAD IS IN COMPRESSION.

The king post is under tensile stress and also receives loads from its braces. The wood of the frame is stained oak; the ceiling boards are red cedar.

Shear and bending moment A pair of scissors perfectly demonstrates shearing action: Two forces slide by each other and destroy the material in between. Shear stress in horizontal timbers can be vertical (across the grain) or horizontal (along the grain). Unlike masonry materials, which are comparatively weak in resistance to shear forces, wood is so resilient that vertical shear failure almost never happens unless the timber is defective or eventually rots. It would occur if the load were so massive that the timber actually broke, with the wood fibers torn apart at the point of connection. Since the strength of the timbers at their joints is critical to frame strength, the joints must also be designed to resist vertical shearing. An example of a situation in which vertical shear might be a problem would be in a garrison frame, in which the beam cantilevers beyond the first-story wall and carries the weight of the upper post and roof beyond the support of the lower post (see drawing below at left). If the overhang were very short—short enough to eliminate bending problems—cross-grain shear would be a significant concern. Especially because of joints in the beam at the intersection of the lower wall and the overhang, this situation requires careful evaluation.

Horizontal shear (along the grain) is a much more common problem and results from adjacent wood fibers being pulled and pushed in parallel but opposite directions. This kind of shear failure in a timber would probably be the result of an extreme load having produced an excessive bend (or bending moment). Bending subjects the upper and lower portions of the timber to conflicting forces of tension and compression; horizontal shear, or a slipping of fibers along the grain, usually occurs in the neutral zone between the two forces. But the great elasticity of some species allows even a timber with a long span and an excessive load to bend quite a bit, like a bow, before failing. Actually, shear failure along the grain is more likely to happen when beams are relatively stiff and are forced to bend. Support a yardstick on chairs 30 in. apart and it will bend a great deal under a load; put a large load on the yardstick with a 12-in. span and it is much more likely to break. So horizontal-shear analysis takes into consideration relative stiffness and structural properties of the species as well as the load.

When establishing the size of horizontal timbers, three possibilities must be considered: shear stress (most probably causing horizontal splitting at the beam ends); deflection, a value of elasticity set by building codes to ensure that structures will be stiff enough to be serviceable; and bending stress, which could cause fiber failure. Fiber failure occurs in a timber when the tensile stresses caused by bending become too great, so the fibers simply break across the grain. Pure fiber failure is not very common and would probably be accompanied by some shearing along the grain as well.

Vertical shear situation

POST CARRYING
SIGNIFICANT LOAD

BEAM CANTILEVERS PAST
FIRST-STORY WALL.

VERTICAL SHEAR FAILURE
COULD OCCUR HERE.

Horizontal shear and bending moment

UPPER PART
OF BEAM
IN COMPRESSION

NEUTRAL AXIS

LOWER PART
OF BEAM
IN TENSION

FIBER FAILURE
COULD OCCUR HERE.

Loads and loading   The transfer of loads through frame members is an essential engineering consideration in timber framing. Understanding how loads are absorbed and the way in which the tribulations of one timber are distributed to others is critical to a well-designed frame. Because the load is transferred at joint intersections, much will need to be explained about the functions of various kinds of joinery, which we'll do later. The point to note here is that all the components of the frame must work individually and collectively to gather the loads and direct them to the posts without staggering under the effort.

All the horizontal timbers carry a load, if only the weight of the timber itself. In most cases, they also carry the weight of other materials, such as flooring, roof planking and shingles. These materials make up the dead load on the frame, which is almost always evenly distributed over the surface. In addition to dead load there is live load, which consists of all those things other than the building materials—snow, people, furniture and wind. The number to plug into the equation for live load is determined by the local building code. Beams that bear simple live and dead loads would be floor joists, summer beams, purlins and connecting girts.

Because loads pass through the frame like streams converging on a river, many timbers must accept more than one type of load. For example, when a post bears on a beam, it could be transferring a significant load from another area of the frame to that one point. In other cases, there might be two or three points along a beam where loads are applied through vertical or diagonal members. Concentrating the load in this manner further complicates beam sizing because the load type (evenly distributed, one-point, two-point or three-point) must be considered as well. Beams within a frame might support posts that could support other beams that perhaps support a floor, so that when the load is finally accumulated, the beam that must bear it all is asked to perform a formidable task. To do this, it will probably need to be a formidable beam. If, when designing a frame, you try to avoid such extremes with simpler, more direct load routes, the frame will be stronger and easier to build.

You can't begin to consider timber sizing without a decision about the wood for the frame, because there are dramatic differences in the load-resistance values of different species. A relatively weak species (red cedar, for example) can certainly be used, but it should be designed with short spans—it would be silly to design a frame with 16-ft. spans and then decide to use pine or cedar. Aesthetics of the different species also have a bearing on frame design. Timbers made from light-colored wood and clear grain might be more closely spaced than those made from a more dominant wood, such as oak or fir. For these reasons, design the frame to fit the wood and not the other way around.

Never be afraid to oversize a timber-frame member, and never underestimate what a frame might have to withstand. If a frame could be isolated within a protective bubble, it would only have to be strong enough to hold itself together, but real life demands that frames be designed with the assumption that snow will be on the roof, wind will blow against the walls and people and things will weigh heavily upon the floors. We are also asked by code and by common sense to plan for the worst: Someday the snow may be hip deep and very wet; someday the wind might be a hurricane; on any day, the inhabitants might hold a raucous party, and certainly the kids will jump from beds. When sizing timbers, err on the side of endurance, and you probably will not have erred at all.

Light-colored woods are less likely to appear overbearing than dark woods, even when spaced closely together. The timbers in this bedroom, here still under construction, are white cedar treated with a clear penetrating oil. (Brock Simini, Architects.)

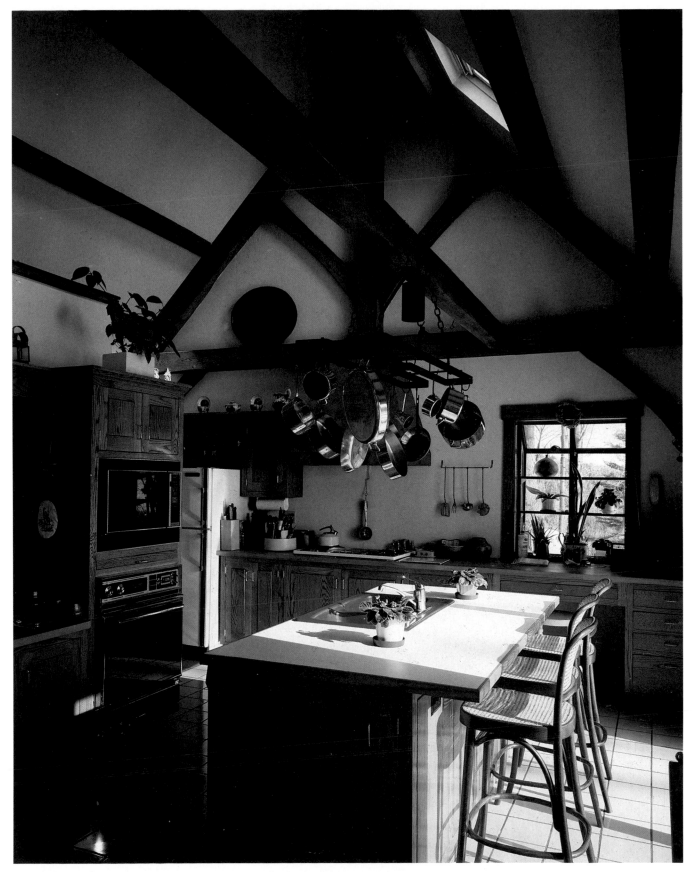

The darkly stained oak in this house dominates the decor. The beam spanning the kitchen is 16 ft. long. (Photo by Bob Gere.)

The roof system

More than any other factor, the arrangement of timbers in the roof determines whether a frame will be built with walls or bents. Indeed, frames are often defined by the type of roof they support. The roof is usually the most difficult aspect of the frame, and figuring the angles and the lengths of the pieces is almost always the most demanding mathematical calculation. In addition, the roof generally contains the most challenging joinery and can require sophisticated engineering. Therefore, we'll consider the structure of the frame from the top down.

There are four classic timber-frame roof types: principal and common rafters, principal and common rafters with purlins, common rafters, and principal rafters with purlins.

Deciding which to use might only be a matter of personal preference, but more commonly the choice involves structural factors, including the shape and pitch of the roof, loading, wood species, available timber length and the floor plan.

The principal and common rafter roof In this system, the principal rafters are directly in line with the principal posts so that their burden is directly transferred. Smaller common rafters are spaced evenly between. The rafters either connect to plates that ride on top of the outside wall posts or are interrupted by a principal purlin (or sometimes two) on each roof slope. Of course the rafters

The roof structure is usually the most challenging aspect of the frame, requiring difficult joinery and complex mathematical calculations. The turned post and collar ties form the center of a cross-shaped building.

are sized according to loads and spans, but it would not be unusual to use principal rafters that were 8x10 (or even larger) and common rafters as small as 4x6 spaced about 4 ft. apart.

This system makes the most sense to me when used with purlins. First, using purlins makes it possible to break up the span of the common rafters, so shorter (and more readily available) timbers can be used. Second, by spanning from bent to bent, the purlins absorb even increments of the roof load and transfer it toward the principal posts. Some of the burden carried by the common rafters is also transferred by the purlins to the principal posts, with the remainder bearing on the plates. In this type of roof, the purlins might well be the largest timbers because they are typically unsupported in their span between rafters.

The problem with a principal and common rafter roof with purlins is that it demands some tricky assembly, since the purlins have to be joined to the principal rafters before the common rafters can be installed. To position the purlins thus requires that a couple of brave (or foolhardy) individuals shinny up rafters that are not stiffened by any other members. Also, the lower common rafters can be hard to install because the joints to the purlin and the plate have to be engaged simultaneously. Still, the interplay of timbers is beautiful, and the system is without structural compromise.

Principal and common rafter roof with purlins

The common rafter roof This type of roof is easy to install, but has a different problem. Here the rafters are joined to the plates at the bottom and at the top either to a ridgepole running the length of the building, or simply to each other in pairs. Each rafter needs to be long enough and strong enough for the entire span. The rafters are usually spaced 3 ft. to 4 ft. apart, with no particular regard to the location of principal posts. The problem is that there is no interaction between the roof timbers and the timbers in the rest of the frame. With only one possible timber running perpendicular to the rafters (the ridgepole), it isn't easy to stiffen the roof in that direction, and the timber frame begins to act as two units rather than one. Beyond the collar tie, common rafter trusses don't usually contain additional timbers for reinforcement against spreading; therefore, there is a tendency for increased outward thrust at the plate. Because of these considerations, common rafter roofs are most suitable for small buildings.

Common rafter roof

COLLAR TIE

COMMON RAFTER

PRINCIPAL POST

PLATE

POSTS NEED NOT FALL UNDER RAFTER FEET.

BENT GIRT

The principal rafter and purlin roof This last roof option is the most popular with our company. Here rafters join directly to the tops of principal posts and are connected to each other with a series of purlins spaced about 4 ft. apart. The system has many benefits, not the least of which is that it eliminates the need for top plates. It's difficult today to get timbers that are adequately long or stable for these plates, so they often have to be scarfed together. When the forests were filled with tall, virgin trees and timbers were hewn by hand, it was almost always possible to make plates to span the length and width of any building, and it would not be at all difficult to get any number of timbers of rafter length. With this kind of material available, and with so much handwork involved, the joiner's concern 200 years ago was not timber length but the number of timbers required. Because a common rafter roof

uses many fewer pieces than a purlin roof, I suspect this was the main reason it was favored at that time. (A 36-ft.-long frame with 20-ft.-long rafters would require 20 common rafters on 4-ft. centers, but with purlins and principal rafters the frame would need about 33 members.)

We stay in business because we have a measure of practicality: Our timbers are purchased from a sawmill rather than hand-hewn. Our sawyer can easily handle purlins, which are usually no longer than 16 ft., but if we asked him for two 42-ft.-long plates, four 30-ft.-long bent girts and thirty-two 26-ft.-long rafters, he'd probably try not to laugh, but he would know for certain that we had given over completely to fantasy. If he could get timbers like that he wouldn't be able to saw them, and if he could get them and saw them, it's likely they would be of questionable quality.

Integrating the rafters into the bents allows the raising of large, complete units as well as greater possibilities in bent design. These bents have been assembled in preparation for a raising by crane.

So we use principal rafters and purlins, and benefit from the other advantages of the system. Because the rafters are part of the bents, we can raise large, complete units. (If there were a plate between posts and rafters, the bents, plates and roof would have to be assembled separately.) By extending interior posts to the roof, we can support splices in the rafters if they are needed to make up the complete length. Also, because the rafter ends join directly to the tops of the principal posts, the frame does not shrink in height. If you remember that wood shrinks considerably across the grain but very little along the grain,

you can see that the height of the building would change as the top plates shrank, as shown in the drawing on p. 31.

Other roof timbers Regardless of the roof system used, rafters generally require the assistance of other timbers both to bear loads and to resist spreading at the eaves. Roof load is calculated as the hypothetical weight of the materials plus the potential load of the snow or wind. The amount of outward thrust at the eave is a function of the load and the angle of the rafters. As the angle gets shallower, thrust increases. In a simple situation, with relative-

The principal rafter and purlin roof eliminates the need for top plates by joining the rafters directly to the posts.

ly short rafters and a small load, a collar tie is often sufficient to limit both sagging and spreading, although it is unlikely to do both simultaneously. The collar tie works in compression to reduce rafter sag and works in tension to bind the pair of rafters together and reduce their tendency to push outward on the walls. The burden of the load remains with the rafters, but the collar tie helps them support it. When principal rafters are used, a collar tie (or other system) is almost always necessary because the loads are so large on these few timbers. With common rafters, collar ties are sometimes used only with every other rafter pair. A horizontal timber joined between queen posts, called a straining beam, performs like a collar tie (see drawing, p. 23). Diagonal struts joined from a bent girt to the rafters limit outward thrust while allowing the central area between rafters to be kept clear of timbers for use as storage or living space.

As the width of a building increases and the rafter spans lengthen, it becomes more difficult for a collar tie to do either of its tasks effectively. To hold the rafter feet together, the collar tie must be low enough in the roofline to prevent outward thrust, but this requires that its length increase along with the width of the building. And the longer the collar tie, the more difficulty it will have supporting compression loads without buckling. The solution is to bring in additional timbers to support the rafters.

There are some relatively standard combinations of posts, struts, braces, girts and ties used to make the roof structurally stable. A king-post truss uses a central single post, as shown in the drawing and photo on p. 26; if it joined to a collar tie instead of to the rafter peak, it would be a crown post. The king post is usually connected to a bent girt, but might only span between the peak and a collar tie instead. The classic king post has diagonal braces joining to the rafters, creating a triangle that works to make the assembly function as a single roof truss. Since the lower horizontal beam of the truss (known as the bottom chord) is hung from the king post, there is no need for an intermediate support post.

Queen posts are similar to king posts, but they work in pairs. Typically, they rest on the bent girt and join either to a collar tie or directly to the rafters. Queen posts are commonly used when it is necessary to create living space under the central area between rafters. Because queen posts transfer the roof load directly to the bent girt, they must be placed carefully so the point loads they impose do not overburden the girt. It's best to position them as closely as possible to the supports beneath the bent girt. If the queen posts do not join to a collar tie, a straining beam between posts would serve the same purpose. Knee braces are used between the queen posts and the straining beam to support loads and stiffen the assembly.

A collar tie, a horizontal member used to bind rafters together, helps the rafters resist spreading, but can also serve to prevent them from sagging. These collar ties are in turn supported by pairs of queen posts.

In another type of roof assembly, elaborate bracing is used to create trusses that span the width of the building without interior supports or a horizontal beam connecting the walls. The hammer-beam truss and the scissors truss are two examples. The finest examples of these techniques were executed in the great cathedrals of Europe, and demonstrate how complex structure and intricate decoration can combine to turn a common craft into art of the highest order. The most notable example of a hammer beam, in Westminster Hall in England, spans 65 ft. and the mechanics of it have yet to be fully explained. Basically, tension and compression forces are passed through a series of timbers and resolved at the base of the rafters and in the outer wall without the need for a bottom chord or collar tie. The scissors truss was used as a way to frame a vaulted masonry ceiling between timber rafters.

Each of the arrangements we've just discussed is designed to keep the roof from sagging or spreading, to get the load from the rafters to the principal posts efficiently. It's that simple. But when the needs of the structure are put in the pot with aesthetic considerations, an endless variety of savory combinations can be served, and often the arrangement of timbers in the roof becomes the most pleasing and dramatic part of the frame. There's something exciting about the way the forces are pulled in by one timber and passed off to another—the interplay can't help but become a focal point of the frame. In other types of construction, the roof is an unattractive assembly of gussets, steel plates and nails that has to be hidden. Because of this, the space under the rafters is often either totally unused or used only as an attic. When this happens, you not only lose space that was figured into construction costs, but you also lose an area of high visual appeal. The interest created by the roof framing and the extra space under the eaves are two distinct attributes of a timber-frame house.

The hammer-beam truss was developed in the Middle Ages for use in cathedrals. In modern timber framing, the concept is revived for large, open living areas.

Scissors truss

TIMBER RAFTER

MASONRY VAULT

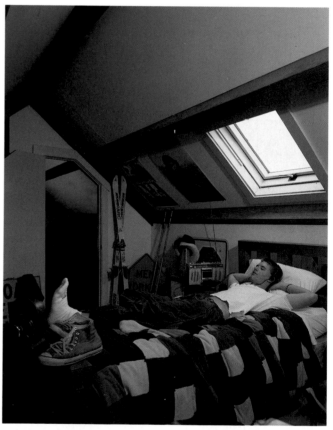

Very little space in a timber-frame house is wasted. Rooms under the roof often have interesting shapes and offer many decorating possibilities. (Photo by Brian E. Gulick.)

The bent and wall systems

Stretching up to shoulder the load from the roof are the principal outside posts. These are tied to the beams of the wall and bent structures. A principle of timber-frame design is that the burden should get to these posts with the least possible effort. When the force is passed from the rafters to an intermediate post and then through a beam in order to get to its destination, it could be necessary to use a beam of considerable size to prevent bending at the point of transfer.

A better way to avoid overloading horizontal timbers is to design intermediate posts within the bent to reach from the deck to the rafters, as shown in the photo on p. 33. (You see this type of bent design a lot in barn construction, because it's an easy and practical way to gain great strength.) Intermediate posts also keep the bent from hinging at the rafters, something we've learned a great deal about in the raising of our frames. Lifting a bent from a horizontal to a vertical position applies stresses the bent may never see again, but it's a fair indication of the strength of the structure. There's a tendency to design a frame in layers simply because the floor plan is usually designed that way, yet when you look at the frame as a complete unit, it's obviously much stiffer if vertical members pass through the levels. In addition, the natural triangulation between the sloping rafters and the long interior posts enhances the frame's resistance to loads exerted against the gable ends and the walls. If you push against a side of a triangle, the adjacent side resists your force by acting in compression, making it nearly impossible to distort the shape. As a matter of fact, a triangular structure can't distort dramatically unless one of the connections fails. Push against a rectangle and the result is much different. The only inherent strength in a rectangle is at the corners, which cannot possibly bear up under a large force.

Structural triangulation is also the reason knee braces are so important in timber framing. Normally located at the upper ends of the posts, the braces connect diagonally to the joining beam and form small triangles at timber intersections. Under load, they work to keep the angles rigid and prevent the building from racking out of square. To ensure that the frame is braced in every direction, braces are always used in pairs on opposite ends of a beam. When one of the pair is in compression, the opposite brace is obliged to be in tension—the brace in compression is attempting to close and the opposite one to open. (See the drawing on p. 26.) The brace in compression has to crush wood to fail, but the brace in tension only needs to pull the joint apart, a relatively easy task. Therefore, while all the braces are necessary, in any given racking-load situation it's probable that the braces in compression are doing the bulk of the work.

Corner posts are the most in need of bracing and the rest of the outside posts are more important to brace than interior posts. Braces are usually made from 3x5s or 3x6s and are generally between 30 in. and 50 in. long. It's hard to get very scientific about brace sizing because there have been no studies on the subject relative to timber framing. The general rules we follow are these: The long side of the brace should be a little less than half the length of the post it braces; braces are always used in pairs; a pair of braces should be used for approximately every 10 ft. in height and no more than every 16 ft. in length around the perimeter of the building. Be much more wary of under-bracing than over-bracing. These are not hard and fast rules, but we try to maintain a conservative stance. After the rigidity of a frame is ensured, the location and size of the braces can become an aesthetic decision.

Typical brace layout

DIAGONAL DIMENSION OF 3X5 OR 3X6 BRACE IS A LITTLE UNDER HALF THE LENGTH OF POST IT BRACES.

If long, reversed braces can be used without interfering with the other needs of the building, a strong case can be made for joining the brace bottoms to a horizontal timber and their tops to a post. The first brace to encounter the racking load therefore responds immediately with that very effective compressive resistance. (The typical situation, shown in the drawing on p. 26, requires that the first brace to receive the force should work in tension, which is not by any means its forte.) Still, you can't just brace the bottom ends of the posts, leaving the upper 4 ft. or 5 ft. unsupported, and normally it isn't practical to have a 10-ft.-long brace consuming the wall surface. But it makes sense to look for opportunities to use reversed braces, since their efficiency and strength can make it possible to reduce the total number of braces required.

Though diagonal braces primarily oppose lateral forces on the frame, they also help the frame bear vertical loads. The normal floor loads in a frame are first carried by the horizontal members—the joists, girts and summer beams. We determine the dimension of these timbers by first calculating the pounds per square foot to be borne by the timber using figures given to us by the local building codes. By calculating sizing formulas and evaluating the span of the timbers and the way in which load is distributed, we can assign a structural contribution to every timber in the frame once the wood species has been determined. If a beam were to fail, it would probably sag greatly first, then break. We dislike breaking, so we exercise careful control over deflection. But as the span of a timber increases and/or the imposed load becomes heavier or more centralized, to control bending we must generally either reduce the span or use a bigger timber. If knee braces help support the span, however, it should be possible to choose a timber that would otherwise be borderline. Braces channel the vertical load from beam to post, changing the reaction to the forces from bending to compression. And since wood is much more resistant to compression than bending, that's the good news.

The bad news is that although performance and common sense lead us to believe that we understand how diagonal braces work, when engineering the frame we are still not able to assign quantitative values to their load-bearing function. There just isn't enough data yet to put the effectiveness of a brace into the formula. And so, until more testing and analysis can be done, we calculate the size of the timbers as though the braces weren't there. The result is that frames have another built-in guarantee of durability.

Reversed braces give a compressive resistance to racking loads. Because of the placement of the intermediate connecting girt, these braces can be relatively short; if the girt weren't there, the braces would need to stretch from the top of the posts to the floor, making them impossibly long.

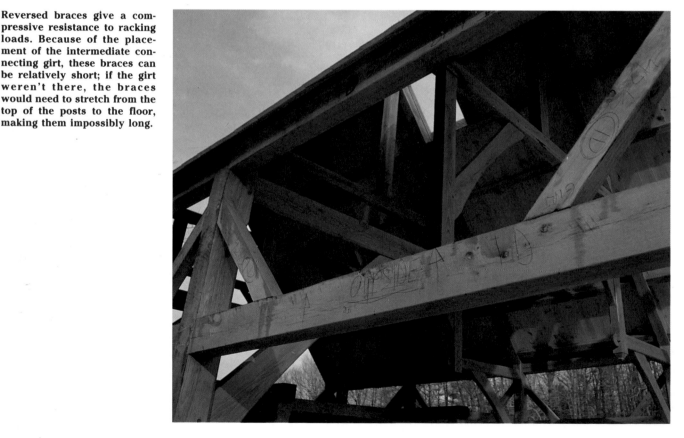

The floor system

The timbers in the floor support the loads applied in the spaces between the bent and wall beams. You can therefore look at each space as needing an individual floor system, with the following considerations bearing upon the arrangement and size of the timbers: the distance to be spanned, the loads to be carried, the structural capacity of the joining timbers, and the design goal of laying out the floor plan with a positive relationship to the timbers.

A major requirement of a floor is that it be stiff. Each timber should support its intended load with minimum acceptable deflection. A bouncy floor is an insult to the rest of the frame, and comparable to putting a Chevette engine in a BMW. To avoid bounciness, it is important to make sure that floors are not designed with extreme spans. A study of old barns in England shows that 16 ft. is the most common distance between bents; the study conjectures that the reason for this is to allow two yoked oxen to walk side by side in the bay (the space between bents). After a number of years in the framing business, I am convinced the real reason is that 16 ft. is the maximum practical span for a timber carrying a floor load. Beyond this, the timbers would have to become very large to limit deflection.

There are several common ways to arrange the timbers in a floor, as shown in the drawing below. Using parallel joists spanning between bents or walls is probably the simplest approach. The joists split up the floor load evenly and, at the same time, provide an understated look. But when the loads and spans demand that the joists be excessively large (anything above 6x8, in my view), timbers arranged this way can also seem overbearing. It is then usually more desirable to focus the loads onto a few large timbers. Large spanning timbers such as summer beams are especially useful if they join to posts, thus directly transferring the floor loads. Like other major timbers, these beams can also be used to define living areas. For most situations, we like the interplay between large and small timbers and actually work to divide the floor with large timbers into visually manageable subdivisions. The large spanning timbers often are embellished to give the frame some formality and refinement.

In addition to their load-bearing function, the timbers of the floor actually tie the frame together. If the distance from outside wall to outside wall is more than the length of a single timber (which, of course, it almost always is), there needs to be additional connection to keep the bents from spreading. When good joinery is used, floor joists or summer beams serve this purpose adequately, providing continuous support.

Some floor-framing options

CONNECTING GIRT

FLOOR JOIST

BENT GIRT

SUMMER BEAM CONNECTS TO POST.

SUMMER BEAM

FLOOR JOIST

SUMMER BEAMS

Depending on the size of the timbers, parallel floor joists can be either subtle or overbearing. These, made from fir, affect the feeling of the room without being dominant.

Good joinery is the basis of fine timber framing. Here the continuous post is flared on two levels to receive beams for the second and third floors.

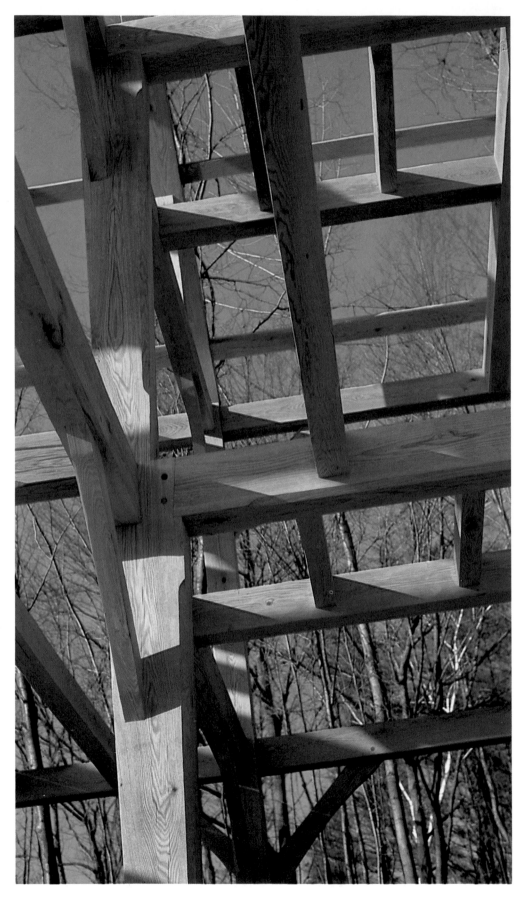

Joinery

In timber framing, joinery is practically the definition of the product. Without joinery, there is a structure made with posts and beams, but it is not a timber frame. It was the discovery of simple joinery that made the first frame possible, and it is intricately worked, complex wooden joinery that holds together some of the great architectural masterpieces of the world. Joinery is a complex subject, and here I'll just summarize a few basics. Look to the bibliography for more information on selecting and cutting timber-frame joints.

An important guideline in timber-frame design is that none of the joints should be more complicated than necessary. The loads and stresses of the building need to be supported by the frame and the entire frame should be securely connected through the joinery. But beyond these rules, design concentrates on using joints that can be made efficiently and that are within the skills of the joiner. Without going out of the way to pursue esoteric or convoluted joints, you will invariably find enough surprises and challenges to keep the hands and mind occupied.

Most timber joints are variations on the mortise-and-tenon—a tongue on one timber is received by a slot in the other. The simplest version of this joint is used to connect vertical timbers to the frame and for joining two beams with minimum loads; knee braces and collar ties generally use an angled variation. Mortise-and-tenon joints are locked with rounded pegs driven through holes drilled through both parts of the joint, although some sophisticated joints rely on wedges and geometry to lock. The other broad category of joints used in timber frames consists of lap joints, such as dovetails and scarfs. Variations of lap joints can be used in many parts of the frame, as we will discuss later. Some of them rely entirely on their angular shapes and the weight of the timbers to lock, others are overlapped and then locked by wedging them through mating notches.

Which joint to use where? Joints must be chosen on the basis of the tasks they are to fulfill, including locking the frame together, bearing weight and transferring forces and building loads from one timber to another. A timber transferring a compression load will need a joint with enough bearing surface to withstand crushing. A timber in tension must be firmly bound with a joint that can prevent its withdrawal. If a timber is exerting an outward thrust, as a rafter exerts on a collar tie, it needs to be restrained by buttressing within the joint.

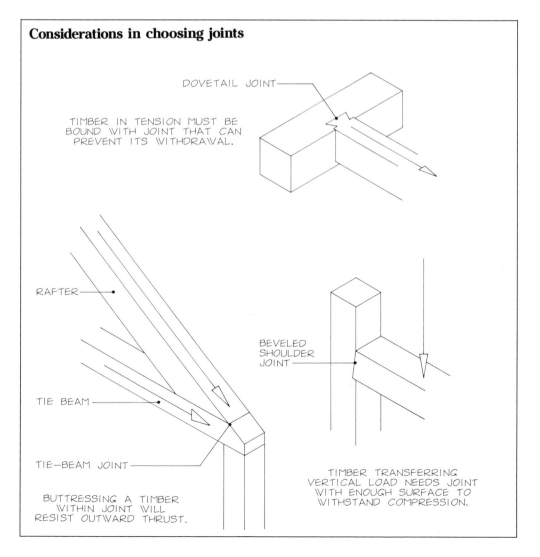

Considerations in choosing joints

DOVETAIL JOINT

TIMBER IN TENSION MUST BE BOUND WITH JOINT THAT CAN PREVENT ITS WITHDRAWAL.

RAFTER

TIE BEAM

TIE—BEAM JOINT

BUTTRESSING A TIMBER WITHIN JOINT WILL RESIST OUTWARD THRUST.

BEVELED SHOULDER JOINT

TIMBER TRANSFERRING VERTICAL LOAD NEEDS JOINT WITH ENOUGH SURFACE TO WITHSTAND COMPRESSION.

The mortise-and-tenon   The simple mortise-and-tenon can be very effective in resisting both tension and compression forces. We'll look at tension first.

In tension, there are three ways a joint can fail: The pegs can break, the wood between the end of the tenon and the pegs can pull out, or the fibers can fail between the edge of the mortised timber and the pegs. The perfect joint would have no one of these factors more likely to fail than the others under extreme tension—all three failures would occur simultaneously. Practically, however, we lean toward making sure there is enough wood between the pegs and the end of the tenon, because this second type of failure is abrupt and fatal; the others are gradual. For most woods, the mortise should be a minimum of 4 in. deep and the centers of 1-in.-dia. oak pegs should be placed about 1½ in. in from the edge of the mortised timber. Mortise-and-tenon widths in hardwood timbers work well at 1½ in. and should be 2 in. in softwoods.

To increase the tensile strength of the joint, increase its depth and thickness and use additional pegs when the width and length of the tenon allow. For instance, in a collar tie it might be important to increase timber depth just to increase the surface area of the tenon, allowing more pegs and leaving more wood to surround the pegs. But balance this with a consideration for other joinery and a judgment about the amount of wood removed from the receiving timber. If three beams meet at the same spot on a post, enlarging the mortises might weaken the post to an unacceptable degree. It is critical to remember that very often increasing the strength of one part of a joint decreases the strength of the other. Unless the two parts are balanced, the joint is faulty.

The ability of a joint to bear weight depends on the amount of surface area involved. Imagine for a moment the ideal situation of a load from a beam being transferred to the top of a mid-span post through a mortise-and-tenon. The joint here needs only to lock the two pieces together, and the entire remaining surface area of the connection—the shoulders of the tenoned (vertical) timber—transmits the load. The joint poses little compromise to the strength of either beam or post and, with the full width of the beam in the middle of its span bearing on the post, the beam is in little danger of shear failure.

The situation changes drastically, however, when the beam bearing the load is joined to the length of a post rather than to its top. The weight borne by the beam is transmitted through the base of the tenon, and as the load increases, it becomes necessary to find a way to increase the surface area at the base of the joint or shear failure of the tenon becomes a possibility. In a simple mortise-and-tenon, the load-bearing capacity of the joint is thus limited to the shear value of the tenon alone. (Wood species with lower allowable shear stresses would require larger timbers and also larger tenons to support the same load.) Of course there is a limit to how much a tenon can be enlarged, for the larger mortise required to house it can compromise post strength drastically.

The small bearing area of the tenon not only reduces the potential strength of the beam under load, it also gives the connection only superficial ability to resist eccentric loading, which can cause torsion. Torsion is a rotational force caused by overloading a member on one side or the other. Floor joists connected to only one side of a beam, rafters connected to a plate, and a queen post off-center on a bent girt are all examples of situations that could cause eccentric loading and resultant torsion. In fact, such conditions are much more likely to contribute to failure than is the inability of the base of the tenon to support the load.

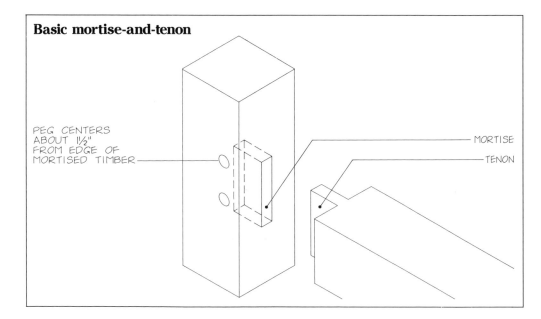

Basic mortise-and-tenon

PEG CENTERS ABOUT 1½" FROM EDGE OF MORTISED TIMBER

MORTISE

TENON

To make the mortise-and-tenon significantly stronger in resistance to shear and torsion, we increase the surface area of the joint by letting the beam's width into the post. When the joint is angled so that only the bottom surface of the beam rests on the post, it is called a beveled shoulder joint; when the post is notched to allow the entire beam end to be received, it is called a housed joint. We generally use either a beveled shoulder or housed joint to connect all load-bearing beams, such as bent and connecting girts and summer beams, to posts. Angled variations can be used where principal rafters join to posts and for diagonal braces. We determine how much of the beam should be let into the post based on loading, torsion, other joinery in the area and wood species. We have found, for instance, that spruce tends to twist while drying, and so in frames built from this wood we house all the joints. When beams are housed or shouldered, remember that tenon depth needs to be increased or tensile strength will suffer. Remember also that while it is necessary to get sufficient bearing for the beam, it is also necessary not to weaken the post unduly. (Beam-to-beam joints are particularly problematic because very often neither can afford the strength reduction.) It's up to the designer to evaluate the problem and figure out the best compromise.

Shouldered joints

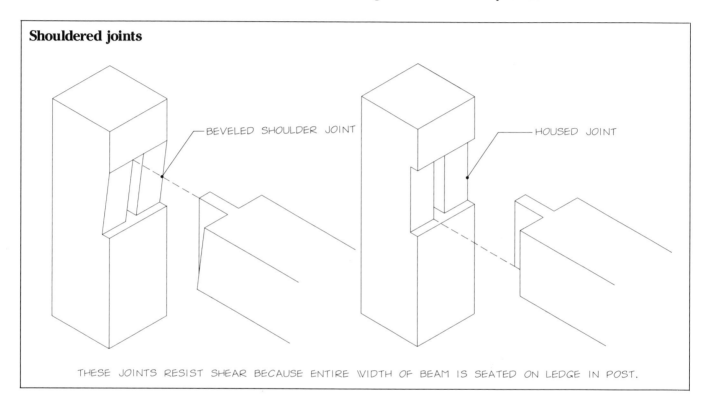

BEVELED SHOULDER JOINT

HOUSED JOINT

THESE JOINTS RESIST SHEAR BECAUSE ENTIRE WIDTH OF BEAM IS SEATED ON LEDGE IN POST.

Tusk tenons and soffit tenons are housed mortise-and-tenons used primarily for beam-to-beam connections. In both joints, mortises are cut parallel to the grain in the receiving beam to allow peg holes to be drilled across the grain. The English have a number of names for these joints, depending on the location of the tenon and the type of housing. For example, it is called a "bare-faced soffit tenon" when the tenon is cut at the bottom of the timber, a "central tenon with soffit housing" when there is a square housing at the bottom, and a "central tenon with a soffit spur" when there is a beveled housing at the bottom. In our communication with each other in the shop we don't use complicated names, so we think of the general class as either tusk or soffit tenons, with soffit tenons being those having the tenon at the beam base.

In beam-to-beam connections, where the mortise is cut mid-span on the supporting timber, it is necessary to ana-lyze loads carefully. The goal is to support the tenoned timber adequately while conserving the bearing capacity of the mortised member. Tusk tenons are useful because the mortise can be located toward the neutral axis of the timber, between the compression and tension zones (p. 27). Stronger still is a soffit tenon, because it puts the tenon and the support at the base of the beam. When the depth of the supporting beam is great enough to allow a soffit tenon to align with a mortise cut in the neutral axis, this most efficient kind of joint can be made. We have come to feel that the soffit tenon is usually the best beam-to-beam joint, and we try to use it wherever we can. The limitations on its use are based on raising technique and sequence. Obviously, it is necessary to carefully plan the raising to engage this joint on both ends. Dovetail joints, described on p. 46, are much more easily assembled than are soffit tenons.

Tusk and soffit tenons

SUPPORTING BEAM

PEG HOLE DRILLED ACROSS GRAIN

CENTERLINE

NEUTRAL AXIS SHIFTS BELOW CENTERLINE BECAUSE OF WOOD REMOVAL.

FULLY HOUSED TUSK TENON

SUPPORTING BEAM

PEG HOLE DRILLED ACROSS GRAIN

CENTERLINE

NEUTRAL AXIS

FULLY HOUSED SOFFIT TENON

An open mortise-and-tenon (sometimes called a tongue-and-fork) is often used to connect rafters at their apex and sills at the corners. (Lap joints, alternate but inferior connectors at sill corners, are discussed on p. 46.) It's actually the mortise that is open, cut completely through the end of the timber. The tenon is cut as usual, but is larger than in most other situations. When used for rafters, the mating members simply lean into each other and are pegged—the weight of the rafters and the roofing materials help keep the joinery secure. An open mortise-and-tenon at sill corners can be exactly the same joint, but placing it there is complicated by the fact that the sill usually receives a post at that location. Load is not a problem because there is full support from the foundation. The best solution would be to use a square tenon from the post to lock the corner. Another possible variation is to make the tenon in the shape of a dovetail, a design that provides further locking, as shown below.

Open mortise-and-tenon joints

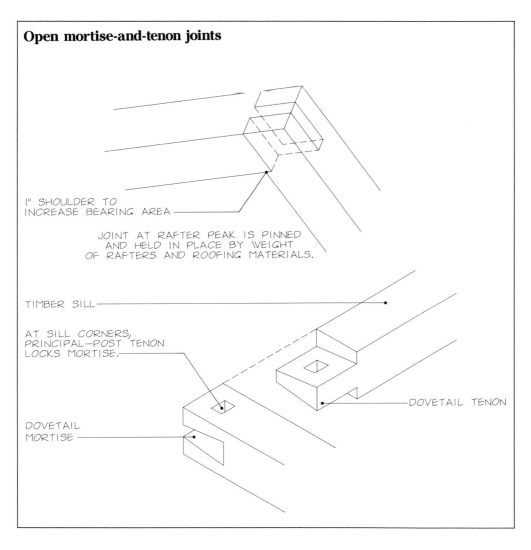

1" SHOULDER TO
INCREASE BEARING AREA

JOINT AT RAFTER PEAK IS PINNED
AND HELD IN PLACE BY WEIGHT
OF RAFTERS AND ROOFING MATERIALS.

TIMBER SILL

AT SILL CORNERS,
PRINCIPAL-POST TENON
LOCKS MORTISE.

DOVETAIL TENON

DOVETAIL
MORTISE

Lap joints The other broad category of joints are those that lap one member over another. The receiving timber is notched to accept a tenon, or lap. Unlike the mortise-and-tenon joint, the tenon is not completely surrounded with wood when the joint is engaged; the joint is secured either with pegs or through the use of locking geometry. My own theory about lap joints is that they evolved in response to raising techniques. Early English frames, for instance, which use a great number of lap joints, were most often made by small groups of professionals and assembled one piece at a time. In this case, it would have been almost impossible to engage a mortise-and-tenon joint simultaneously at both ends, so lap joints were used instead. But as timber frames evolved in this country, most raisings involved the entire community, and raising methods and joints were developed to take advantage of this manpower. Large sections of the frame were joined together on the ground to be raised at once, using primarily mortise-and-tenons. Lap joints, which are often inferior to their mortise-and-tenon counterparts, were kept to a minimum, and usually used only for the smaller members of the floor.

Today we use lap joints primarily for beams in the floor and purlins in the roof. They can be straight laps but are more often dovetailed to resist withdrawal. These joints are frequently made with a housing or a spur to give the timber more support. The obvious problem with lap joints is that wood is removed in the compression area of the receiving beam, which can greatly reduce strength. Laps should never cut entirely across the top of the beam; even if joints are received from both sides, at least 2 in. should be left in the center. When a dovetail is used, it need not penetrate deeply into the receiving timber for good locking—perhaps no more than 2 in. If a straight lap is used, however, the tenon has to be deep enough to hold a peg, which is usually a mimimum of 3¼ in. long. The dovetail can therefore do the job with the least compromise to the supporting member. But the problem with the dovetail is that as the wood shrinks the joint becomes less effective in preventing withdrawal of the timber, which can be extreme when green timbers are used. To make sure the joint is securely locked and to reduce the effect of shrinkage, we use a tapered dovetail and drive dry wedges on both sides.

Knee braces and collar ties are also sometimes joined with straight or dovetailed laps. The best use of a diagonal dovetail lap is for the joint between a collar tie and a rafter when the tension forces will be significant. The biggest drawback to using a lap joint for knee braces or collar ties is that it has little ability to resist torsion, which could cause the joint to pull apart.

Types of lap joints

PEG

STRAIGHT LAP

WOOD REMOVED IN COMPRESSION AREA OF TIMBER REDUCES STRENGTH.

HOUSED DOVETAIL LAP

WEDGED DOVETAIL LAP

TENON IS TAPERED BOTTOM TO TOP. MORTISE IS ¼" LARGER THAN TENON AND THE WEDGES ARE DRIVEN HOME AFTER RAISING DAY.

Scarf joints are lap joints used to splice two or more shorter pieces into one long timber. Plates and sills most often demand scarfs because they tend to be the longest continuous members in a frame. There are hundreds of variations of scarfs, with varying degrees of complexity and effectiveness. Because so much surface area must be cut to fit, all scarfs are relatively difficult to cut, making them challenging and fun for the joiner. On the other hand, no amount of precision can fasten the halves together without compromise. A scarf-jointed timber is not as strong as a solid one and scarfs shouldn't be used to support floor or roof loads if they fall in a span between posts. The best position for a scarf is directly over a post, where it can splice effectively without compromising the load-bearing capacity of the beam. (The post tenon can be used as a key to keep the halves from slipping apart.) It is also possible to support a scarf joint with a knee brace. With various types of keys and wedges to lock the halves together, scarfs are strongest when employed to resist tension. Given their difficulty and limitations, it is sensible to minimize the number of these joints in the frame.

One of the most fascinating joints used in timber framing is actually a combination of joints used to connect several members. The intersection of a principal post, a plate and a tie beam is known as a tying joint. Although there are many variations, almost every one includes at least two perpendicular tenons on the post, one to join to the plate and the other to join to the tie beam. The tie beam is then further connected to the plate with a dovetail lap; it is also mortised to receive rafters. This type of connection was so prevalent through much of the development of English carpentry that to not find a tying joint in a surviving timber frame is somewhat remarkable.

Scarf joint

CENTER WEDGES COMPRESS AND LOCK SCARF.

SIDE VIEW

Tying joint

8X8 RAFTER

TENON (NOT VISIBLE)

RAFTER-FOOT MORTISE

8X8 TIE BEAM

DOVETAIL LAP (NOT VISIBLE)

PEG

DOVETAIL MORTISE RECEIVES TIE BEAM.

8X8 PLATE

PLATE TENON

TIE-BEAM TENON

8X12 GUNSTOCK POST

This scarf joint is supported by a post. The joist is connected with a tenon that falls between the scarf halves, helping to lock the joint.

III. Frame Design

The timbers of the frame should be used as a design tool and meshed with the overall floor plan. The goal is to develop floor and frame plans simultaneously.

In the preceding chapter we covered a lot of theoretical ground, and now it's time to put it into practice with a series of exercises. We'll start with a somewhat traditional saltbox shape, and then sort through a range of frame options within that shape—the objective being to integrate a good frame with the desired floor plan. In reality the frame plan and the floor plan would be designed simultaneously, as discussed in the next chapter, but before you attempt that process, the following background information will be helpful. It is important to know that for any given frame there are many options available, each having benefits and trade-offs.

The frame is actually a more flexible element of the house than you might think. It has to fulfill its structural function, but it can do so in any number of configurations. It makes absolutely no sense to determine the frame according to arbitrary criteria and then squeeze the floor plan into it. To bring the magic of the frame to the living space, the timbers should be used as a design tool, their full palette of possibilities explored. And of course a great frame design would fall flat if it were not within the ability of the maker and if resources were unavailable.

As we analyze the frame options in the rest of this chapter, we'll be looking at the following issues.

Strength Of course you would not deliberately design a weak frame, but it is surprising how easy it is to overlook the details. Many times a small modification yields a big improvement in terms of increasing strength. For instance, moving a summer beam a few inches might make a big difference in the amount of wood that's left between two joints. Moving a post even a foot could radically affect a beam span, eliminating a deflection problem. The frame also must be designed for a specific species of wood—what is good in oak may be a problem in fir.

Timber length and size It's extremely frustrating to find that you have designed a frame around timbers that aren't available. If you are uncertain, check with the sawmills while designing. Most mills have definite limitations; small ones often can't cut anything longer than 16 ft. The trees themselves have their own natural limitations. Northeastern species, such as red oak, grow much shorter than Douglas fir and southern pine, for instance. Loggers also play a role in the availability of long timbers. If they are accustomed to cutting for veneer or furniture stock, they habitually cut long, beautiful logs into short sections. We once gave 25-ft.-long measuring tapes as Christmas presents to a few loggers, feeling certain theirs stopped at 12 ft.

Complexity Do everything you can to make the frame simple and practical to cut. Justify every complication. By all means be certain that making the frame is within the capability of the joiner.

Raising method   While designing the frame, plan the raising. Will you be lifting bents or walls? With a crane or by hand? Will there be separate roof trusses? It's necessary to know something about the site to determine what is possible. We once arrived on a much ballyhooed "beautiful" site only to discover that, yes, it was just a few hundred feet from the road, but it was practically straight up. We had a difficult enough time getting tools on the site, never mind the timbers. We seriously considered a helicopter, but finally wound up transporting the timbers one at a time with a bulldozer. The raising proceeded slowly as we hung from trees and invented lifting mechanisms.

Raising sequence and connections   Place timbers so good joinery is possible. Be certain that each piece can be placed into the frame and pegged without undue difficulty. One of the biggest mistakes you can make is putting a timber in a position where other beams, posts or rafters make drilling or driving the pegs impossible. Don't ask how I know this.

Now we'll look at some bent options for the house shape shown below, which is a traditional saltbox except for the unevenly pitched roof. The change in pitch might have been selected purely for aesthetic reasons or because of the need for more headroom. All of the bent plans in this chapter work with this shape. Because so much of the frame is dependent on the bent timbers, we can initially study the entire frame by looking at bent plans. Major connecting timbers are indicated as darkened areas.

Option 1   In colonial times, the saltbox was often created by adding a shed onto an existing building. This bent plan therefore represents the approach that you might see in an old building.

In this option, the A, B and D walls each have plates, so the frame would be raised as walls instead of bents. After the walls were raised and the lower bent girts and post C were in place, the tie beam would be positioned on the walls and the rafters raised.

ADVANTAGES   This type of frame is easily broken into small sections for a hand-raising. Even the walls could be raised as two or three units.

The tie beam serves as the lower chord of the rafter truss, working in tension to prevent outward thrust. This is stronger tension resistance than could be achieved simply with a timber tying between rafters. The weakness in the tie beam would be the scarf joint, but the post tenon could pass through it to prevent separation.

DISADVANTAGES   Unless there is a specific need to detach the shed from the frame, the frame would be stronger if the shed were integrated. On the other hand, if the shed is to be a solarium, this design would facilitate a switch to a wood that would be suited to the excess heat and moisture. (See p. 184.)

Option 1

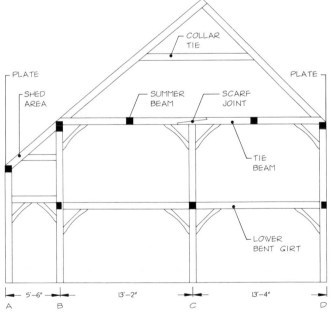

The roof is quite distinct from the rest of the frame, and unless the roof has wind braces, there will be little to prevent it from hinging.

There may be some shrinkage in total building height as the tie beam and plates shrink and the rafters settle. With the tie beam and three plates traveling the length of the building, there will be either a great many scarf joints or some extremely long timbers.

It's common for summer beams to fall mid-span between posts, but it is a condition to avoid. A mid-span point load could well require an increase in the size of the tie beam, especially when the frame is of a weaker wood.

Diagonal wind braces, here joining from the rafter to the purlin, are sometimes needed to prevent racking perpendicular to the bent.

Option 2 The big difference in this design is that the rafters sit on top of posts instead of plates; connecting girts span from post to post between bents. Here the mortise-and-tenon joints between the upper bent girt and posts will need to resist tension forces from the rafters. Struts assist these joints, creating triangulation and thereby rigidity.

ADVANTAGES Even if you could not get a timber long enough for the upper bent girt, only one scarf would be needed in each bent.

The bents could be assembled and raised as a unit, or raised lower section first, then rafters.

DISADVANTAGES The roof and the shed are still not well integrated with the frame. By now you should understand that the word *integration* is not meant to define a socially conscious concept, but is used to describe whether the frame has sufficient transverse members at central points for connection and rigidity.

Intersecting joinery makes it difficult to put the connecting girt at the top of the wall, which means sheathing has to span between this connector and the roof sheathing.

Option 3 The difference here is that the *C* post passes through the upper bent girt and joins to the collar tie.

ADVANTAGES Because the *C* post spans the hinging point at the top of the other posts, the bent is much more rigid here than it would be in Option 2.

The large braces joined to the collar tie support the rafters, preventing sagging and helping to limit outward thrust. I would feel safe letting these braces replace the struts in the previous bent.

Without a scarf joint on the tie beam, it is relatively easy to join the summer beam to the *C* post, which not only gives the summer beam better support, but allows the upper bent girt to be smaller, since it would not be supporting any beams mid-span. Here all major beams are supported by posts—a situation rarely achieved, but always a design goal.

DISADVANTAGES A 22-ft.-long timber is required for the *C* post, which might have to be as large as 8x10 to receive the bent girts and summer beams. A timber this size could be hard to get, and would certainly be hard to handle.

With so much of the bent interconnected, this structure would be difficult to break into small units for a hand-raising. It begs to be completely assembled on the deck and raised with a crane.

Option 2

Option 3

Option 4

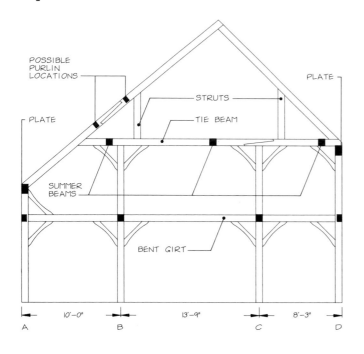

POSSIBLE
PURLIN
LOCATIONS

PLATE

PLATE

STRUTS

TIE BEAM

PLATE

SUMMER
BEAMS

BENT GIRT

10'-0"   13'-9"   8'-3"

A   B   C   D

Option 4 Here we go back to the same general theory as Option 1, except we move the posts to accommodate some hypothetical requirements of the floor plan. To create more headroom on the upper level, we also replace the collar tie with struts. The rafter load passing through the struts would have to be carefully calculated and the tie beam sized accordingly. (A difficulty with the lexicon of timber framing is illustrated here, where the tie beam on the *D* side looks more like a collar tie on the *A* side. Since it seems to be supporting more than tying, I call it a tie beam.) The knee braces extending from the *B* and *C* posts give good support. The rafter load on the part of the tie beam cantilevered over the *B* post would also need calculating. When there is a scarf joint mid-span between supports, as there is here in the *A*-side rafter, assume that the area of the scarf can carry almost no load. This scarf is therefore in a vulnerable position. If the rafter is accepting additional loads from purlins, the purlins should be positioned away from the joint.

ADVANTAGES The shed is integrated with the rest of the frame, not only strengthening the bent, but lending more possibilities to how rooms might be arranged with posts.

DISADVANTAGES The *A*-side rafter passes through the bent levels and is theoretically a better transverse tie, but the scarf joint reduces the strength of the connection.

There is still the problem of hinging between the rafters and the tie beam, especially on the *D* side.

The tie beam is another long or scarfed timber.

The summer beams on the tie beam don't align with posts. This might happen as a result of a desire to avoid the complex joinery necessary to bring a beam into an area already consumed by a scarf. It also might fulfill a need to get load-bearing timbers close to the eaves to support the third floor. In any case, they put a strain on the tie beam, especially between posts *B* and *C*, where the span is greatest.

The summer beam between posts *C* and *D* is a big problem. Because it is directly under the rafter, the joint could not be pegged if it were a mortise-and-tenon, and there is not enough space between the rafter and the beam to position it from above, as with a dovetail. Therefore, unless it was joined prior to the placement of the rafter, the only other alternative would be to use a rather exotic blind wedge or a through tenon with wedge. This is yet another lesson I learned the hard way.

This is a complicated assembly to raise. Try to imagine the sequence: First the two outer walls are joined by the lower bent girt along with the *B* and *C* posts; then the tie beam is placed over three posts; then the *A* side rafter is installed in one or two pieces; finally the *D* side rafter. The only advantage to making a raising this hard is to satisfy sadistic impulses.

Option 5 First, terminology. The tie beam that looked a little like a collar tie now looks like a bent girt on one end, so I'll refer to it as an upper bent girt. There are three important changes in this option: The first is that the *B* post joins to the rafter, helping to tie the bent together and reducing the length of the bent girt. The second change is that the *C* post has been moved so that the greater span is between *C* and *D,* to complement the hypothetical floor plan. Within the limits of acceptable beam spans, moving the posts doesn't always create structural problems. The third change is that the connecting girts substitute for plates.

ADVANTAGES With the upper bent girt reduced from 28 ft. to 22 ft., the probability of getting a full-length timber is greatly increased.

Eliminating the scarf joint means one of the summer beams can fall on a post.

The load on the *A*-side rafter is transferred immediately by the *B* post instead of going from the strut through the tie beam first, as in the previous option.

Support for the rafter scarf is improved by placing it directly over the post. (Option 4 might have been improved by placing the scarf over the strut.) In each case, the rafter would be improved if there were no scarf.

With the plates removed, this bent can be assembled on the deck and crane-raised as a unit. Besides being more efficient and ensuring better fits, a crane-raising is much safer than a hand-raising.

DISADVANTAGES Although the scarf in the upper bent girt has been eliminated, there is still a requirement for long timbers—a 20-ft. post and a 22-ft. girt.

If a hand-raising were desired, it would be hard to separate the rafters from the rest of the bent, because you would have a scarfed 26-ft.-long rafter on one side and an 18-ft.-long rafter on the other.

Between *C* and *D* on the upper bent girt, the summer beam produces a one-point floor load almost exactly on the middle of the beam. Only one foot away is another point load from a strut, which will transmit a significant rafter load to the same beam. This would need careful analysis and it's certain that a large beam would be needed.

Because the upper bent girt lies between the rafter and the post on the *D* side, there is potentially more shrinkage here than on the *A* side where the rafter joins directly to the post. This is called differential settling, and it is a problem to be avoided in bent design.

Option 5

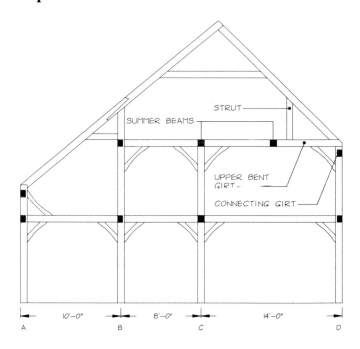

Option 6 Here the *C* post has been moved a couple of feet toward post *B*. Perhaps the narrow aisle-like space this creates would define an area used for the chimney, stairs and halls, providing access to the large space between *C* and *D* posts. Even though the beam span between *C* and *D* posts is large, I wouldn't hesitate to use this option if it clearly benefitted the floor plan.

ADVANTAGES Most of the major beams are still supported by posts.

By bringing the *B* post through the rafter, we've eliminated the scarf joint. This simple change in joinery means that the upper roof section is more detached and can be raised as a unit after the rest of the bent is erected.

DISADVANTAGES The longer beam spans created by moving the *C* post require larger timbers. If the frame were made from a wood with low structural values, spans such as these might not be practical. It would depend on how the floor interacted with the bent and the resulting timber size.

Although the bird's-mouth joint used on the *B* post might be an advantage in raising, it doesn't provide the lateral strength of a long scarf joint. Once again, there is less integration of the roof with the bent.

Since the lower girt, horizontal strut and rafter all join to the *B* post, the shed is again quite distinct from the rest of the frame.

The strut and summer beam still produce a significant load in one area. The position of the summer beam is better because it is closer to the support of the knee brace but the span has also been increased, which makes the two-point load more troublesome.

Differential settling is still a concern.

Option 7 I would consider this the most desirable arrangement of timbers for this bent. The simple change is that both the *B* and *C* posts join to the rafters, but doing this really solves some problems.

ADVANTAGES The vertical connection on both ends makes this bent extremely strong. There is no place where it could hinge.

The rafters join directly to posts for a strong connection and direct transfer of load. This would be a good design for some of the weaker woods because the spans are broken up and all the major beams are supported by posts.

Wood shrinks most across the grain, and because end grain joins to end grain at the rafter-post connection, shrinkage in the height of the building is reduced to an absolute minimum.

The upper bent girt is now a manageable length.

Ceiling height on the second floor is not confined to the height of the outside post. The upper bent girt can be placed anywhere along the length of the *B* and *C* posts.

Because the horizontal bracing used between the *C* and *D* posts is strong, it can be used as a design element to frame windows, divide living spaces or act as shelving.

The vaulted space between the *A* and *B* posts and the *C* and *D* posts can be used to bring a feeling of space and light, via roof windows, to the second-floor living area. This was true in other options as well, but because of the *B* and *C* posts, the outer areas are more defined.

Option 7

Option 6

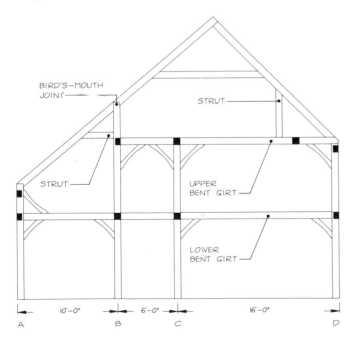

DISADVANTAGES   The major disadvantage is the need for long posts, in this case 22 ft.

This bent, almost without a doubt, would have to be crane-raised.

On raising day the connecting girts have to be joined to the upper ends of the posts. Someone has to be up on the bents to insert the tenons and one of the bents must be spread apart. It's hard work and tough on the nerves.

Carrying the central posts to the rafters has numerous structural advantages, such as allowing loads to be transferred directly.

Option 8 This option has exactly the same post layout as Option 7, with most of the same structural advantages, but it is put together with plates instead of principal rafters and purlins. It could be raised either as complete horizontal walls or as bents, with the plates and rafter installed after the bents were raised.

ADVANTAGES If for some reason the purlin system was not aesthetically desirable, this would be the most obvious out. Using plates, a common rafter roof or a principal and common rafter roof are possibilities.

It would be easy to break this frame into small units for hand-raising.

When enclosing the frame from the outside, the plates give nailing surface for the sheathing, so there's no need to span between the upper connector and the top of the rafter, as there would be in Option 2. Plates also make finish work easier from the inside because they create a logical transition between the walls and roof.

This would be the system to use if you needed a framed gable-end overhang. Extend the plates beyond the posts and join common rafters to the plates and you've got it.

DISADVANTAGES Perhaps the biggest problem is that this option requires two timbers (the plates on the *B* and *C* walls) that are completely unnecessary in Option 7. In addition, the plates on the *A* and *D* walls have to be large enough to support the weight of the roof from the rafters, a structural requirement also unnecessary in Option 7. The total amounts to a great deal of extra wood.

Raising day would have all the problems of Option 7, plus there'd be additional plates to raise.

Scarf joints or timbers the length of the house are probably required for all four plates.

When joining rafters to a plate, you can't expect to develop much tying strength. Mortise-and-tenon joinery is impractical from the rafter to the plate; there is usually only a notch with a face peg. It is important with this type of framing system to make sure that the bent is strong independently of the rafters through good connections between the posts, ties and bent girts.

Option 9 This bent demonstrates that there is flexibility in positioning posts when using the plate system. Note that with the greater span between the *C* and *D* posts, we have gone back to diagonal braces. An obvious difficulty is getting the extremely long *C* post in addition to the long plates. A frame such as this would be ideal for woods such as fir, larch or southern pine, in which long timbers are generally available. Otherwise, the advantages and disadvantages are the same as for Option 8.

Option 9

Option 8

Option 10 With the addition of a king-post truss at the roof, this is the same basic design as Option 7, and has the same advantages and disadvantages. The truss adds rigidity and strength to the rafters, although one could legitimately question whether it is necessary. But it's attractive, and might be nice if the second floor were left exposed to the roof. With braces from the king post to the rafters, the roof has good longitudinal rigidity. Placing beams on different levels avoids multiple joint intersections on the posts and opens up some interesting floor-plan possibilities.

Option 10

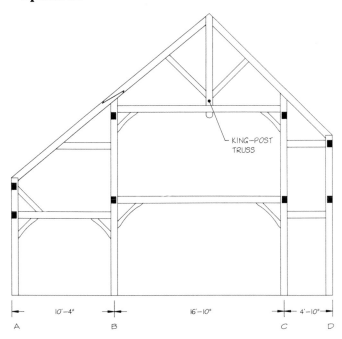

Option 11 By passing the king post to the lower bent girt, you might be able to use that member to create a natural division between rooms on the second floor. Although a king post with braces is able to join and tie rafters, generally giving adequate resistance to sagging and spreading, here I would want to assume the worst case, which is that the lower bent girt bears some of the rafter load.

ADVANTAGES The only advantage of this layout over Option 10 has to do with relating timbers to the floor plan.

DISADVANTAGES There is a potential, depending on the quality of the joinery and loads on the upper bent girt, for the lower bent girt to need to be inordinately large to bear the one-point load for the king post.

Option 11

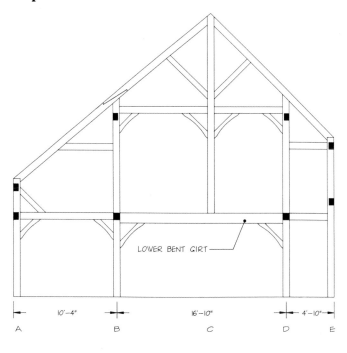

Option 12   This option employs a change in ceiling height without detriment to the strength or shape of the frame. Ceiling height is quite flexible with timber framing, as bent girts can be put anywhere along the length of the posts. In platform framing, people often feel compelled to stay within the normal 8-ft. stud length to keep costs down, which means ceiling height tends to fall within this range. While a great many studs will be required to frame the partitions in a timber-frame house, we try to align the partitions with major timbers; stud length is thus determined by the distance between the floor and the bottom of the timbers. Because of this, we can increase ceiling height to between 8 ft. 8 in. and 8 ft. 10 in. without going to a 10-ft.-long stud for interior partitions.

ADVANTAGES   The king post and collar tie combination strengthens the rafters and helps connect them. A tenon from the king post passes through the collar tie, keeping it from deflecting under load. The king post is also an attractive feature for a cathedral ceiling in the second floor.

Plates are used, but this bent could also be framed with a rafter-to-post connection, with a connecting girt replacing the plate. The collar tie and the diagonal strut would play a major role in limiting outward thrust at the *D* post.

DISADVANTAGES   The problem is that what is gained in ceiling height on the first floor is lost to the second.

Option 13   This bent forms a narrow aisle in the center of the house, which can work as an effective design element.

ADVANTAGES   The bent is strong and the parts well integrated; the *B* and *C* posts span nearly to the ridge.

The upper connectors on the *B* and *C* posts allow bracing near the top of the building in the bay direction, helping to keep the entire frame rigid.

All the major beams are joined to posts.

DISADVANTAGES   This frame requires very long timbers. The *B* and *C* posts would need to be 24 ft. The *A*-side rafter should not be scarfed until there is adequate support, so it would need to span 22 ft. from the *A* post to the scarf.

The long span between the *A* and *B* posts could also require some large timbers, especially if one of the weaker woods were used. The load from the strut is probably significant and would have bearing on the size of the beam.

Option 13

Option 12

Options 14 and 15 An asymmetrical bent plan might become necessary if the post-and-beam arrangement on the first floor needed to be different from that on the second floor. Neither of these frame plans would be my first choice, but I wouldn't hesitate to use them if it would greatly benefit the floor plan. The biggest problem is the introduction of an intermediate post on the second floor, which transfers a one-point roof and floor load to the bent girt; this timber would therefore need to be quite large. If the wood used for framing did not have good structural capacity, this option might prove to be impossible.

Option 14

Option 15

IV. Home Design

Getting from the frame to the floor plan is not a leap of faith, it's a heap of planning. In this interior, the hammer beams allow the living room to be spanned without posts, to create a cathedral ceiling. Timbers also frame the staircase, hallway and built-in shelves. (Photo by Bob Gere.)

The frame is such a dominant part of a timber-frame house that it's easy to infer that a good frame automatically makes a good house. It's all too tempting to first design the frame, to make it strong and theoretically good-looking, and to superimpose the floor plan upon it later. There's a comforting linearity to this way of thinking—you take care of the "important" issues, such as timber size, joinery and beam spans first, before turning to the "niceties." And indeed, if you work this way, you will probably be rewarded with a very nice frame. You also run the risk of creating a pretty miserable home. For the "niceties" (the aesthetic and practical requirements of the occupants of a house) are more necessary to good design than might at first be apparent. To neglect these requirements is to risk making a house that sits awkwardly on its site, that has an irresolvably poor traffic pattern, or that simply fails to be attuned to people and the environment.

Good house design is hard work, made more so by the fact that the path to it is not clearly mapped. You can enter any library and find volume after volume about construction procedure, with endless detail on how to make a house strong and safe. But how to make it look and feel good? How to make it work well with the needs of the people who live in it? This is much more subjective stuff, rife with theories and opinions. Perhaps the only generalization you can make on timber-frame house design is that timbers are not necessarily a decorative benefit, and if

they enhance and simplify instead of cluttering and complicating, you can bet it was planned to be that way. It didn't just happen.

In this chapter, I'll share what I know about designing timber-frame houses, beginning with the all-important preliminary work. Although much of this material does not contain the word *timber,* I do not digress, for good timber-frame house design is based on principles and practices of design that are good for any house. To do right for the timber-frame house, it is necessary to just do right. After covering these initial design concepts, including the building program and site study, we'll look at generating floor and frame plans. Finally, I'll backtrack a little to explore some ways to use the natural spaces created by timbers, and to discuss some of the design options that various arrangements of timbers provide both for the whole house and for each room. Of course it's impossible to learn to design a house from reading one chapter in a book, but there's much to be gained from developing an understanding of each element in the design process.

Ruling notions and the building program

It may seem obvious, but nothing is quite as important in design as understanding and addressing the reasons why a building needs to be built. Every house is born as a notion, and this original ruling notion is the seed from which the plan of the house grows and is ultimately defined. The first

Good house design balances needs and desires with budget and site requirements.

step is therefore to open that notion to discussion. It may be lofty or mundane; it may concern stylishness or a desire to conserve energy. It may express how a family wants to live or focus on a relationship with the outdoors, with artwork or with furniture. Most often there are several notions working in concert, but too often there is one that dominates all the others and paints its colors into every corner of the house.

A few examples illustrate how diverse and powerful ruling notions can be. One of the most common notions I see establishes a particular architectural style as a design prerequisite. In other words, the house is already a cape (or a ranch, or an underground house) before there is any understanding of the site or the living requirements of the occupants. This may seem innocent enough, but it's not. For while the strongly vertical lines of alpine architecture look great in the mountains, they look out of place on the plains. And while sprawling horizontal architecture may fit a family's image of expansive living, it might not fit their craggy hillside site. People will probably always have a preferred architectural style, but this should be considered an ambition of the design and not a ruling notion.

Another ruling notion I frequently see concerns the timber frame itself. People often approach us for a frame of a particular size and shape, but don't have any idea of how the frame will relate to the living areas—this will be worked out later, we're told. We try to point out that "a

24x36 saltbox frame" is not the right starting point for a home. Under these conditions, the features of the frame can turn into obstacles and the building process will turn into a remodeling project as the floor plan is forced to weave around existing structural ingredients.

A recent ruling notion I encountered focused on a very fine, very large Oriental rug, inherited by our clients. They had never been able to enjoy the rug because their living quarters were too small, so when they approached us about a house, they wanted to make sure there was plenty of room for the rug. A second notion was that the master bedroom should be on the first floor—no more going up and down stairs for them. Now these people were not wealthy and could not afford a large house, so you can imagine the difficulty of designing a small house with room for a 24x30 rug and a downstairs master bedroom. All early renditions of the plans had small, elongated spaces (kitchen, dining, entry, master bedroom and bath) gathered around the rug. It finally became essential to spend some time talking about these ruling notions. The rug stayed, ruling as ever, but the master bedroom went upstairs.

Good house design attempts to balance function, economy, form and energy performance into a unified package. But unless the ruling notions of a project are diagnosed and their consequences projected, the design will probably be thrown off center. Plans can still be drawn, and the house can certainly be built, but strong forces will be at work and they will elbow their way into the design time and time again. Obviously, overlooking economic realities could mean that the ceremonial first meal is cooked on a hibachi in a drafty shell. A house built to satisfy an artistic compulsion might well be better to look at than live in. Energy conservation is important, but there is a big difference between living on the inside of a solar collector and being comfortable. After defining the ruling notion, put it on the back shelf, address the many other design issues, and come back to it later. If it survives as the dominating force, it deserves to be.

The next step is to create a building program. A building program is nothing more than a list of requirements for the house, the landscape and exterior activities. It should include not only physical requirements, but also personal ideas about lifestyle. It might be important, for instance, that the living room be large enough for two settings of furniture, receive direct sunlight and have easy access to an exterior terrace. If it is important that the master bedroom be completely separate from other bedrooms and that it have enough room for morning exercise, this should be noted on the building program. After the program is completed, it's much easier to look at practical construction issues—how the house will be sited, how the rooms will be arranged—and the many decisions relating to materials.

Potential homebuilders should use the sample building program at the end of this chapter (p. 84), and think carefully about each answer. Be sure that when you've finished you have described the home you aspire to build. This does not mean that the final design will satisfy every whim. It simply means you determine the trade-offs while the plans are being drawn instead of discovering them later as faults. So be prepared for the compromises that you will inevitably have to make.

The site study and the bubble diagram

When the building program is complete, it's time to study the site and roughly describe the house that will sit upon it. Understanding the site is an essential part of design, and having a complete house design prior to a knowledge of where it will be built is like buying the pants before you know who will be wearing them. Placement of the house should be sensitive to land contours, forestation, flora, views and sunlight. At the same time, seek summer shade, protection from the wind and isolation from noise. Economics suggest careful consideration of the location and expense of the driveway, septic system and water supply.

Laying out a building on a site is mysterious work. Whether the site brims with potential or is featureless, there is always one place for the house that is better than any other. You wander about the property like a lost divining rod in search of that precious spot. It will help, during this part of the work, to take an analytical approach. Begin by drawing a site plan that shows all the major features of the land, an example of which is shown on p. 63. The easiest way to start the site plan is to photocopy or trace the site survey map. (If a site survey does not exist, consider having one made.) At the very least, use a description from the deed and draw the site and its contours from your own measurements and observations. Show on the plan all positive and negative features, such as the trees that should be saved, lowland or swamps, creeks, views, roads, potential access directions and neighboring houses.

Of paramount importance in siting is access to the sun, so also include on the plan the direction of solar south. Achieving a good relationship with solar south is probably the simplest part of siting because it can be done scientifically and reaps measurable rewards. Using only good orientation and proper proportions of glass and insulation, passive-solar houses are no longer considered difficult or

Listing all physical and lifestyle requirements in the building program gives the designer direction. For example, in this house sufficient mounting had to be provided for the hunting trophies, and space had to be reserved for the jukebox.

awkward. Their design begins with the two basic siting rules that follow.

To receive the maximum amount of solar heat, the house should face as closely as possible toward solar south. Solar south is not the same as magnetic south, because of longitudinal differences and variations in the earth's magnetic field. There is a simple method for determining solar south. Go to the site at solar noon (exactly halfway between sunrise and sunset, usually listed in a local newspaper). Hang a string with a weight to make a plumb line, and mark the direction of the shadow, which will be cast toward solar north; the opposite is solar south. Determine the compass heading of solar south so you can locate it in the future. It may not be possible to orient the building directly toward solar south, but a rule of thumb is to stay within 25½ degrees, because within this range you lose less than 10% of the potential solar gain through vertical glazing.

The next rule is to try to eliminate winter shading. The angle of the sun's arc changes throughout the year, being highest in June and lowest in December. Placing yourself in the position of the house, try to follow the path of the sun from sunrise to sunset as if it were a December day. The arc you would follow depends on your latitude. (For instance, at my house the sun follows an angle of about 24½ degrees to the horizon on December 21 at solar noon.) Better yet, get out there on a December day and watch what happens. You are looking for anything that obstructs the sun, such as hills or trees. Depending on what you find, the house may have to be moved or trees may have to be thinned and pruned.

While trying to eliminate December shading, you will be grateful to have some in summer. If there are deciduous trees, the house might be positioned so it is shaded by the crown of a tree in June, but less obstructed after the leaves have dropped off in the fall. But remember that even bare branches can cause heavy shading. These may have to be pruned to allow sunlight to pass through.

A thorough understanding of the site is then blended with the building program to create the basis for the house plan. Try to fit all the important elements of the home onto the site with a bubble diagram, as shown below. In addition to living areas within the house, also locate the driveway, parking area, garage, woodshed, septic system, terraces, gardens, barn, pasture and any other required feature. The process of completing this diagram will naturally spur some decisions about the floor plan. For example, if the driveway needs to be to the east of the house to complement features of the land and reduce expense, it

Sample site plan

NORTH

DOTTED LINE DEFINES AREA ENLARGED IN DRAWING.

1300' ELEV.

TREE LINE

SOFTWOODS

CONTOUR LINE

TOWN ROAD

SWAMP

COUNTY ROAD

Sample bubble diagram

MAGNETIC SOUTH

SOLAR SOUTH

NORTH

TOWN ROAD

DRIVEWAY

GARAGE   BREEZE WAY   KITCHEN   SOLARIUM

LAUNDRY BATH   DINING   LIVING

FORMAL ENTRY   STUDY

would not make sense to put the garage on the west. If the parking area were toward the north of the house, it would not make sense to put the main entry on the south. And if it were possible to site the house to capture a view, you would probably rather see it from the living room than the laundry room. Likewise, it is not usually prudent to waste solar-heating potential on a little-used bedroom when it could be better used in a major living area.

With the position of a few essential ingredients, many other parts of the house follow. For instance, because you would be going from the car to the house on the east side, it makes sense to put the kitchen to the east so groceries would not have to be carried across the house. For convenience, the dining area should be close to the kitchen. The kitchen is roughly located toward the southeast and the living room is toward the southwest, with the dining room in the middle. Laundry, bath and other utility areas are shifted toward the northeast, opposite the kitchen, to keep plumbing areas together and separate them from the living room. The rather extravagant formal entry falls adjacent to the living area. Eventually, a meaningful design begins to emerge, which combines the wistful desires of the building program with the attributes and limitations of the site.

Also arising out of this process should be insight into the general shape of the house. Once again, it is important to be sensitive to the land rather than to rely on preconceived notions. Obviously, the shape of the house must accommodate the living areas and their relationship to the outdoors. It should be open to the sun, buffer winds and make the views available. Perhaps most importantly, it must consider economics and energy conservation. These two concepts fit together because they have a similar goal: to pack as much as possible into a structure with a small total surface area. As a building is stretched out and convoluted, its foundation area is increased along with the surface area of the walls and roof, creating a need for more labor and materials. The additional surface area also allows more heat to move from the inside to the outside. Still, good architecture demands that we try to find a balance. The shape and form of the house should have intrinsic aesthetic value.

For timber-frame houses, intrinsic aesthetic value means that the shape of the building should be true to the language of the material. Remarkable symmetry and beauty are almost inevitable when timber framing is practiced well in its simplest form, and there can be no doubt that it begs to create rectilinear buildings that directly reflect the shape of the timbers. To ask the craft to shape a curvi-

Classic building forms, such as this story-and-a-half colonial, are almost automatic in timber-frame construction and are seldom design failures. At right is an interior view of the same house. (Photos by Brian E. Gulick.)

linear building, for instance, risks that the timbers will become awkward and clumsy and perhaps that the joinery will be stretched beyond its limits. Very complex buildings having numerous corners, layers, jogs, angles, turrets and dormers (as in highly decorative Victorian-style buildings) are best constructed with frames that have their fudge-factors hidden behind plaster walls. Timber-frame buildings of such complexity need difficult joinery, require the best efforts of the finest timber craftsmen and cost like the dickens.

Let the dictates of the site and the building program be the greatest influence on house shape and style. At every turn, choose simplicity over complexity—there is no shame in simple, classic building forms, which seldom disappoint and almost never fail. Most of the traditional styles that dominate architecture were born as timber-frame structures; they were refined through the centuries as the skills and aspirations of the builders evolved, but it was an evolution with no radical leaps. Instead, the master builders were confident enough in the formula, or "pattern language," that they used the same styles to construct both cottages and cathedrals. Within this ancient language lie flexibility and variations that are as suitable for 20th-century buildings as they were hundreds of years ago.

A Standard Set of Plans

1. **Site plan**
2. **Foundation: plan, sections, details**
3. **Floor deck: plan, sections, details**
4. **Floor plans: each level**
5. **Elevations: all sides**
6. **Building sections: where necessary**
7. **Interior elevations: where necessary**
8. **Typical wall plan**
9. **Kitchen plan and elevations**
10. **Chimney (masonry) plans and sections**
11. **Stair plans and sections**
12. **Exterior roof and wall trim details**
13. **Interior trim details**
14. **Garage plans and sections**
15. **Exterior deck or porch plans and sections**
16. **Greenhouse or solarium details**
17. **Electrical plans: each level**
18. **Plumbing plans and necessary sections**
19. **Bent plans: every bent**
19. **Timber wall plans: every wall**
20. **Timber floor system plans: each level**
21. **Panel plans (where applicable): each elevation and each roof side**

Notes on design

Generating floor and frame plans is the next step, but before embarking on this, consider these additional points.

Be prepared to do (or have done) the most meticulous, complete set of final plans possible. Houses are simply too expensive and too complicated for decisions to be left to a carpenter on a coffee break. The bitter reality of housebuilding is that it is like getting mugged by a thief; the house will demand the entire bankroll and frisk you again before the job is finished. The route from the bank to the completed house must thus be carefully mapped, and only with a full set of plans can you know that the house will meet your expectations and do so within budget. A full set of plans means that every item in the house has been accounted for and every detail in the assembly has been precisely explained—from the depth of the foundation hole, to the configuration of each joint in the frame, to the mounting of the last closet pole. This detailing defines the material and labor necessary before the project commences and is the only way to control costs.

At left is the standard set of plans that we use. Creating such a set of plans is likely to be quite expensive (between 5% and 10% of the total building cost), but there is no better investment. We have worked with a few homebuilders who have done a fine job with their own design and planning, but most people do not have the skills or time necessary to do a good job with blueprints. Homebuilders choosing this course should be wise enough to know what they don't know and, at the very least, retain professionals who will act as consultants.

Homebuilders choosing to work with a professional architect or designer should select this person carefully. The ability to create good architecture out of the simmering pot of information collected on the site and from the building program is a talent that does not come to every person. A good designer can stir it all together and bring to the house those tasteful lines that go down easily with the ecology of the site and the geography of the area. Enduring designs are born in humility, of the understanding that very few buildings are an aesthetic improvement over no building at all. Unfortunately, this is not a concept stressed by schools of architecture. Too often, architects emerge from their educational dens and immediately attempt to capture the world with the latest artistic snares. At the very least, make sure the designer you choose is familiar with the timber-frame system—suggest this book and others in the bibliography. Also make sure the designer has a copy of your building program and refers to it often. At interim meetings, you might even want to go over the list together as a way of analyzing decisions that have been made. And remember, working with a professional does not mean noninvolvement. A designer should not be expected to put together a house design without a great deal of input from the clients.

Of course, an alternative to designing your own home or hiring a professional designer is to use a stock design as offered by some timber-frame companies. This may seem like the ultimate design crapshoot, but if you start by going through the preliminary design steps discussed earlier and then search to find a plan that fits your requirements, the process can work quite nicely.

Generating floor and frame plans

This stage of design is a little more complicated than the previous steps, because the designer must decide on dimensions and precise spatial relationships, and address how the house is expected to work. While I discuss the rudiments of developing frame and floor plans in this section, the details on arranging the timbers within the house are covered in the two following sections, beginning on p. 69. I chose this organization because I wanted to cover basic design methodology before going on to the more refined aspects of using timbers in a floor plan. Make sure you read those sections before charging into design work.

The birth of the floor and frame plans out of the notations in the building program, the wanderings on the site and the musings about the bubble diagram are rather magical events. Out of the chaos comes order, and sometimes no one person involved is quite sure what made it happen. But if the groundwork has been accurately laid, even the first efforts at a floor plan can be pretty accurate.

Begin with a block diagram, as shown at right. Modify that as necessary and draw a floor plan, locating major posts and beams. In these first attempts, the goal is to find an acceptable arrangement of rooms and timbers, and to see if the sizes of the spaces seem adequate. To be truly useful, however, the early floor plans should quickly evolve to include some finish and construction details, although there is no need for exhaustive detail at this stage. Stairs, chimney, partitions, closets, cabinets, plumbing fixtures, and door and window locations should be shown because the plans can't be properly analyzed otherwise. The bathroom space won't make much sense unless it is seen in relation to potential fixtures. The kitchen must be seen with cabinets, and bedrooms should have closets.

Locating the posts and beams in even the very earliest renditions of the floor plan makes sense both structurally and aesthetically. Posts can't be located without anticipating the relationship they will have with intersecting beams and studying the impact of these timbers on the overall plan. But while it's necessary to consider the floor plan, the frame plan and indeed the shape of the building as a unit, it's also important to realize that all these components should be able to stand on their own merits. This means that if it is helpful to change the building's shape to suit the floor plan, this should not be done at the risk of creating a house that is awkward or ugly. And while beams and posts can be moved to accommodate design goals, these decisions should neither cause the frame to become structurally deficient nor make the frame overly difficult to assemble. This may seem obvious, but it is the most common pitfall in timber-frame design. It's all too easy to remove a critical timber or brace, to stretch a beam beyond its normal capacity, or to contort the frame into an uncomfortable position.

To avoid these failings, it's necessary to keep redrawing floor and frame plans as you continue to refine and alter the design. Creating initial frame plans requires a concept of the shape of the house, an idea born from aesthetic judgment and an understanding of the site and the potential living spaces. The skills and intuition of a good designer are essential here. In its crudest form, the initial frame plan can be a stick representation of potential bent plans

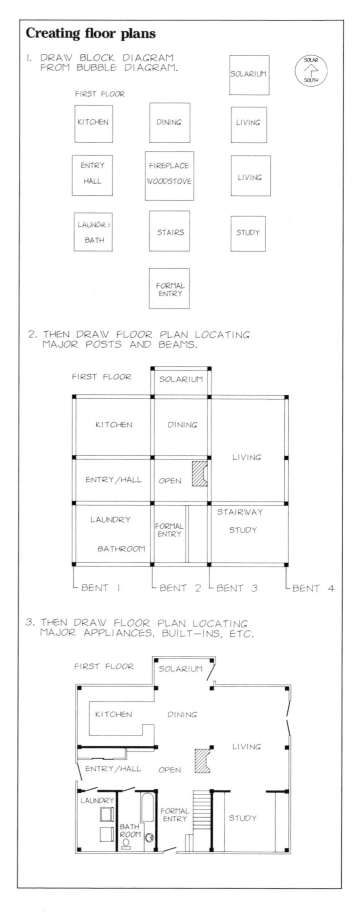

Creating floor plans

1. DRAW BLOCK DIAGRAM FROM BUBBLE DIAGRAM.

2. THEN DRAW FLOOR PLAN LOCATING MAJOR POSTS AND BEAMS.

3. THEN DRAW FLOOR PLAN LOCATING MAJOR APPLIANCES, BUILT-INS, ETC.

as posts and major beams are positioned on the floor plan. As design progresses, show the relationship of bent girts, summer beams and connecting girts to the floor plan with dashed lines (as shown in the drawing below). It is not necessary to go into further detail on beam arrangement until the plan is more finalized, but it is useful to shade the posts on the floor plan to show they consume space.

As illustrated in the previous chapter, the development of the bents is critical. Bents are usually the dominant structural element in the frame and they also determine the shape of the building. The way timbers are placed in the bents affects ceiling height as well as the feel of the spaces in the house. So not only should each bent be structurally sound, but as you juggle post length, beam heights and rafter intersections, you need to think about the use of space. As the floor plan becomes more defined, the frame plans should likewise develop into a complete set of plans to prevent oversights and structural inconsistencies. Eventually the bent plans must show all members, with accurate dimensions on timber locations and lengths.

As the design develops, also sketch onto the bent plans the location of windows and doors. Most people strive to center these on a wall for symmetry, using the floor plan to determine their positions. But in fact, windows and doors are best centered between braces, which aren't even visible on the floor plan. Sketching them on the bent plans makes it easier to remember that, when viewed from the inside, windows and doors are actually seen in relation to the timbers in the frame.

Designing a floor plan is filled with uncertainty because dreams finally meet hard reality. It's a time for listening to common sense and practicality. Do not design beyond the budget. Pay attention to the movement of the sun and the direction of the wind. Conserve energy. Consolidate pipes. Give people a place for privacy as well as places to congregate. Above all, even if the decisions seem complex, the floor plan should not be; you will never go wrong if you simplify. Eliminate unnecessary partitions. Straighten convoluted paths and get rid of clutter. The house can be intriguing without being mystifying.

Preliminary floor and frame plan

WINDOWS AND OTHER MEMBERS DRAWN AS DESIGN PROGRESSES.

INITIAL FRAME PLAN CAN BE SIMPLE REPRESENTATION OF POTENTIAL BENTS.

Bays, aisles and whole-frame systems

While designing, it's important to have a good understanding of the spaces naturally created by timbers and how they can be used for maximum aesthetic and pragmatic benefit. A major objective of timber-frame design is to use the timbers for more than structure, to integrate the living areas with the timbers in a balanced and harmonious way.

The natural spaces in timber-frame houses are bays and aisles. (These spaces are shown in the drawing on the facing page.) Bays are the areas between bents, and are the dominant spaces. They run from the front to the rear of the house on each level. Most timber-frame houses have between two and four bays, the common width of which ranges from 6 ft. to 16 ft. Most typically there are three bays, with the outer two being wider and containing the bulk of the rooms. The narrower central bay contains the entrance, hall, stairway and chimney. Each of the outer bays is designed to hold compatible rooms. For instance, the more formal and private areas would be placed together in one bay, while the work and utility areas would be grouped together at the opposite end of the house. The rooms on the other levels are organized to be compatible with the rooms on the first level. Rooms with plumbing would be stacked, for instance, and second- and third-floor rooms requiring privacy would be placed over the more private rooms of the first floor. This commonsensical approach is why traditional timber-frame homes are a model for many modern designs, even for non-timber-frame houses.

A bay may contain one room, such as a living room or large bedroom, or several rooms. In the latter case, intermediate posts and summer beams or joists are used to define the areas and to provide attachment for partitions, although very often several rooms function in a single bay without partitions; here timbers suggest the transition from one space to another, as detailed in the next section. Kitchens and dining spaces work well this way, as do living

Looking from bay to bay in this home, we see a division of spaces defined by bents.

Within a bay there can be one room or several. The timbers in this bay, as well as the low ceiling over the dining room, distinguish the living areas.

rooms and study or TV areas. It's also common for areas to be open to each other among several bays—we have built a number of houses that have almost no partitions on the first floor. A single living level might contain the kitchen, dining area, living room, study, several entry halls and a bathroom. The bathroom would be enclosed, but all the other areas would be defined only by timbers. A benefit to an arrangement as open as this is that heat can move freely throughout the house, but the obvious drawback is the lack of private space.

Running perpendicular to the bays are the aisles, which, like bays, are usually not much wider than about 16 ft. If a frame is designed as a series of walls instead of bents, aisles are the more natural spaces. The posts in the walls would have to be parallel to each other, but in the bent direction interior posts would not have to align, which would offer design flexibility. If defining the spaces with aisles is more beneficial to room layout, this is the best reason of all for designing a frame with plates.

Barns are often arranged in aisles, having a central entrance for vehicles at the gable end, which allows the unloading of equipment and animal feed into the outer aisles. Most timber-frame churches and halls are also built like this, but in houses the proportion of common living area to

The living area in this house is arranged in an aisle space instead of a bay. A portion of the middle bay is left open for dramatic effect and for air circulation.

overall house area is usually more conducive to the use of bays. To illustrate this point, imagine a building about 30 ft. wide by 36 ft. long with equally spaced posts, creating three bays and three aisles. The bays would be 12 ft. on center and the aisles 10 ft. It is a lot easier to think of a potential room being half a bay (12 ft. by 15 ft.) than half an aisle (10 ft. by 18 ft.). While a living room might well consume a whole bay, for it to consume an entire aisle (10 ft. by 36 ft.) would be absurdly out of proportion.

Ease of assembly and raising also often dictate that frames be designed as bents rather than walls. Most of the rooms thus fit within bays, with one or two spaces being defined in aisles. (Since most frames have identical bents, aisle spaces are almost always available.) When the house is oriented with a south-facing eave, we often design a solarium by continuing the roofline of the main living area to create an aisle with sufficient glazing for good collection, as discussed in Chapter IX. As long as the posts continue through the frame in the same alignment, living spaces can be stacked in aisles just as they are in bays. When a room is on the outside eave wall of a building with a post length shorter than 16 ft., the space is left open to the roof for drama, but also because there would not be a great deal of added living space close to the eave anyway.

The most efficient way to use space within a house is to stack living areas from outside wall to outside wall in each bay and aisle. But what is most efficient is not always most desirable. Often it is advantageous to leave areas open through several levels, or to change floor and ceiling levels in certain areas to improve proportions or create visual divisions. We like to leave a portion of a central bay open to allow heat to travel into the other living levels, but (thinly disguised) this is also an excuse to create a view of more of the frame and to introduce a feeling of spaciousness and drama to a home. It's also possible to leave an entire bay completely open, both vertically and horizontally. This is especially effective in an otherwise small and tightly organized house. Taken to extremes, efficiently used space sometimes feels miserly and cramped, but just a small touch of playfulness can change that entirely.

Level changes in a floor plan can be used effectively to follow the slope of the site or to alter the feeling of a room. Because in timber framing we are not confined to common stud lengths, within a given timber bay or aisle it is possible to have floors (and ceilings) on several levels. This also avoids the problem of several joints intersecting at the same spot on a post, which would weaken the post. The builders of old barns almost always put floors and haylofts

This aisle solarium was created by extending the roofline in two of three bays. The principal rafter is supported by the solarium plate.

on several different levels, as joinery dictated, and there is no reason why this framing consideration can't be used as a design feature in houses as well. Public spaces and places for entertaining, such as living rooms, family areas and dining rooms, should have higher ceilings than places for contemplation or intimacy.

When bays and aisles are not large enough in themselves to adequately serve a design purpose, it's possible to use an entire frame to enclose an area. Used with a trussed roof system, not only is it possible to create a large, unobstructed area (usually with a cathedral ceiling), but in such a space the decorative effect of the timber frame blossoms. In most situations, the truss would have beams spanning the width of the space—a king-post truss is a good example. The drama of the open roof is best suited to living and family rooms, but we have used it for bedrooms, entries, kitchens, porches and even baths; the extra volume in the open roof might be an inefficient use of space (depending on whether there is enough area to be considered usable), but it is surprising how easy it is to trade a little economic folly for a fine feeling. Remember that just because this option calls for a whole frame,

there's no reason why the frame has to be large. The idea works just as well with small spaces.

Whole-frame areas can be either completely separate, attached to the rest of the house from just about any angle, or integrated into the other bents—same shape, different arrangement of timbers. (See Chapter IX for more details.) It's typically easier to keep the frame separate, because you can then fit it to the house without having to align it with the other bents. When all living areas will be on the same level, the entire floor plan can use whole frames. Since no living space would be needed under the roofline, the pitch of the roof could be decreased to reduce wasted space, and the trusses could be designed primarily for beauty. Living areas can be arranged any number of ways, but more variety is possible if smaller wings are appended to a larger central core. If bedrooms, baths and utility rooms can be moved into attached, appropriately sized frames, they will not have to find definition inside the main structure. Obviously, consolidation of the floor plan is indicated when the desire for heat efficiency is strong or the state of the owners' finances is weak.

Designing with whole frames

Timbers and room design

The timbers in each wall and ceiling of a house exert enormous influence on the feel and use of the rooms. The way timbers are arranged within a room is therefore influenced as much by the occupants' planned usage and ambition for the overall mood of the house as it is by structural requirements. As we've already seen, timbers can make a space feel expansive or cozy, public or private. They can also enhance impressions of massiveness or airiness, formality or playfulness, even brightness or darkness. The wood species and general finish treatment of the timbers further heighten the effects created by their arrangement—rough-sawn pine timbers left natural will add rusticity, whereas planed oak timbers stained and oiled to a glossy finish will give the house elegance.

Some insight will inevitably be gained and ideas will no doubt be refined while you work through the building program. Narrow the choices by thinking of the rooms and their potential contents as a three-dimensional still life, with the timber frame working as a picture frame. You probably would not want to imprison a Frederic Remington in a heavily embossed gilt frame, nor would weathered barn boards suit a Renoir. If the desired ambience of the house is formal and the furniture will be ornate, give the frame that quality, too.

We have a rule that we follow to achieve the ultimate integration of a timber frame with the living area. We apply this rule to large rooms and small, important and secondary. We use it on rooms with partitions and those that will never have walls. It is a straightforward rule, stating simply that to give a space boundaries, each room must be defined with timbers. This means that rooms should always be designed with a post in each corner and beams around the perimeter, as illustrated by most of the interior photos in this book. Under the roofline, this might mean having a pair of rafters at each end of the room. As well as offering visual advantages, this rule also makes sense from the standpoint of construction. A carpenter can easily attach plates and studs for partitions to timbers in simple, rectangular wall sections. If timbers are not arranged this way, partitions often must weave around them, causing both studding and finish work to become unnecessarily complex. Of course there will be cases where it's not possible to design a post in each room corner, but these should be exceptions.

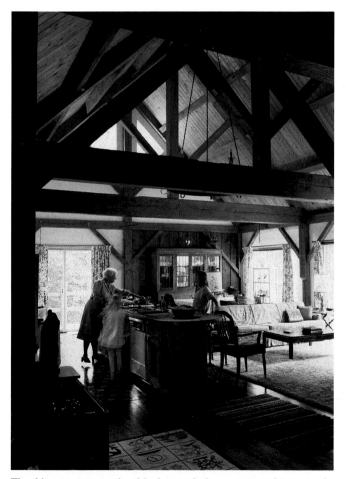

The king-post truss in this house helps create a large unobstructed space that is used here for the kitchen, dining and living areas.

Under the roof, spaces are usually defined with rafter pairs on two sides.

To further understand available options in timber arrangement, let's explore several ways to manipulate some of the framing members in the floor plan below. (This is the same house that was generated earlier by the bubble diagram.) Notice that the bents start out exactly the same, with Bents 2 and 3 having an extra post each to frame the solarium. The changes we'll be making, shown in full on p. 81, don't alter the basic floor plan, but they do affect the timbers and the use of space.

Let's look first at the passage between the kitchen and dining room on the south side of Bent 2. The posts, braces and beam form a clear and elegant division between the two spaces, a doorway without a door, a partition without a wall. Curving the braces softens the angles and makes the arch more formal. Larger braces make a stronger, bolder statement. For an even more distinct separation, we could eliminate the braces, frame the passageway with two posts and then add built-ins for china between the door frame and the outside posts. Integrating finish details in this manner helps keep the house uncluttered. We'll choose this option for our final floor plan.

When changing members of the frame, remember to pay attention to the structural requirements. In this case it's okay to remove the knee braces, because the reversed braces above the bent girt add rigidity (see the drawing on p. 79). Knee braces are sometimes used for looks where they're not needed for strength, but it is important to know for a fact when they're necessary and when they're not.

In Bent 3, we have several framing options. The original design (shown at the top of the drawing on p. 75) suggests the transition between living and dining rooms, but to further define it (and for convenience), we might add a wood-storage bin next to the chimney. For the visual benefit of the frame we would keep the bin shy of the ceiling, and if

we felt that the masonry didn't integrate well with the frame, we might add a post to the bin edge, creating a narrower passageway to the living room. We'd balance this with a post on the opposite edge of the chimney. While considering these changes, we'd look at the dining area, since the posts in Bents 2 and 3 would no longer be aligned. Must they? No, for while the bents should be bal-

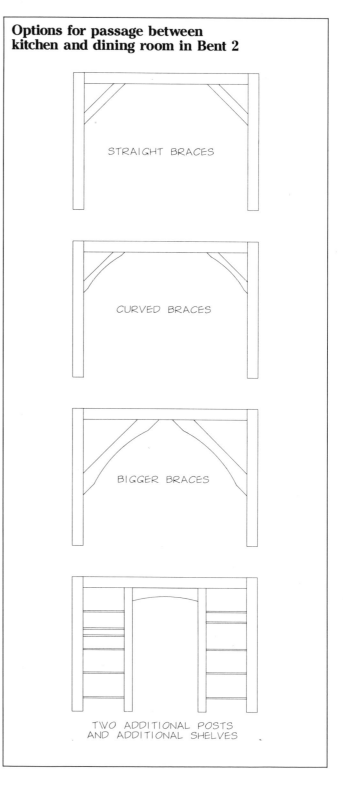

Options for passage between kitchen and dining room in Bent 2

STRAIGHT BRACES

CURVED BRACES

BIGGER BRACES

TWO ADDITIONAL POSTS
AND ADDITIONAL SHELVES

First floor

SOLAR
SOUTH

SOLARIUM

KITCHEN

DINING

LIVING

ENTRY/HALL

OPEN

LAUNDRY

FORMAL
ENTRY

BATHROOM

STUDY

BENT 1

BENT 2

BENT 3

BENT 4

anced, in this case the concept of integrating some of the functional necessities of the house into the frame is a balancing agent in itself. Besides, both passageways would have an archway created within the original frame. So for our final floor plan, we'll choose the last option.

The drawback to this series of changes is that the dining room now has hard boundaries, which will make it smaller.

(See the final revised floor plan, p. 81.) Without the extra posts and wood bin, the east and west sides of the dining room had more space for traffic and to accommodate an extended dining table for large groups. But given the new boundaries, the extended dining table will probably have to be arranged in the north-south orientation, with large crowds spilling over into the solarium.

Options for passage between dining and living room in Bent 3

Framing a French door

TIMBERS ADD FEELING OF WEIGHT, CONTRADICTING FEELING OF DOORS.

SIMPLY CENTERING DOORS BETWEEN BRACES IS BEST SOLUTION.

On the south end of Bent 4 there is a French door leading out to a deck. There are two choices here. The door can be framed with timbers or simply centered between braces. I favor the latter approach, because timbers around the door add a feeling of weight, which contradicts the intent of the door. By contrast, the arch formed by the braces suggests an opening. Simplicity wins out on this one. I would keep the door trim as soft as possible, either opting for no trim at all or painting a simple wood trim the same color as the walls.

The north end of Bent 4 is identical to the south, except there is a window instead of a door. But before making any decisions, we should consider the other ingredients in the study. Are there bookshelves and built-ins? Is there wainscoting around the perimeter of the room? Should this room have subdued light? Assuming the answer to all these questions is yes, we might consider framing this wall differently from the one having the French door. To stick with our theme of integrating finish elements within the frame, we'll cap the wainscoting with a small timber made from a compatible wood. Timbers will frame the sides of the window, and bookshelves will be built in between the window posts and the outside posts. The darkening effect of the extra timbers will also benefit the room by keeping the light from being overbearing. For symmetry, the window is centered.

On the opposite wall of the study is our first interior partition. When interior partitions align with timbers (as they should), you have to determine the side on which the knee braces will be visible. Splitting a timber with a partition requires that partition framing be individually fitted around the braces—a time-consuming task. Usually we expose the braces to the central areas to give the house more continuity. This particular wall is a toss-up because one side faces the privacy of the study and the other is somewhat hidden by the stair. What clinches the decision in favor of the stair wall is the floor-to-ceiling cabinet in the

Framing a window

BUILT-IN SHELVES

SMALL TIMBER CAPS WAINSCOTING.

TIMBERS FRAME WINDOWS.

study that would cover the braces anyway. So the best thing to do is to build the partition on the study-side of the braces, leaving their full thickness exposed to the stair. Still, the brace that falls on the upper part of the stair and the posts will cause some difficult finish work, because the stair parts will have to be scribed around them.

The wall of the main entry opposite the stair is a plain partition wall. For plumbing reasons (see Chapter VIII), and because so little of the frame would be visible anyway, it makes sense to move this wall toward the bath and expose the frame to the same degree as the opposite wall. When finished, this would be just a wall with timbers and braces, perhaps useful as a place for a small gallery of art.

The downstairs bathroom in this house is neither large nor luxurious, and we don't care if we lose the effect of timbers there. In the laundry room, we throw aesthetics out the window and allow the needs of the room to dictate timber and window arrangement. The only inhibiting factor is the symmetry of the exterior wall—the window should be centered between the braces.

This brings us back around to the east wall of the kitchen. Here the ingredients that need to interact with the frame are a window and the base cabinets. We want as much morning light as possible, so the window is large. To keep the arrangement simple and consistent with our other changes, we might choose to simply center the window between braces with simple trim. It would be possible to frame a timber backsplash between the posts, but it certainly would not be necessary.

East wall of entry

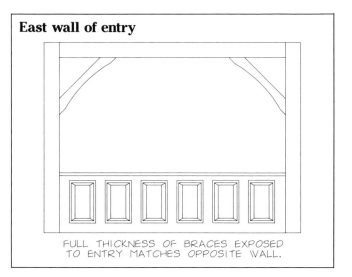

FULL THICKNESS OF BRACES EXPOSED
TO ENTRY MATCHES OPPOSITE WALL.

Two sides of a partition wall

CORNER BOARD

FULL THICKNESS
OF BRACES
EXPOSED
TO STAIR

WEST WALL OF ENTRY

TIMBER POST

BUILT-INS COVER
PARTITION WALL.

EAST WALL OF STUDY

The arrangement and size of ceiling timbers should be designed carefully, since they have a strong effect on the feeling of a living space. Large, closely spaced timbers give this ceiling weight and symmetry.

Posts in the walls can be as much as 16 ft. apart, but ceiling joists can rarely be more than 4 ft. apart because they generally support loads from the floor above or from the roof. The impact of such closely spaced timbers (and not insignificantly, over your head) is strong; the way a room feels is greatly influenced by the ceiling beams. If they lack symmetry, the room will feel disjointed, and if the ceiling is low, the beams will make it feel lower. The structural requirements are defined by the loads that must be carried, but there is almost always a variety of ways to satisfy the requirement. In the kitchen, for instance, we could simply span between the two east-west timbers with joists. The span would be less than 10 ft., so the joists would not be large. By using a simple, repetitious pattern and increasing the span between joists as much as possible, the least expressive treatment is created.

On the other hand, if the kitchen would benefit from a focal point, particularly if there were a working island in the center, a large summer beam would be a great addition. It would further subdivide the space, allow the joists to be smaller and might even prove handy for hanging kitchen implements.

The ceiling for the living room also deserves examination, and with the first stroke of my pencil I would raise it. I want more volume for this space, partly because it ought to feel different from the other living areas and partly because I think different ceiling heights are just more interesting. Of course this could cause some finishing difficulties on the second floor, but it might be worth it. The first step in changing the height is easy—we simply move a series of bent girts and connecting girts up to another level. Bent 3 will have the greatest change because it will need to have girts on the common level for the study while also receiving the timbers for the raised living-room ceiling. But this is not difficult or complicated. The study is introspective while the living room is expansive; the change in feeling is accentuated by having these two different kinds of areas side by side.

Raised living-room ceiling in Bent 3

THESE RAISED GIRTS SUPPORT BAY 3 FLOOR JOISTS.

THESE GIRTS SUPPORT BAY 2 FLOOR JOISTS.

Kitchen ceiling framing options

FLOOR JOIST

SUMMER BEAM

With that done, let's look at four different ways of framing the living-room ceiling. The first is a series of equally spaced joists, spanning from bent to bent, a simple but dull approach. Also, because each joist would probably have to be fairly large (approximately 5x7 in oak and 6x8 in fir), this option could easily be too overbearing for some tastes.

The next arrangement uses one large summer-beam timber in the middle of the room. The ceiling is now much more interesting, and the joists can be smaller. The problem is that this solution ignores the fact that there are two other posts that could also carry beams. So I think this option would look odd, especially since the reason for the extra post is to define the fireplace—a major ingredient in the room. The next logical step would therefore be to lo-cate a summer beam on each fireplace post. This strong, asymmetrical arrangement would influence potential furniture settings, but it could work, especially since the room seems to be aligned in this direction anyway. If this system were chosen, I'd want to keep all the joists the same size even though the shorter spans could use smaller timbers, since varying joist sizes would be visually disruptive.

The final possibility would be to add a summer beam over the wood-bin post in Bent 3, for greater symmetry. All the joists now could be quite small, which would further emphasize the summer beams. With the higher ceiling in this room, I would choose this last option, feeling the proportions of the room would benefit from the relatively close grouping of large timbers.

Living-room ceiling framing options

EVENLY SPACED JOISTS

SINGLE CENTRAL SUMMER BEAM

SUMMER BEAM DEFINES FIREPLACE

SUMMER BEAM INTO EACH POST

The completed floor plan is shown below. I am not endorsing it, nor do I intend to imply that good timber-frame house design requires extreme manipulation of the frame. On the contrary—very often the simplest route is best. The points I wish to illustrate are that it's worthwhile to work to make the design right, and that the construction system need not be an obstacle to that pursuit. Consider function and resources in every corner of the house, for every surface, in every room; aspire to make art. There's no shame in falling short, but it's silly not to try.

Revised floor plan

Two more floor plans

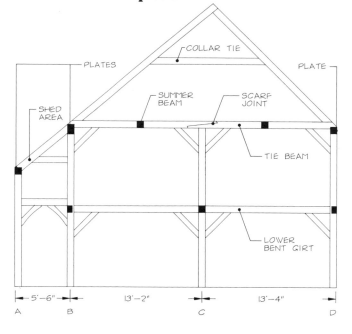

In Chapter III we analyzed 15 different bent plans of the same overall shape. Now I'd like to go back to Options 1 and 13, giving each a hypothetical floor plan to see how design requirements and floor plans might have evolved together. I'm using these only to demonstrate how floor and frame plans can work together, not to represent ideal designs. Also, these plans depict a rather large house, but this is only because the bents used in Chapter III needed to be large enough to show detail. Remember too that design begins on the site and includes many personal considerations, including budget. Different people with different sites and budgets would come up with different, but equally serviceable, plans.

The floor plan shown below follows the design logic described in this chapter, depicting a classic three-bay house oriented toward solar south. The central bay houses the stair, foyer and solarium, and gives access to the outer bays on both floors. On the first floor, only the bath and closet have partition walls; all other living areas are clearly defined by bays, timbers and other features. The south kitchen cabinets, for instance, align with bent posts and a summer beam, establishing the boundaries of the kitchen without walls. The middle bay, chimney and stairway help isolate the living room from other areas. The solarium falls between the A and B posts and could be separated from the rest of the plan if necessary. Because the shed part of the frame is distinct, it would be possible to use a different wood species for the solarium.

Since the bathroom and closet are not particularly well separated in the third bay, it would probably be helpful to add additional posts between the D and C posts to further define the partitions at the corners. I would also want to look for ways to integrate the fireplace mass and the stairway into the frame more definitively.

The second floor follows the first, with plumbing stacked and bedrooms falling over the major areas of the first floor. A rather steep stairway to the third floor could be located over the stairway to the second floor, but Bents 2 and 3 would have to be designed without collar ties to allow passage from the central bay to the outer bays between rafters. Queen posts would probably do the job, if it was certain they would not overload the tie beam.

This plan falls into place without a struggle, partly because it is large and simple, but mostly because it is based on a "pattern language" that has been used for timber-frame houses for centuries.

The floor plan shown below is quite different, even though the arrangement of bents and bays is basically the same, because living areas are defined primarily by aisles. The main entrance is through the gable end instead of the eave side of the building. Like the other plan, this one is organized to capture the sun in the major areas, but the southern orientation is toward a gable instead of an eave. The impetus for this arrangement would have been derived from siting considerations—in the morning the breakfast area and the kitchen would receive the sun; you would see it set in the living room. The central aisle houses the entrance and the stairway. Only the dining room and the study fall within bays. Since the stairway is already outlined with posts and beams, it offers a great opportunity to be completely integrated into the frame. Overall, the floor plan is well defined by timbers. Only the division between the study and the bath/closet area is a problem, but a large beam could be used to cap the partition.

Probably the biggest problem with the first floor is that the fireplace is poorly positioned in the living room. It would have been better to center it on the room's east side, but since the masonry can't go through the bent, it had to be placed on one side or the other. With further work, perhaps the fireplace could be pushed to the south, with the flues and mass corbeled toward the middle bay after the firebox.

On the second floor, the master bedroom falls in the aisle over the living room, but the other bedrooms and the bath fall in the outer bays. All the second-floor rooms work quite well with the frame. The biggest problem is that the bath is located over the breakfast area, creating some plumbing problems (see Chapter VIII for a complete plumbing discussion). A chase could be developed in the cabinets, but it would be easier if the bath were located over a convenient plumbing wall.

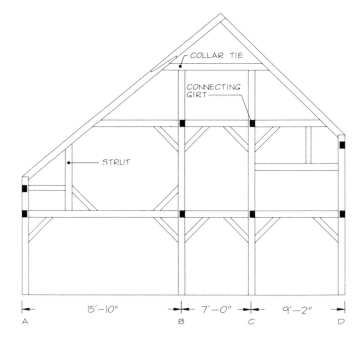

The stair is in a good location to provide access to the third floor but, as in the other plan, Bents 2 and 3 would have to be rearranged to give headroom for passage along the length of the building. An easy framing solution, given the availability of long timbers, would be to extend the *B* and *C* posts to the rafters.

Both of these plans represent good starting points for the development of frame and floor plans. They mesh well with each other, even in this rough state. As design continued, I'd expect both the floor plans and the frame plans to be altered, reflecting further integration and refinement.

Sample Building Program

Part I

The following will help you consider the pragmatic design aspects of your home. The proposed sizes of rooms, their function, and the needs and activities of the occupants will determine the layout and dimensions of your house. Your answers to the questions below will help to determine design priorities, as well as identify any extras.

1. List projected occupants (family members, relatives, etc.).
2. List pets, livestock, etc.
3. Projected time of occupancy of each occupant (life, to 21 years, seasonal, etc.).
4. What transportation vehicles, construction equipment, farm equipment, etc., do you need to store, and what kind of shelter is required?
5. Have you determined the approximate total square footage of required living areas? If so, what is the square footage? How did you arrive at this size (existing situation, family size, number of bedrooms/baths, future needs, furniture arrangements, etc.)?
6. List any circumstances particular to you or your family that may affect design (handicapped people, medical needs, noise considerations, lighting, air quality, temperature control, etc.).
7. Should expansion flexibility be a consideration? Do you know what rooms will need to be added and how large they might be?
8. List activities and amount of time to be spent in rooms/spaces below, and approximate space required. Reference to and measurement of the spaces in which you now live may be helpful. Keep in mind furniture, equipment, storage requirements, etc.

Living	Bedroom 2
Family	Bedroom 3
Kitchen	Bedroom 4
Dining	Guest
Sunspace	Study/library/den
Baths	Project room
Utility/laundry	Basement
Pantry/storage	Garage/shop
Bedroom 1	Other

The following suggests other possible rooms and spaces to consider:

Closets	Playroom
Greenhouse	Breakfast nook
Airlocks	Porch
Mudroom	Patio
Darkroom	Hot tub
Powder room	Pool
Broom closet	Sauna
Linen closet	Exterior wood storage
Dressing room	Courtyard
Interior wood storage	Barn

Part II

This group of questions is intended to help you pinpoint how you would like your life and your living space to interact. Try to consider how things feel as well as how they look, and remember the flow of people, things and food through the environment. Indicate the things that you find disturbing and the things that have a relaxing effect.

Bedroom

1. Do you like to wake up in a bright and/or sunlit room?
2. Do you like to be able to look outside while lying in bed?
3. Do you prefer the bed to be a particular height off the floor?
4. Do you prefer windows, a fan or an air conditioner for ventilation?
5. What are the privacy requirements of the bedroom from the outside and from the rest of the house?
6. What are your storage requirements? Give size and general description of items.
7. Do you like a separate dressing area?
8. Does the bedroom also need to function as a study, T.V. room, sitting room, etc.?
9. What sleeping accommodations will be necessary for other family members or in the future? (Use the first 8 questions as guidelines.)
10. Would you feel comfortable if the bedroom had a cathedral area or would you prefer a flat ceiling?

Bathroom

1. What are the special qualities you like in a bathroom? Does it need to be especially bright or roomy?
2. Should there be a bathroom attached to one or more bedrooms?
3. How private should the bathroom be from the rest of the house and from the outside?
4. Do you need a bathroom easily accessible from the outside?
5. Do you prefer fans or windows for ventilation?
6. Do you like to be able to see out a window while showering, washing or using the toilet?
7. Do you use the bathroom in a hurried or a leisurely manner?
8. Do you prefer showers or baths?
9. Do you bathe with others?
10. When you take a shower or bath, do you use the bathroom to dress or undress?
11. Do you have a preference for a particular brand of fixtures?
12. What requirements do you have for mirrors?
13. What are your storage requirements?
14. What sort of bathing accommodations are necessary for other family members now or in the future? (Use the first 13 questions as a guide.)

Kitchen

1. What times of day and to what extent do you use the kitchen?
2. How many people should be able to use the kitchen at the same time?
3. Will the kitchen be used for eating as well as for food preparation?
4. What appliances are necessary?
5. Is there a particular appliance/fixture arrangement that suits you best?
6. Do you like to be able to look out the window while working in the kitchen? If so, from what area?
7. Do you like a bright or sunlit kitchen?
8. Is it important to have an exhaust fan in the kitchen?
9. How do you prefer to deal with waste and garbage?
10. Where and how would you like to store your food?
11. How much cupboard or drawer space do you need?
12. Do you like pots and pans, dishes, utensils and food to be visible or hidden?
13. Would you use timbers to hang pots and pans?
14. What non-food items do you store in the kitchen?
15. What other items (such as desk, T.V., fireplace) would you like in the kitchen?
16. Should the kitchen be separate from the rest of the house or linked to other areas?

Dining

1. What sort of feeling should the dining area have?
2. Is the dining place a single or multipurpose area?
3. Is there a need for a guest dining area separate from the normal family dining area?
4. How many people should the dining area accommodate?
5. Is natural or artificial light, or both, appropriate?
6. What is the best way to get food and dishes to and from the dining area?

Living

1. How do you want the living area to feel?
2. Should it be separate or integrated into other living areas?
3. What activities go on in the living area?
4. How many people should it accommodate?
5. Should it have partitions and doors?
6. Should it be bright during the day?
7. What sort of artificial light is compatible with your image of the living space?
8. Is a fireplace desirable?
9. List any equipment you think should be in the living space (stereo, books, video, etc.).
10. How do phones and T.V. figure into your life?

Miscellaneous

1. What should the predominant feeling of the house be (rustic, informal, elegant, etc.)?
2. How would you describe the style that makes you feel most comfortable (modern, colonial, etc.)?
3. What are the attributes of the timber frame that would help to achieve the above requirements?
4. What other rooms or activity areas are necessary (study, playroom, darkroom, shop)?
5. What guest accommodations are necessary?
6. Is additional storage space necessary?
7. How much interaction between the indoors and outdoors is desirable?
8. Do you like transitional spaces (porches, decks, etc.)?
9. Do you see the exterior landscape as formal, casual or natural?
10. What requirements do you have for outdoor activities and accessory buildings (pool, tennis, gardens, horses, basketball, etc.)?
11. What is your attitude toward dirt? Where do you mind it and where is it okay? How do you clean it up and how often?
12. How many vehicles do you have and how do they fit into your life?
13. Do you have pets? How many and what kind?
14. Plants? How many? Special requirements?
15. What sort of textures do you like?
16. What colors do you like?
17. List the things you can't do in your present environment that you would like to do in your new environment.

V. Skins and Frames

The development of insulation systems in this century has changed our expectations of interior comfort. Higher R-values make it possible for passive solar heat to be retained for long periods. (Photo by Brian E. Gulick.)

Through most of human history, people expected temperatures in their homes to rise and fall with the temperatures outside, to be only moderations of exterior extremes. But the development of insulation systems over the first two-thirds of this century changed that, and homeowners today expect to have full control over the weather in their rooms. Both ends of the country have been made more habitable because we have found a way to manufacture comfortable air with machines that heat, cool, humidify, dehumidify and even purify the air; it is now possible to live in both cold and hot climates without suffering. The problem, however, is that the control is illusory in most cases, achieved through the consumption of wood, coal, oil, gas and electricity. The temperature in the house is transformed temporarily, but it soon passes through the walls, roof and floors into the outside atmosphere. Our machines deliver newly tempered air before we discover the escape of the old, but while this may keep us comfortable, we all know that energy once used is forever gone.

For a few crazy years (most notably between 1925 and 1975), the actual cost and true value of fuel were far apart, and our precious energy resources went up in flames. During this time the average American home was a poorly designed energy sieve lacking only a funnel on top to make the pouring in of fuel easier. Frank Lloyd Wright himself contended that insulating the walls of a house was hardly necessary. He felt that it would be worthwhile to insulate the roof, "...whereas the insulation of the walls and the air space within the walls becomes less and less important. With modern systems of air conditioning and heating, you can manage almost any condition" (*The Natural House* [New York: Horizon Press, 1954], 155). Indeed. Why worry about conserving energy when fuel is cheap and when you can get a heating unit that "can manage almost any condition?" Unfortunately, there are homes everywhere that still use the monsters Wright was talking about.

When the energy crunch hit in the mid-1970s, it was natural to turn to the sun and wind to replace oil and gas. It wasn't immediately clear that the basic precepts of house design might need to be re-evaluated, so liquids were pumped, air was pushed and heat was stored in every conceivable medium. That's when we discovered how wasteful the average American house is. We found that solar collectors and wind generators, no matter how technologically sophisticated, are like a spit into the wind when heat is passing through the house at a full gallop.

Engineers and architects generally agree that the way to reduce energy consumption is to design houses that naturally collect heat during cold seasons and reject it during hot seasons. Then you install the best possible insulation so desired temperatures can be retained without assistance for long periods of time. It's a concept that works in both warm and cold climates, reducing heating and cooling requirements, and so theoretically simple that you really have to wonder how we managed to stray from it in the first place. But like so many other simple solutions in this era of high-tech, this one is often bypassed, for we are easily seduced by the outer limits of human understanding and tend to rely more on mysterious laws of physics and impressive mathematics than on the primal senses. My dad tells the story of the Oxford professor who was halted in his march across the campus by a couple of students who were eager to clarify some details from the classroom discussion. When the conversation was completed, the professor turned to one of the students and asked, "By the way, which direction was I coming from before you stopped me?" The student pointed down one of the paths. The professor smiled and said, "Well, good, then I've had

my lunch." Lost within the labyrinth of our own single-mindedness, it's easy to forget where we are coming from and where we are going.

Perhaps the largest barrier to reducing fuel consumption in our homes is that conventional stud-framing methods are inherently contrary to good insulating practice. They were simply not invented with insulation in mind. In the mid- to late-1800s, when stud framing was being developed, people achieved thermal comfort primarily by drawing closer to the hearth: No thought was given to the system's compatibility with insulating materials because there were no insulating materials. So stud framing evolved with the single purpose of making construction easier. But because the framing, fiberglass insulation and sheathing in

Stress-skin panels are applied to the outside of the frame, surrounding the walls and covering the roof.

stud construction are all installed separately, each component compromises the other. Studs suffer a reduced life because moisture from air trapped in the fiberglass causes them to rot. The fiberglass insulation would be much more effective if it weren't interrupted every 16 in. to 24 in. by a stud. The whole unit would be a better air seal if it weren't composed of hundreds of individual pieces. To prevent air infiltration through the gaps, the studs and insulation are covered with a flimsy, vulnerable sheet of plastic that is immediately punctured with thousands of screw or nail holes made in attaching the sheathing.

In addition, the fiberglass itself is not the best insulating material. It's relatively inexpensive and easy to stuff into the spaces between framing members, but unless it is more dense than the typical product, it doesn't trap air very well. Insulation value is provided by pockets of dry, still air, and the fact is that air moves through fiberglass quite easily, which is why it is used in other applications where the goal is not to trap air but to filter it. By today's energy-conserving standards, the typical batt of fiberglass amounts to being a pretty good sweater but not much of a coat.

Builders and architects are working hard to circumvent the inherent insulative deficiencies of stud framing, but most of the new solutions demonstrate that we really

ought to try thinking in new ways. For example, one popular system uses two parallel stud walls with batts of insulation in both walls and more in the space between—three layers of insulation, two walls and a highway for mice. Another method is to build a conventional stud frame and then attach a light plywood truss to the outside to carry additional insulation. When completed, the composite is a fortress wall 12 in. to 16 in. thick. Stud framing is dominant throughout the world and it won't soon be replaced. But outside of the housing industry, people have developed effective insulation systems precisely because they haven't had the constraints imposed by this construction method. Walk-in freezers, coolers, thermos bottles, energy-efficient hot-water heaters and liquid gas tanks are all examples. Each one of these devices uses a continuous, uninterrupted membrane of rigid-foam insulation, a simple and sensible alternative, but one that was impractical for housing until the recent development of the new rigid foams.

In 1976, after building a few timber-frame houses and feeling limited by conventional building materials, I began to search in earnest for a better insulation system. At the time, we were using a built-up enclosure of horizontal 2x4 nailers and rigid insulation board (p. 95), and while this is still a viable technique for some projects, I was convinced

Typical stud wall

FIBERGLASS INSULATION
(VAPOR BARRIER
OMITTED FOR CLARITY.)

2X4 STUDS 16" O.C.

PLYWOOD SUBFLOOR

2X10 JOIST

½" PLYWOOD
SHEATHING

BOX SILL

2X8 SILL

FOUNDATION WALL

that we needed something wholly different if timber-frame homes were truly to make a comeback. For our built-up method was no improvement over conventional insulation, in that it was labor-intensive and suffered from thermal breaks. In addition, it was wasteful, because a properly built timber frame can withstand all building loads without relying on sheathing for rigidity or infilling for support. In fact, what we were doing was building a frame around a frame. I knew that if we could take full advantage of the self-supporting nature of the timber frame, our buildings would be more economical to construct and the insulation values would be greatly improved.

Endless phone calls, some library research and several trips over quite a few months led me to query people who specialized in making walk-in freezers. These were people with no particular ties to any kind of product, whose business depended on using the finest insulation. Two companies were receptive to my questions; one was especially helpful and invited me to visit its research laboratory. The technicians there gave me a short course on insulation, demonstrating why interrupting it with framing members is not good practice and why fiberglass is really second-rate stuff. By using a dyed vapor and changing the atmospheric conditions on either side of a test wall, they were able to create convection currents inside the wall cavity, which caused air to filter through the fiberglass.

For its insulating walls, this company preferred a composite of materials called a stress-skin panel. The panel is nothing more than a sandwich of a thick core material bonded to two thin outer skins. According to the U.S.D.A.'s *Wood Handbook* (see bibliography, p. 229), "The facings resist nearly all the applied edgewise loads and flatwise bending moments. The thin, spaced facings provide nearly all the bending rigidity to the construction. The core spaces the facings and transmits shear between them so they are effective about a common neutral axis. The core also provides most of the shear rigidity of the sandwich construction." What this means is that the structural principle

behind a stress-skin panel is similar to that of an *I*-beam (below). The outer skins perform the same role as the beam flanges, while the foam core functions like the *I*-beam web. As in an *I*-beam, the skins resist tension and compression while the core carries the shearing forces and supports the skins against lateral wrinkling. Even if the core of the panel were not insulative, stress skins use materials economically, gaining strength without heaviness or great expense. Cardboard and hollow-core doors are examples of stress-skin panels used for light weight and efficiency of materials.

Panels used in refrigerated warehouses and freezers utilize rigid foam for the core and, usually, galvanized sheet metal for the skins. In freezers, as with timber frames, the panels support no loads. While it was exciting to see a proven product with features so perfectly suited to the needs of timber framing, a panel with metal skins is not exactly appropriate for residential construction. Our challenge was to find a way to make a panel with skins that could serve as interior finish and exterior sheathing surfaces. (For reasons of economy, we immediately dismissed the idea of screwing drywall and nail-base sheathing to the metal skins.) There were also a number of construction details to work out before stress-skin-panel technology could be successfully integrated with timber-frame homes. For instance, we would have to find a way to run wires, install windows and doors, and attach trim and finish materials. We were even uncertain about the best method for attaching panels to the frame and to each other. It was alternately exhilarating to see the potential and overwhelming to be confronted with so many obstacles.

Luckily, I wasn't alone with the thought that stress-skin panels might be suitable for residential construction. Several companies became interested in developing the panel for the burgeoning timber-frame industry. It was because of their intense efforts at the beginning of our experimentation, and continuous improvements in the performance and quality of the product, that we are now able to use stress-skin panels with confidence.

How a stress-skin panel works

The typical panel we now use has oriented-strand board for the exterior surface and plaster-base drywall for the interior finish surface, although we occasionally use panels having oriented-strand board on both sides. (See "Selecting stress-skin panels," p. 99.) Like a human skin over a skeleton, panels are almost always applied completely to the outside of the frame, surrounding the walls and covering the roof. The frame and the insulating membrane are therefore separate, resulting in big benefits. Because the interior finish, insulation and exterior sheathing are all installed simultaneously, several construction processes are combined into one—on-site labor is saved and the building is closed in quickly. Another benefit is the absolute protection given to the frame. Since no part needs to be buried in a wall cavity or exposed to the elements, the frame is not subject to deterioration from weather or moisture. Using this system, the panels take the beating; in time, they could be replaced if necessary, but the frame should survive the ages unscathed.

Urethane and expanded polystyrene are the two foam types currently used for the panel core. Urethane cores can be laminated to the skins with an adhesive or injected in liquid form between separated skins, but expanded polystyrene cores can only be laminated to the skins. A typical core thickness for a urethane panel is 3½ in., yielding an R-value somewhere between 26 and 30, while a polystyrene core has to be 5½ in. thick to achieve a similar R-value.

Conventional wisdom suggests there should be more insulation in the roof than in the walls, so at first it might not seem to make much sense to have such high R-values in the wall panels. Theoretically, because warm air rises, air in the upper regions of the house will be substantially warmer than that at the lowest level. When heat is lost through the roof, convection currents draw up more warm air, resulting in a continual temperature differential between the upper and lower areas of the building—witness the uninsulated attic on a hot summer day. We are discovering, however, that as we slow heat loss through the roof, the temperature differential from the peak to the floor narrows to within a few degrees. What makes this especially remarkable is that most of the houses we build are open to the peak, so the distance from the top of the ceiling to the floor might be over 25 ft. In a house insulated with stress-skin panels, heat is lost only through conduction, not convection, and at a very slow rate because the rigid foam in the panels is a poor conductor. It makes sense to us to keep the entire thermal envelope at approximately the same insulative level, because if the temperature next to roof and wall surfaces tends to be about the same, R-value should be at least proportionately equal.

Out of curiosity, one of our Massachusetts clients recently monitored the winter temperature in his home for one week with a series of thermometers hung between the 25-ft.-high peak and the floor. He found that the maximum temperature difference was 5°F and the average of the period was 2°F. With the introduction of a small fan, he was able to reduce the temperature differential to one-half a degree—quite an achievement and an excellent testimony to a good insulation system.

But as effective and successful as stress-skin panels are, they are not universally correct for every circumstance. Three factors should influence the choice of enclosure system for any particular timber-frame project: structural integrity, energy performance and cost. The system needs to be strong and durable, able to resist wind loads on the walls, snow loads on the roof and the awesome load of time. Energy needs should be reduced to the lowest practical level, keeping in mind that it doesn't make much sense to spend ten dollars to save one. Relative to its value as a fuel miser and as a tough shell for the house, the system must warrant the cost of construction.

The most difficult of these criteria to determine is energy performance. Too often, there is R-value myopia, and judgments are made entirely on the basis of what the manufacturer's wrapping says you have stuffed in the cavities. Unfortunately, the wrapping goes without the warning that your actual performance may vary. A value of R-50 would be a poor joke if it were used on a north wall that was 60% glass, and all the insulation in the world won't save a house that is riddled with air leaks. I recently went to examine one of our houses that wasn't performing up to expectations, although everything seemed to be in place and done according to usual procedure. But because the windows seemed colder than normal, I decided to remove the side casing. Sure enough, not one window, door or skylight had any insulation or caulking between the jamb and rough opening. Added up, the uninsulated area amounted to a 4-ft. by 4 ft. hole in the house. Good insulation, bad workmanship; the system tilts.

There are really quite a few factors that need to be in proper balance to achieve good energy performance. Because it is so important to analyze all issues in relation to each other and because the calculations are so complex, a local engineering firm does a computerized audit of all our homes early in design. Such audits are available throughout the country (they are required by the building department in some states), through utilities, heating suppliers or private engineers. I personally like to work with a firm that expects to make money doing the audit, but not afterward.

The energy audit considers wall- and roof-surface area and orientation, window- and door-surface area and orientation, volume, available degree days, infiltration values, below-grade treatment and insulation, and heat generated by occupants and fixtures. Estimated auxiliary energy requirements are estimated on a yearly, monthly, daily or even an hourly basis. Both gains and losses are estimated. Once all data about the house is entered into the program, it is simple to manipulate values to see the effect on the bottom line. For example, we might try on paper a house with triple glazing or low-E (emissivity) glass and find that the added cost doesn't warrant the slightly improved performance. When the most desirable option is determined, the energy audit can also predict what the fuel cost will be on a yearly basis for each type of available fuel. Even if the audit does not perfectly reflect actual fuel consumption, I have found that it is usually quite accurate, if conservative. I agree with those states that have made an energy audit a requirement. If building departments are going to insist that electric outlets be no lower than 14 in. (my pet peeve), then they ought to slow the flow of fuel as it pulses through the veins of our houses.

An energy audit is also the best method to weigh the cost of the enclosure system against the cost of the heating system and the fuel to run it for the next ten or twenty years. If the long-range numbers are anywhere near close, it makes sense to choose better insulation now rather than bet on the future price of fuel. We strive to pinpoint the measures that bring us to the point of diminishing returns, the very top of the proverbial efficiency curve, so that we'll feel confident when additional insulation or better windows cannot be justified in light of the small gain.

Following the energy audit, and after a careful analysis of each component of the building's envelope and another look at the bank account, the optimum enclosure system is chosen. I discuss the selection, installation and manufacture of stress-skin panels later in this chapter, but first we'll look at a few alternate types of enclosures.

With good insulation, rooms with high ceilings have little temperature differential between the roof and floor.

Alternatives to stress-skin panels

I can think of several reasons why a person might choose not to use stress-skin panels.

1. Small buildings under 1200 sq. ft., having little volume and surface area, are likely to reach the top of the efficiency curve with a less expensive enclosure than panels. For some buildings, we conclude that panels would be useful and cost effective on the roof where there is little waste, but that the walls should be treated differently. There are usually many penetrations in the walls for windows and doors, which generate a great deal of scrap and cause installation to be more difficult. I am not suggesting that insulation values be compromised, only that depending on the situation, it may be possible to achieve optimum performance with an alternate system.

2. High-quality panels are not readily available in all regions, and trucking them from one end of the country to the other isn't very practical. If the project is in an isolated backwater, it may be necessary to do some low-tech manufacturing or use an alternate system.

3. Panels might be too costly for the budget. We have found the installed cost of panels less expensive than the installed cost of any system with a competitive performance value. Although the cost of panels is relatively high per square foot, the installation labor is reasonable because they go on so rapidly. For most of the alternate systems the materials are less, but installation is labor-intensive. Builders who don't place a high value on their labor might therefore find other systems attractive. We've raised frames for several clients who decided to use an enclosure system they could manage with their own resources.

4. Some people simply have an aversion to the inorganic nature of panels. Or they can't believe panels can offer the permanence and security provided by using wooden materials for sheathing attachment. For these people, no words are persuasive. I offer only my empathy with the sentiment, and alternatives.

5. A building not occupied all the time, such as an office, shop or vacation home, might not justify the insulating value typical of panels. By using one of the alternatives (and lowering performance standards greatly), a lot of money can be saved. Still, it makes sense to err on the side of energy conservation.

6. Timber framing is an ancient method of construction and people often want to use it to create a historical reproduction. Panels are inappropriate in this situation because the added thickness outside the structure does not reproduce the look of early timber-frame homes.

With all the alternatives that follow, keep in mind that you already have a building that structurally supports itself. The insulating system needs to be stiff and offer good

Infill stud system

TIMBER POST

BRACE OFFSET ON POST BY AMOUNT EQUAL TO THICKNESS OF FRAMED WALL PLUS INTERIOR FINISH.

FIBERGLASS INSULATION (VAPOR BARRIER OMITTED FOR CLARITY.)

2X4 STUDS 16" TO 24" O.C.

PLYWOOD SUBFLOOR

JOIST

PLYWOOD SHEATHING

1½" RIGID FOAM

BOX BEAM

2X8 SILL

FOUNDATION WALL

thermal value, but its structural requirements are small. Also remember that with these systems, the roof and walls will probably be treated differently. Stress-skin panels allow them to be treated identically because the same premanufactured components satisfy the requirements of both. But when built-up systems are used, it makes sense to customize the materials and treatment to the specific situation—timber frames typically have widely spaced timbers on the wall and only a wind-load consideration, while roof timbers tend to be more closely spaced and the loads more significant, depending on the area. Refer to the energy audit to determine if the chosen insulation values suggest using a greater R-value on the roof.

The infill stud system for walls This is the most difficult, least effective way to enclose a timber frame. It's also the way that most old timber frames were enclosed, so it's the method usually used when an owner wants to replicate the appearance of an old house. Basically, infilling is the process of building stud walls between the timbers and packing them with fiberglass insulation. The walls are then wrapped on the outside with a layer of 1½-in.-thick rigid foam. Because the walls are attached between timbers and not to the outside of the frame, the entire thickness of the timbers is not revealed to the living space. In addition, the timbers wind up fitting poorly to the adjacent studs after movement and shrinkage, allowing great air infiltration. It stands to reason that there is also a potential for condensation to occur in the cavities where this air infiltration is taking place. A building publication recently reported that many of the posts and beams in a four-year-old timber-frame house enclosed with this method already had significant moisture damage. The infill stud system should only be used if the timbers are dry or if the occupants are prepared to be vigilant about caulking the gaps that develop.

Probably the one advantage of this method is that it requires only conventional materials and simple carpentry. Because the walls don't support any compression loads, single top plates are fine; headers and sills need only be a single stud. All framing can be 24 in. on center. Infilling is made much easier if the timber framer joins all minor members, such as knee braces, toward the inside of the building by the thickness of the framed wall, including the drywall. If the frame is built this way, each stud wall can then be assembled and nailed on the deck and raised as a unit. The infill stud system can be greatly improved by extending 1½ in. of each 2x4 outside the frame, allowing 1½ in. of rigid foam to be placed over the timbers and then another 1½ in. of rigid foam over the entire assembly before the exterior sheathing.

For the infill stud system to work easily, push the braces toward the inside of the building so they won't be obstacles to studs and finishwork.

The exterior stud system for walls By simply moving the stud walls to the outside of the frame, the problems created by infilling can be avoided. The timbers can now shrink or move without causing infiltration or compromising insulation quality; finish work no longer has to fight the frame. Walls can still be conventionally framed, although as in the previous method, many structural members can be reduced or eliminated because the timber frame is self-supporting. Installation is somewhat backward, because the drywall and vapor barrier are attached to the outside of the frame first to avoid infilling between timbers. (Choosing to install the drywall after the studs means that each post will need a stud adjacent to it for sheathing attachment.) At this point the drywall will be attached only to the sills and girts of the timber frame, and will be quite flimsy. If the studs will be on 24-in. centers, choose ⅝-in.-thick drywall (instead of ½-in.) to maintain stiffness. Before the stud frame goes up, tack the vapor barrier to the drywall.

There are some inherent problems with this system. First, the drywall must be protected from the weather, which means you must work quickly and take fastidious precautions. The best protection is to have the roof on first, but if the eaves project well beyond the walls it will be hard to make a good connection to the top plate. Until the roof is on, it's a good idea to keep a tarp rolled up at the peak of the building to pull down over the drywall when necessary.

The second problem is that the stud walls can't be pushed up into position as units, because the drywall blocks the path. So whether the walls are fabricated on the deck or another level surface, they'll have to be carried to the outside of the frame and hoisted into position. It's thus best to keep the walls to a manageable size—that is, not much longer than 16 ft. or taller than 8 ft. to 10 ft. Achieve this by planning for walls to meet at the centerline of posts and girts. When the walls are positioned on the frame, toe-nail them wherever there is sufficient nailing with 20d galvanized nails. Also, spike the studs to the timbers with barn spikes at 4-ft. intervals, penetrating softwood timbers by 2 in. and hardwood timbers by 1½ in. To keep the studs from splitting, pre-drill a ¼-in. hole before spiking.

After the stud walls are in place, install the wiring and electrical boxes. Then pack in the fiberglass. For improved performance, nail sheets of rigid foam over the stud frame. If rigid foam is not used, horizontal siding can be attached directly to the studs. If the studs are 24 in. on center, the siding has to be at least ¾ in.; overlap shiplapped boards to create a conventional clapboard appearance. Vertical siding would require that horizontal furring strips be attached to the studs first.

Exterior stud system

TIMBER POST

DRYWALL AND VAPOR BARRIER (OMITTED FOR CLARITY) APPLIED TO OUTSIDE OF FRAME BEFORE NAILERS.

BARN SPIKES AT 4' INTERVALS INTO TIMBERS

2X4 STUDS 24" O.C.

PLYWOOD SUBFLOOR

JOIST

PLYWOOD SHEATHING

1½" RIGID FOAM

FIBERGLASS INSULATION

BOX BEAM

2X8 SILL

2X12 SILL

FOUNDATION WALL

The horizontal nailer system This method consists of 2x4 nailers attached horizontally to the timbers with rigid-foam insulation in between. It takes full advantage of the nonstructural nature of the enclosure wall; the light-duty nailers exist only to stiffen the wall and to provide attachment for the interior and exterior sheathing. For good support, a 2x12 sill is absolutely essential. Because the sill is also the bottom nailer, it must extend beyond the frame by the same width as the other nailers.

As in the exterior stud system, the drywall and vapor barrier are applied to the outside of the frame first. Then rough window and door bucks are pre-made and toe-nailed to the 2x12 sill and timber girts on the outside with 20d galvanized nails. Rigid-foam insulation is ripped to a width that allows the nailers to be 24 in. on center—if the nailers were 1½ in. thick (typically the actual thickness of a 2x4), this dimension would be 22½ in. If you're using plywood for exterior sheathing, make sure the top edge of each 4x8 panel falls on the centerline of a nailer. For a higher R-value per inch and a better perm rate, I would choose either extruded polystyrene or urethane foam. It should be ¼ in. to ⅜ in. less in thickness than the width of the nailer to allow the exterior sheathing to breathe.

Begin application of the foam by laying a bead of caulking on the 2x12 sill. Two 1-in.-thick foam boards separated by a 1x3 spacer can be used between the sill and next nailer to create a convenient wire chase (a solid foam block would have to be routed for wires). Then lay a bead of caulking on top of each layer of foam and put on a nailer, forcing it down against the foam and toe-nailing it to the timber frame or to window and door bucks. Repeat the procedure all the way to the top of the wall. At the end of each wall, use a vertical stud to cover the ends of the spacers. Applying additional sheets of rigid insulation over the whole system, when all nailers and insulation are in place, is a good way to compensate for thermal breaks. Then screw or nail the drywall to the nailers. Wiring and electrical outlets should be run while the insulation is being installed so cuts in the foam can be made easily. Check your building code. Some will require the wiring to be in a conduit because it will be exposed to the weather for a while. Vertical siding can be nailed directly to the nailers, but horizontal siding will require vertical furring strips first.

An advantage of this method is that installation is easy and can be done one piece at a time. A crew of two can manage the entire process. In addition, layering horizontally takes advantage of gravity and makes it significantly easier to get a good seal between materials—because you have to run up and down the ladder so much, constantly trying to push the stuff together, this is difficult to do with

Horizontal nailer system

DRYWALL AND VAPOR BARRIER (OMITTED FOR CLARITY) APPLIED TO OUTSIDE OF FRAME BEFORE NAILERS.

TIMBER POST

2X4 NAILERS 24" O.C.

PLYWOOD SUBFLOOR

JOIST

2X8 SILL

3" RIGID FOAM

¼" TO ⅜" AIR SPACE BETWEEN FOAM AND PLYWOOD SHEATHING

PLYWOOD SHEATHING

2 LAYERS OF 1" RIGID FOAM

1X3 SPACER

2X12 SILL

FOUNDATION WALL

vertical studs. High-quality foam performs better than fiberglass, and caulking improves the seal. Still, there are a number of breaks because of the nailers, and the system is labor-intensive indeed.

This is a good alternate enclosure method, and you can vary the thickness of the insulation to keep costs in line. Our shop was built with a variation of this system, using furring strips for nailers with 1-in.-thick expanded styrene between them. The interior and exterior finish are vertical boards. The system gave us a decent finish, minimal insulation and minimal cost.

The Larsen truss system for walls and roof The Larsen truss was developed by John Larsen specifically to address the difficulty of retrofitting older buildings with better insulation. Acknowledging that the buildings did not need additional support, just more insulation, he set out to create a rather nonstructural framework to contain insulation and hold sheathing. The solution is a light truss that uses 2x2s as flanges and plywood for the web. These trusses can be made by anyone with a tablesaw, glue, clamps and a little patience. They can be made to span the height of the walls or the length of the rafters and are lifted and managed easily by one or two people. Because the width of the plywood web is variable, you can use as much insulation

as necessary without a great deal more expense for wood. The web is usually only ⅜ in. thick and does not need to be continuous, so there isn't high conduction through the material. For a new timber-frame structure, this option would make sense only where rigid-foam plastics were either totally unavailable or totally unpalatable to the client.

Installing a Larsen truss is similar to installing exterior-stud walls except that the truss is always attached a section at a time. Drywall goes on the frame first along with the vapor barrier. A truss is then secured to the timber posts by nailing the exposed edges of the inside flanges with galvanized nails that penetrate the posts by at least 1½ in. Wiring is run and electrical boxes installed, then the fiberglass insulation is applied as tightly as possible to the plywood. It's not necessary to use additional rigid foam on the outside. Exterior sheathing is nailed directly to the outside flanges.

The principle of the Larsen truss is that it makes a cavity for a great thickness of insulation at a low price—from 12 in. to 15 in. of fiberglass is not unusual. But most of the difficulties with the system stem from this thickness, for the distance between the inside edge of the frame and the outside edge of the truss is so great that they bear almost no relationship to each other. The trusses will therefore ap-

Larsen truss system

PLYWOOD WEB

2X2 FLANGE

TIMBER POST

DRYWALL AND VAPOR BARRIER (OMITTED FOR CLARITY) APPLIED TO OUTSIDE OF FRAME BEFORE TRUSSES.

PLYWOOD SUBFLOOR

JOIST

PLYWOOD SHEATHING

FIBERGLASS INSULATION

PLYWOOD BASE

2X8 SILL

FOUNDATION WALL

pear as unnatural appendages to the building if they over-hang the foundation, or the foundation will have to be re-considered to accommodate the trusses. I endorse the latter option. A simple solution is to design pilasters into the foundation wall to support the posts and use the wall itself as a base for the trusses. (See p. 119 for a discussion of pilasters.) Besides the aesthetic problem of the exterior walls overhanging the foundation by 12 in. or more, it's also hard to seal and protect the bottom of the insulation cavity.

Extreme wall thickness also creates some difficulties at exterior windows and doors. Jambs need to be as wide as the wall is thick, causing extra expense for materials and labor. Extreme depth at the jambs might also restrict light from spreading well as it enters the house. The condition can be eased by beveling the jamb sides back at an angle, a nice but expensive touch.

On the roof, Larsen trusses can also be used effectively. But because fiberglass roof insulation must be ventilated to avoid potential moisture buildup, the thickness of the truss and insulation must be planned to allow an air space of at least 2 in. between the insulation and exterior sheathing. The air flow must pass from the eave to the peak; holes will have to be drilled for each cavity at the eave and a ridge vent will be necessary at the peak. (Commercial ma-terials for eave and ridge vents are available through most lumberyards.) Begin by attaching the drywall and vapor barrier to the outside of the roof timbers. To install the trusses, snap a chalkline along each eave and lay the truss-es on 2-ft. centers, their bottom edges aligned with the chalkline. Trusses can be fixed to each other at the peak and the inside flanges should be attached to the timbers in the same manner as on the walls. Cut the bottoms of the trusses perpendicular to the slope of the roof. Attach planking to the bottom edges of the trusses to cap the cav-ity. To avoid having roof trim the same width as the truss-es, attach jet blocks to the box, as shown below.

Using Larsen trusses on the roof

2" AIR SPACE ABOVE INSULATION
INSULATION TRUSSES
TRUSS
DRYWALL AND VAPOR BARRIER

PEAK DETAIL

JET BLOCK
JET BLOCK
WALL SHEATHING
JET BLOCK

EAVE DETAIL

(EXTERIOR SHEATHING OMITTED FOR CLARITY.)

Foam boardstock roof insulation In this technique, sheets of rigid foam are laid over 2x6 planks within a box built around the roof perimeter. You use planking instead of drywall because the interior roof sheathing must be able to support its own weight between timbers without sagging.

The planks are applied directly to the roof timbers, and the box frame is built from stock that is as wide as the insulation is thick. A vapor barrier is tacked to the planks, sealing the sides of the box. All seams should be sealed or taped. The insulation is then installed in the box. Choose insulation thickness by analyzing the relative values of the foam; to prevent crushing or deflection in high-load situations, the foam should have a density of at least 2 lb. It is certainly possible to use foam not much thicker than 3 in. or 3½ in.

After installing the insulation, caulk all voids or fill them with expanding foam and tape the seams. To make an air space between the foam and the exterior sheathing, attach 2x3 or 2x4 nailers every 2 ft. on center, perpendicular to the roof timbers. Nail through the foam to the frame using the guidelines suggested for panels on p. 107. Then put on the exterior sheathing. Roof overhangs can be established using the planks and/or the nailers for support.

Foam and nailer roof insulation If you want to use drywall as the interior finish instead of planking, you'll have to use a system with nailers. The basic rule here is that the nailers run perpendicular to the roof timbers (vertically over purlins and horizontally over rafters). After that, the system is similar to the horizontal nailer system for walls. Apply the drywall to the frame first, then attach the vapor barrier.

Use a nailer wide enough to allow a 2-in. air space between the foam and the exterior sheathing—if you were using 3½-in.-thick foam, for example, you would need a 5½-in.-wide nailer on edge. Place the nailers over the vapor barrier and toe-nail them to the frame with 20d galvanized nails. Then install a section of rigid foam and the next nailer. When the foam is in place and properly sealed, attach the exterior sheathing to the nailers.

While the drywall is exposed and unsupported it presents a potential safety hazard to the installer. To help prevent serious accidents and damage, work your way across or up the roof, installing all the layers at the same time. This will make it possible to stand on either the sheathing or the frame while materials are being positioned and secured.

Foam boardstock roof insulation

PLYWOOD SHEATHING
2X4 NAILERS 24" O.C.
TAPED SEAM
RIGID FOAM
2X6 PLANKS (VAPOR BARRIER OMITTED.)
PURLIN
2X ROOF BOX

Foam and nailer roof insulation

AIR SPACE
NAILER
RIGID FOAM
PURLIN
DRYWALL (VAPOR BARRIER OMITTED FOR CLARITY.)
CONNECTING GIRT
TIMBER POST

Selecting stress-skin panels

Some of us thought we would never submit to plastic. We saw it come in our lifetime, and when we wanted to point out what was wrong with the modern world we pointed to plastic—tangible evidence of the great deterioration of all good things. Old cars were built like tanks; new cars have too much plastic. My old reliable typewriter is all metal and it still works but I can't remember where it is. There might be metal somewhere in my computer, but all that is visible is plastic. We grumble and complain, but plastic is here to stay. Perhaps a few of us would be wealthier if we had not laughed so hard at Dustin Hoffman's famous line in the film "The Graduate."

It is no coincidence that the timber-frame revival has moved just about as quickly as the development of stress-skin-panel technology. Those of us who craft timbers with mallet and chisel are often a little startled when we are reminded that the panel, a very critical component in most timber-frame building, is made mostly of plastic. The panel is only a core of foam with sheet materials bonded to either side, yet it is asked to play a major role in the construction of significant buildings. Our expectations for panels should therefore be high; they must adhere to the following tough specifications:

1. They have to be strong and stiff. The timber frame can have either purlins or rafters on the roof on approximately 4-ft. centers. Spans between horizontal timbers in the walls are usually no longer than 10 ft. Panels must be able to hold their own in these spaces. This can mean as much as 100 lb. per sq. ft. on the roof and a 100 mph wind bearing against the walls.

2. They must not delaminate. Delamination between the materials would be our worst fears come to life.

3. None of the materials should suffer unreasonable deterioration because of exposure to time, temperature changes or the elements. The panel should be at least as stable as wood.

4. Panels should have a high R-value per inch of thickness, to achieve optimum thermal performance without creating imposing fortress walls.

5. And they should have a low perm rate. Humidity and air pressure in tight houses are higher than normal, and it is more important to prevent the flow of humid air. If this air should penetrate the inside skin, the core material should be water-resistant enough not to soak up the excess moisture like a sponge.

6. They should hold up well under high heat and fire. We are all concerned about flame spread and toxicity. Panels house the foam in an oxygen-free environment, putting a flammable product in the safest possible position, but we still want to know that we would have a chance to leave the building safely should a fire start.

7. The core material should have a sufficient molecular bond to resist creep. Even though the panels are nailed to the frame, creep could cause a more rapid deterioration of the panel system, especially on the roof, where they are unsupported at the base and tend to carry a greater load.

8. The panels must allow practical, efficient installation.

9. Cost must be reasonable or, like many other exotic building products, stress-skin panels will be saved for commercial and public buildings and for the very rich.

Current commercially available panels are made using either urethane or expanded polystyrene as the core material. Extruded Styrofoam is too expensive, although it would make a fine panel. Phenolic foam so far is too brittle and water-absorbent, having a perm rate of 8 per inch. This is clearly unacceptable, because the panel core also has to act as a vapor barrier.

The choice between expanded polystyrene and urethane should be based on an analysis of the attributes and deficiencies of each material. Panel manufacturers tend to specialize in one foam type or the other, and they battle to claim the perfect product. In an attempt to settle the dispute, I hereby pronounce them both in need of further development—the best manufacturers are those who recognize this. Rigid foam has value only in relation to the role it plays as one of the panel components and should be judged on the basis of performance, safety, durability and cost. For more information about expanded polystyrene and urethane, see p. 110.

For the interior and exterior skins, most manufacturers offer several options, and the best option is not necessarily clear. Luckily, the problems inherent in each of the options are not necessarily severe. The most important concern should be whether or not the manufacturer has tested the specific panel to meet the buyer's local structural codes. With this aside, there are good and better choices depending on local conditions and the requirements of the building. A house on the shore of Nantucket Island should be treated differently from a house in the mountains of Colorado. Large loads and long frame spans might suggest the strongest panel; enclosing a swimming pool or a hot tub might force the decision to turn on moisture protection. Remember, too, that while it is in the best interest of the manufacturer to make and sell identical panels to keep the price down, it is often in your interest to get panels made to your specification.

In general, the exterior skin should be strong, especially under compression. It should have good nail-holding capacity for the application of siding and trim. It should be dimensionally stable, not expanding and shrinking abnormally in wet and dry cycles. Finally, it should be a capable vapor barrier, helping to prevent moisture penetration. The usual options are chipboard, oriented-strand board and plywood. Inevitably, there are trade-offs. For strength and moisture resistance, marine plywood would be wonderful, but the cost is prohibitively high. Some of the prefinished plywood sidings, such as Texture 1-11, might be durable enough, but it doesn't make sense to use a great thermal panel with a poor thermal joint—it's almost impossible to have both the expanding foam seal necessary for optimum energy performance and good looks. Regular exterior plywood is not bonded as well as it should be and tends to delaminate. Because the panel leaves no air space between the plywood and the core, moisture gets in and the plies split apart. So that leaves oriented-strand board and chipboard. Chipboard is nothing more than compressed flakes of wood held together with glue. Oriented-strand board (OSB) looks like chipboard, but the grain of the wood chips is aligned and compressed into thin sheets that are then cross-laminated in a manner similar to plywood. The advantage of OSB and chipboard over plywood is that they can't delaminate. OSB is stronger than chipboard, has better nail-holding capacity, is about the same price and has therefore been our preference.

The interior skin should have good tensile resistance to loads and serve as an air/vapor barrier to keep moisture from penetrating the core from the inside. It should also serve as a fire barrier, isolating the panel core from the house interior, and must either be the interior wall surface or be able to support it. The alternatives are usually drywall, blueboard (plaster-base drywall), greenboard or fire-resistant drywall. When we use gypsum board as the interior skin, blueboard is our first choice because it is stronger than regular drywall and holds up well when rain gets to the site before we get the roof on. Blueboard also gives our clients the option of either plastering or painting. The exterior sheathings listed previously can also be used for the interior skin, with the finish interior surface then applied as another layer—we call these panels doublechips. Although more expensive, doublechips have several advantages. First, they're stronger and give a better surface for attaching trim, cabinets and other finish elements. Second, the greater strength of the interior skin helps keep the panel from warping when the exterior skin expands in high-moisture conditions. When we use doublechips, we

specifically request the interior skin be made with little formaldehyde in the glue. Don't forget that a combination of interior panel skins might also make sense, for example, where there are high-wind conditions but little snow, drywall panels can be used for the roof and doublechips for the walls. Or doublechips can be used just in the area where cabinets need to be hung and drywall panels used for all other areas.

There are over 30 different panel manufacturers across the country, most located on the east coast. All panel manufacturers use some variation of the techniques discussed later in this chapter. Read that before deciding on the type of panel that's appropriate for your job. Aside from the differences in manufacturing technique, there are a number of manufacturer-suggested panel-to-panel connections. Several of the most common are shown at right. Panel connection is just as important a consideration as the way a panel is made, because it's the connection at the seams that is really the weak link in the system. The seams are the areas most prone to infiltration and weakness, and also where expansion and contraction are most likely to show. But there's a prevalent tendency to overlook the critical fact that insulation must be tight to be effective. Just because the panels have been pushed together does not mean a seal has been made—in fact, in almost every circumstance,

Plaster-base drywall is generally the interior panel surface. After the panels have been installed, interior finish, insulation and exterior sheathing are completed. The foam visible between panels is in the chimney opening, which will be cut out later.

a good seal has *not* been made. You just can't expect 90 to 200 linear inches of sheathing edge to be joined without some pretty big gaps.

Ease of installation is a big concern for panel manufacturers, many of whom use molded joints or tongue-and-groove joints for precisely that reason. We've found these systems don't give the reliable seal we're looking for, so we use the first option shown in the drawing below. The panels come to us with square edges, which we then rout out to accept two 5/8-in. by 3-in. plywood splines. Our router head is designed to take out a little extra insulation at the foam edge between splines to create a cavity into which we can spray expandable foam. This is done after the panels have been installed by drilling a 1/4-in. hole approximately every 14 in. through the splines to accept the nozzle of the foam can. We fill all roof joints as well as the wall joints. In addition, where panels join over a timber we leave a deliberate gap of at least 1/4 in. during installation, to be filled with foam later. We also foam at the base between the 2x8 and 2x12 sills, at all outside corners, at the eave and rake seams between wall and roof and at the ridge. It may seem like a lot of bother, but these extra steps make the difference between good and great performance.

Some panel-splining options

CUSTOM ROUTER HEAD CUTS PANEL GROOVES.

NAILS ATTACH SKINS TO FRAME.

5/8X3 PLYWOOD SPLINES SCREWED TO PANELS FROM BOTH SIDES. 1/4"-DIA. HOLES DRILLED THROUGH EXTERIOR SKIN OF PANEL AFTER INSTALLATION PERMIT INJECTION OF EXPANDING FOAM EVERY 14".

JOINT CEMENTED TOGETHER AS PANELS ARE INSTALLED.

2X4 SCREWED TO EXTERIOR SHEATHING.

IX3 SPLINES SCREWED TO PANELS FROM BOTH SIDES. I" RIGID-FOAM SPLINE PLACED BETWEEN WOODEN SPLINES CLOSES INSULATION GAP.

Panel installation

In theory, installing stress-skin panels is similar to installing other types of exterior sheathing except that the panels are thicker, heavier and a whole lot more expensive. To keep waste down and installation efficient, it's important to map out a strategy prior to getting started. Because panels are attached to the timber frame, the location of the timbers determines the final lengths, widths and cuts for the panels. Therefore, use a blueprint of the frame plan as the

The location of the timbers in the frame determines the final lengths, widths and cuts for the panels.

basis of the panel plan. You'll need a plan for each wall of the house and for the roof surfaces. Locate the rough openings for windows and doors using the architectural plans for reference—don't draw in any panels yet. The rough openings should be the same as those specified by the door and window manufacturers for stud-frame construction. All locations for openings should be referenced from the edges of the timbers, because the panel installers will have nothing else from which to measure.

After locating the rough openings, draw in the panels. Laying out the panels is a matter of juggling several considerations—strength, panel waste, rough openings and roof overhang. Here are a few guidelines before you begin.

First, check the requirements of the local building code and the loading characteristics of the chosen panel. Most manufactured panels are engineered to span 8 ft. to 9 ft. on the walls and 4 ft. on the roof. Be wary of a manufacturer who cannot provide documentation.

Second, you will not want to risk inordinate panel waste by forcing the spans to work out perfectly. For example, suppose the distance from the 2x12 sill to the centerline of the girt is larger than the 4x8 panels. You could certainly cut the 4x16 panels to fit, but you'd be creating a lot of debris. A better solution would be to position the 4x8 panels from where they had adequate nailing on the box beam to where they had adequate nailing on the girt, keeping in mind that 2 in. is the minimum for good nailing. To do this, you would snap a line along the face of the box beam and nail a ledger to the line to support the panels during nailing. Then you would fill in between the 2x12 sill and panels with offcuts.

When the panels will not reach entirely from the sill to the first beam, nail a strap to the box beam to set a baseline. Panel offcuts are used to fill in over the box beam.

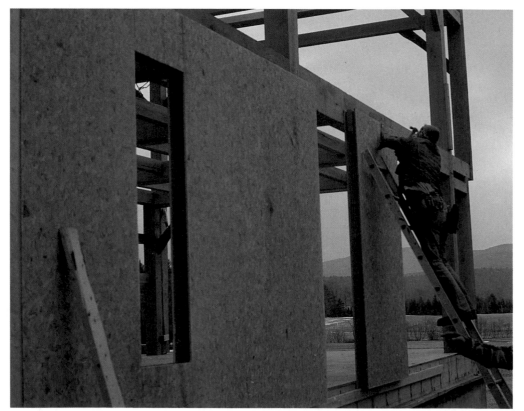

Third, panel joints that fall between the edges of rough openings should be reinforced with a 2x4 used as a spline. (I use 2x4s generically here; of course the nailers would be different dimensions if the panels were thicker or thinner.) Window openings that are wider than 3 ft. 6 in. and taller than 5 ft. and all door openings should be reinforced with a 2x4 on either side that runs from sill to girt. Smaller windows can be cut directly into the panels without a need for this reinforcement. If the window is small enough, try to locate it toward the middle of the panel, leaving 6 in. to 8 in. on either side. But if the window has to be closer to a panel edge, move the panel edge to the edge of the rough opening to put the joint in a place where it can be strengthened with a 2x4. In other words, you don't want just a little bit of insulation between the edge of the rough opening and the edge of the panel because this would create a weak area.

Fourth, non-supported overhangs on the rakes should be limited to 1½ ft. beyond the wall panel and 1 ft. should be the limit at the eave. Using doublechip panels allows an increase in overhang to 2½ ft. on the rakes and 2 ft. at the eave. (If you like, you can run the doublechips along just the roof edges and use standard panels for the rest of the roof.) Some trim details support the eave panels, making it possible to use greater overhangs with the standard panel, as discussed in Chapter X. Doublechip panels are also useful in high-load situations, because the nail-base sheathing is so much stronger in tension than drywall. When using doublechips, you can avoid infilling the interior finish sheathing by nailing it to the outside of the frame before panel installation.

Reinforced door opening

Reinforced window opening

Here are some other things to consider when laying out the panels on the plan: Panels should run vertically on the walls, unless the spacing of the posts is closer than the spacing of the horizontal girts and plates. Next, plan to fill in above and below window and door openings with panel pieces. Work hard to have the tapered factory edges of the drywall meet at all seams, though you won't be able to achieve this everywhere. Use the same procedure on the roof, laying out full panel sections on either side of roof, window or chimney rough openings. You will have to juggle all these factors in an attempt to reduce waste. Dot in the panels over the frame plan, making sure each panel and offcut is clearly marked.

Once the plan is drawn, the panels can be cut and installed. During these stages, try to satisfy the requirements of all three panel components. Interior sheathing must be handled with proverbial kid gloves. The foam core is tougher, but it must be well sealed at all cracks and crevices before installation is finished. The exterior skin is primarily a nail base and you must make sure it provides solid, dependable nailing for all materials applied. Good installation procedure requires vigilance on all these fronts at once.

Information and layout example from a typical panel plan

Although it's not a rule by any means, we usually attach the wall panels first. It is much easier to lift the wall panels into place without the roof panels in the way, particularly if an overhead winch or crane is used to help with lifting, as is typically the case. There are also some situations in which it would be extremely difficult to fit the wall panels under the eave panel and over the 2x12 sill simultaneously. If the eave panels extend over the upper plate or girt, nailing the top edge of the wall panel would be difficult, if not impossible. But the obvious disadvantage of installing the wall panels first is that they will be unprotected and thus vulnerable to the elements until the roof is on. You can see the need for good planning and tight scheduling.

Begin by marking panel breaks and the rough openings for windows and doors on the outside face of the sill and beams. Check that openings coincide with the frame as depicted on the plans. Then string a line along the eave to accurately represent the eave intersection. Using a chalkline or a large *T*-square, draw lines on the panels for the rough openings and all other cuts. Check all measurements before cutting. We usually lay out and cut the wall panels one at a time and precut the roof panels in preparation for crane assistance. The benefit to this system is that you can check your work on the walls as you go, whereas the possibilities of making a mistake on the roof are pretty slim, as there are usually few openings. Always use a mask and goggles when cutting. Panel dust and chips are inorganic and ugly, and should be cleaned up often. My most disturbing experience with our panel debris was when a client's beautiful cranberry bog was fouled with a frost of panel dust. The house needed insulating, not the bog.

Tools for Installation

Panel installation requires only a couple of specialized tools. They are:

- **a circular saw capable of cutting through the thickness of the panels, usually 4½ in. to 5 in.**
- **equipment to cut routs for the nailers and splines. Urethane foam is cut with specially made router heads that fit on portable grinders. We use two grinders so we don't have to change the heads very often. You should expect your manufacturer to help you obtain equipment compatible with the system you choose.**

If the building is large and your crew is small, you may also want to use an electric winch to lift the panels to the higher areas, useful if the building is large and the crew small. If you choose to precut the panels and use a crane to lift them into place, a crane with an operator can usually be rented on a daily basis.

Other useful tools for panel installation are generally found in the typical carpenter's cache:

- **a drill for wires.**
- **a large *T*-square.**
- **a power screwdriver for driving drywall screws.**
- **a bayonet saw for round openings and notching cuts.**
- **ladders long enough to reach the top of the frame.**
- **a good assortment of hand tools: hammer, chalkline, framing square, etc.**

Wall panels are laid out and cut one at a time, after double-checking measurements and layout lines. The window opening in this panel has been routed to receive a 2x4. (Photo by Sarah Knock.)

Panel detail at eave

1" HIGH BY ½" DEEP
NOTCH RECEIVES
EXPANDING FOAM SEAL.

Panel detail at corner (plan view)

8X8 POST

TRIM

NAILER
FOR
TRIM

1" SPACE USED AS WIRING
CHASE, FOAMED BEFORE
SIDING IS INSTALLED.

The panels are heavy, so make all the cuts in a panel at the same time. Panels that will span the full height of the wall should be sawn about ⅜ in. short to make room for the foam. If your saw isn't capable of cutting through the thickness of the panel, cut in halfway from each side—any remaining foam in the middle will break off easily. Tilt the saw base to cut the roof angle. Then cut a notch in the top outside edge about 1 in. high and ½ in. deep for the expanding foam. With the grinder and spline-cutter head, rout all seams that do not fall on posts; panel edges falling on posts are sawn to allow a ¼-in. gap at the seam for the foam. The perimeters of all rough openings for windows and doors are routed to accept nailers (usually 2x4s)—do this with the nailer-cutter head in the grinder set to full depth. Also rout the outside edge on each corner for a nailer. Where the panel edges need reinforcement, as with wide windows (p. 103), the nailer head is set to one-half the width of the nailer, so the nailer can bridge the joint between panels.

After the panels have been cut and while they're still on the sawhorses, install and secure the splines to one edge of a pair of mating panels. Attach the splines first on the exterior side with 1½-in. galvanized screws and then use regular drywall screws on the other side. Screws should be on approximately 8-in. centers. The nailers on the corners of the house may be put in while the panels are on the ground, but don't put any nailers in window and door openings until the panels are installed, because you want the nailers to span the panel seams for extra reinforcement.

Before positioning the panels, start the nails through the exterior sheathing. The nails used depend on the frame

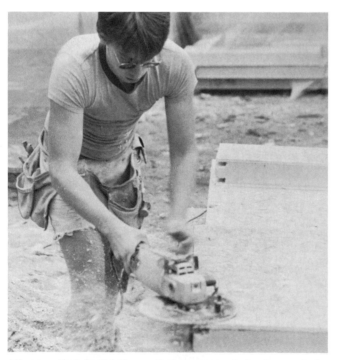

All seams that don't fall over timbers are routed using a grinder with a special spline-cutter head. Goggles and a mask should be used during cutting. (Photo by Sarah Knock.)

Before the panels are lifted into position on the frame, nails are started in the exterior sheathing. In this oak frame, spiral galvanized nails were used to avoid a tannic-acid reaction with bare metal. (Photo by Sarah Knock.)

material. For softwood frames, use an annular ring (pole barn) nail that will penetrate the timbers by at least 2 in. For hardwood frames, use spiral galvanized nails long enough to penetrate the wood by 1½ in. These should be on 8-in. to 10-in. centers around the perimeter. After starting the nails, apply a bead of construction adhesive onto the faces of the posts, beams and 2x12 sill (or face of the box sill) that the panel will be attached to. Starting with an outside corner, lift each panel into place. Slide the panels together horizontally. When installing the top panels in the wall, lift them to the eave string by prying with a flat bar. Drive in the nails.

After the first panel on each wall is in position, you will need to drive subsequent panels together to engage splines. Sometimes it is necessary to do this with a mallet, protecting the panel edge with a block of wood. If the pan-

el length is not greater than 10 ft., it is often easier to drive the splines from above rather than mating the splines edgewise, another reason to put on the wall panels first. In places where panels are stacked on top of each other, use ¼-in. plywood spacers to create a cavity for foam. Make sure to allow at least 2 in. of nailing surface in the timbers for the panel edges. Gable-end wall panels should be shy of the roof panels by the same amount for foaming.

Here the spline is being driven from above. If the panel were over 10 ft. long, this maneuver would not be possible.

These two panels were attached to the frame without pre-installed splines. With the splines in place, the panels often have to be driven together. (Photo by Sarah Knock.)

In this window opening, which has been routed to receive 2x4 nailers, the splines are seen in place. They are screwed to the interior and exterior sheathing. The gap between the splines will be filled with expanding foam later.

Before installing the panels on the roof, snap a line on the purlin or rafter that will be at the first panel seam. Following the line will help ensure that the eave or rake will be straight for the trim. Place a bead of construction adhesive on the roof timbers and the top of the beveled edge of the eave panel prior to placing the roof panels. With the nails already in position, attach the panel when it is aligned with the chalkline. Most roofs require few spline joints because the timbers are on 4-ft. centers. Space the panels ¼ in. from each other with plywood spacers, creating a cavity for foam. If you choose to ignore my instructions about foaming the wall seams, don't carry the illogi-cal thinking up to the roof, for you'd certainly be disappointed with the resulting energy performance.

When all the panels are in position and completely nailed to the frame, install the nailers in all the window and door rough openings and around the perimeter of the roof. Use long, straight material for the roof nailers and set their edges precisely to a string line. This will make installing the roof trim infinitely easier. Secure all nailers with 8d galvanized nails from the exterior skin and screw with drywall screws from the interior skin. Also make sure all the spline joints have been properly screwed and nailed.

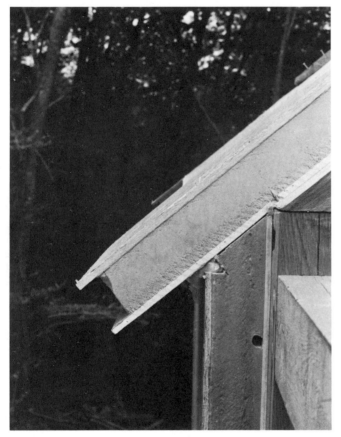

The first roof panel is laid to a chalkline snapped on the frame. Roof-panel edges are routed for a nailer, which is installed when all the roof panels are in place. Note the notch in the wall panel to enable foam to make a good seal with the roof panel.

Nailers are fixed to the window and door openings and to the roof edges after all panels are positioned. Regular drywall screws are used for the interior sheathing and galvanized screws for the exterior. (Photo by Sarah Knock.)

Roof panels are usually lifted into place with a crane. Gaps are deliberately left between roof panels for expanding foam. (Photo by Sarah Knock.)

Now fill all the roof and wall seams with expanding foam. At each spline joint, drill a ¼-in. hole approximately every 14 in. to insert the nozzle of the foam can. Work your way up, not down, the joints. Keep the cans warm and experiment on some scraps before you start because climatic conditions affect foam expansion. We have found that a two-second count on a 14-in. spacing generally fills to the next level quite nicely, but be prepared to adjust the spacing and the count as necessary. After the foam has completely expanded and hardened, scrape the excess from the surface.

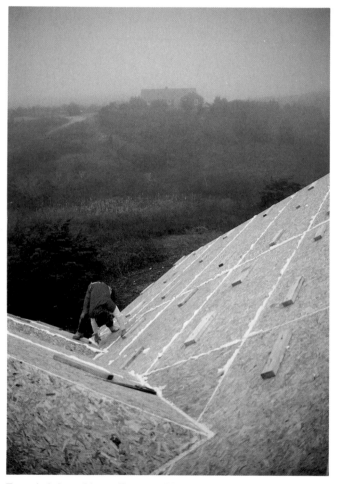

Foam is injected into all seams. Most roof seams are open, since they usually fall on timbers. Seams that fall away from timbers must be splined, and therefore have to be drilled before foam can be injected.

Urethane and polystyrene panels

Urethane and polystyrene are alike in that they both are rigid-foam plastics used for insulation. Thereafter, they are mostly different from each other. Following are some of the advantages and disadvantages of each and a discussion of manufacturing techniques.

Advantages of expanded polystyrene (beadboard)

1. It is easy to manufacture. Polystyrene beads are compressed together under heat and pressure to make a large block, or "bun." The bun is then slabbed with a hot knife to the required thickness.

2. Beadboard is light and easy to work with.

3. Since hot wires are used instead of a router to make cuts, there isn't a problem with dust.

4. Polystyrene accepts various glues and mastics, and generally bonds well to the skins.

Disadvantages of expanded polystyrene

1. Because beadboard panels are so easy to make, too many people are doing it. Panels fabricated under the apple tree are sold alongside those made in well-tooled facilities with good quality control.

2. Polystyrene is a hazard in high heat and fire. It loses its structural integrity at about 180°F and melts at 300°F. In a fire test I witnessed, heat from the fire quickly melted the beadboard into a volatile liquid. My conclusion is that a "Type X" (half-hour fire rating) drywall product should always be used on beadboard panels.

3. Expanded polystyrene panels have potential for radical molecular creep. Dr. Tim Johnson, a technical researcher at Massachusetts Institute of Technology, reports that over a 16-ft. span loaded to 40 lb. per sq. ft. for 90 days, beadboard panel samples shifted 6 in. because of creep. This is a big load and little time; I worry about small loads and lots of time.

4. Most panel manufacturers keep costs down by using 1-lb. instead of 2-lb. density beadboard. Yet a 2-lb. density foam would give better compression strength, a higher R-value and a lower perm rate. Beadboard panels are generally the least expensive, but not because they are on sale.

5. Low R-value per inch means more inches of thickness are necessary for good performance. The lower price of the material is offset when the R-values are equivalent. Window and door jambs and roof edges require more lumber for framing and finish.

Advantages of urethane

1. Urethane has a very high R-value. A panel made to a typical 2x4-stud thickness has an R-value of about 24 to 28.

2. Urethane is typically manufactured at a 2-lb. density. When properly formulated, it is stiff and resilient.

3. Because the panels are fairly thin, they are relatively easy to install. Nailers needed around windows and doors and at roof edges can be 2x4s instead of 2x6s or 2x8s.

4. With a perm rate of 1 or less per inch, the urethane itself acts as a vapor barrier.

5. Panels can be made either by laminating skins to slabbed bun stock or injecting liquid urethane between the skins (called pouring). Panels made from other materials can only be laminated.

6. Good urethane formulations will not support flame. However, they will eventually burn if the fire is fueled by another source.

Disadvantages of urethane

1. Urethane foams are complex. There are hundreds of different formulas and both the manufacturing environment and technique must be precisely monitored. It is rather like Grandma's cake recipe: Leave out one little ingredient and the cake tastes terrible; open the oven for a peek at the wrong moment and it falls flat; and only Grandma knows how to make it right anyway. An increase or decrease in the blowing agent (usually freon) that causes the foam to expand can greatly affect density. If the temperature is too low during manufacture, the foam could be too brittle. There is no generic foam; physical properties change greatly from one company to another. If your supplier hasn't heard of words like isotropic, polyol and isocyanate, you are probably purchasing from the wrong company.

2. Although some formulations do not support flame, most urethane is flammable and the smoke is toxic.

3. Urethane loses some of its R-value as the gases are lost from the cellular structure. Over a period of four or five years, the panel could lose 5 points of R-value. Again, this depends on the particular formula and manufacturing system.

Polystyrene panel construction

Polystyrene panels can be made only by laminating the skins to the slab stock. It's a simple process that helps keep the price down. This panel can literally be made by spreading glue over the surface of the foam, applying the skins, and putting weight on it while it sets.

Laminated-urethane-panel construction

The advantage of lamination is that it isn't technologically as difficult as pouring and the slabs of foam can be pre-cured, meaning the foam should be dimensionally stable and the initial outgassing of propellant should be completed. On the other hand, pouring eliminates the potential deterioration of the adhesive and is much quicker. But because pouring technology is still new, the most important thing for consumers is to buy from reputable manufacturers.

As with polystyrene panels, a laminated urethane panel can literally be made by spreading glue or contact adhesive over the foam surfaces, applying the skins and putting weight on the assembly while it sets. Contact adhesive is used for speed; glue is used when finer technology does not exist. One company I visited used a corps of high school kids to construct giant piles of panels. The kids would mop glue on a skin, place a foam slab on the top, spread more glue and another skin, and so on, until they could no longer reach the top and were ankle deep in glue. Unused buckets of glue were then placed on top to hold down the mountain of sandwiches. The panels actually weren't bad, and though the company went out of business, it wasn't for want of glue.

I have a homespun test for panels. I put samples measuring 4 in. square on the wire cage in a canning pot with several inches of water, and bring the temperature up to 155°F. I leave it there for 12 hours—100% humidity at 155°F, and while not as harsh as what time and weather could do to a panel, it's still a pretty good test. The glue-mopped panels described previously survived the test well, but samples made with contact adhesive failed miserably.

The disadvantages of laminated panels are several. For example, pre-curing often causes tension to build up in the bun stock, resulting in warping. In addition, cutting urethane slabs from the buns leaves a film of dust on each surface because the cellular structure is somewhat brittle. Trying to bond a material to a dusty surface has predictably poor results. In one of the assembly-line gluing processes, the panels are run under a high-pressure pinch roller while contact cement is setting. The pinch roller crushes the cells on the slab surface, making even more dust. It is no wonder that this type of laminated panel almost always falls apart in my canning-pot test in less than four hours. More disconcerting than my private laboratory conclusions have been those occasions when I have found scraps of the material left on the building site that were completely delaminated after only a few weeks of exposure.

Poured-urethane-panel construction

There are two ways to pour panels, vertically and horizontally. In vertical pouring, liquid urethane is injected between two skins set on edge in a form: Vertical simply means that the 4-ft. by 16-ft. or 4-ft. by 8-ft. sheets are standing on edge with the 4-ft. side up. This system requires simple technology and relatively inexpensive equipment, but it is necessarily slow. The skins are placed in the form manually and the foam has to rise 4 ft. before the panel is completed. Because the form has no top, vertically poured panels often show uneven cell structure and therefore would exhibit uneven strength and stability properties.

A bigger disadvantage is that the foam cells rise vertically, and tend to be elongated in the same direction. Considerable compressive strength in the flat direction is lost because of this cellular shape. Think of the cells in the foam as a cluster of eggs. We know eggs to be much stronger in length than width and if they were all lined up lengthwise, this cluster would be easy to crush. When cells are elongated like this, the foam is said to have anisotropic properties, resulting in more strength in the direction of the rise than perpendicular to it. To prevent anisotropism, the foam must have more than 2-lb. density, must be made using the proper amount of blowing agent, and both the urethane and the manufacturing environment must be at the correct temperatures.

In horizontal pouring, liquid ingredients are sprayed between two horizontal skins, one held at the bottom of a form, the other at the top. The foam is thus required to rise only the width of the panel, 3½ in. to 5 in., instead of 4 ft. Cell rise and formation occur in the same direction in which compressive strength is required. Because the foam rise is measureable and consistent, it is possible to make precise adjustments, achieving an isotropic foam and a panel with an excellent bond.

Horizontal pouring also lends itself to automation. Panels can be made on a belted assembly line, giving some assurance that the price will stay reasonable.

VI. Getting Out of the Ground

A timber frame built to last hundreds of years should stand on a foundation designed with the same commitment to longevity.

onstruction of a house begins with bulldozers and ends with 220-grit sandpaper, proceeding from rough to fine, from larger to smaller tolerances. It's a sensible progression. But an unfortunate corollary is the thinking that brawn is needed at the beginning of a job and brains at the end, that it's okay for dirty work to be accompanied by muddy thinking. The roar of heavy machinery, the splash of concrete and the crude piles of dirt are all uninviting, and tend to keep the project planners on the periphery until the "good" work begins. In addition, excavation and foundation work contribute little to the aesthetics of a house, so people are generally less concerned about these stages of the job. This attitude isn't surprising, but it is short-sighted, because the longevity of a building is directly related to the way it sits on the earth. A foundation is a one-shot deal: Once it is in, the die is cast. The building either has a chance to endure or it doesn't. If brains and craftsmanship are applied nowhere else in the house, they should be used to "get out of the ground."

When foundations are taken for granted, their designs are produced for the sole purpose of satisfying code requirements, and the job is usually contracted on the basis of price. On the site, critical decisions are often made by people who are not in a position to know all the criteria that should bear on design and construction. My own experience concerning faulty foundations includes a lesson or two learned the hard way. The excavation for one of our

early projects in northern Massachusetts began in the late fall, well into the time when frost penetration has become a factor to consider when preparing a site. It was my job to lay out the foundation and set the benchmark (the reference point for the top of the wall). Because the site was 70 miles from my home, I left it to the homeowner and the subcontractors to see to it that the work was performed according to our plans and specifications.

On a bleak and forbidding day, a man and a bulldozer worked without enthusiasm or guidance. When they left, the area for the house was roughly excavated, but the tough digging through hard soil and cold weather resulted in an inaccurate job of grading the base of the excavation in preparation for building the footing forms. Nobody thought to protect the newly exposed earth from frost. When the crew showed up to build the footings two days later, they were faced with hard frost, hard soil and uneven terrain. What to do? I can hear them talking: "Why spend the rest of the day working like convicts with picks and shovels because of Bull Dozer's mistakes, when what we need most of all are warmer derrières and fatter wallets?" So they set the form boards without regard for anything or anybody: not for our plans, for the client's house, for the building code, for the laws of physics—not even for their own reputations. At its best, the footing was fully 12 in. deep, as called for in the plans. At its worst, the "footing" was only a 1-in.-thick concrete skim; most of it was between 2 in. and 6 in. thick. These guys had simply nailed some form boards together on top of the uneven, frozen soil and leveled out the concrete in between. To make the story even more tragic, in the next two days another crew came in and poured a wall on this footing. I discovered the crime only after the forms had been stripped. When I went into a rage about the disaster, the owner shrugged, the wall crew pointed to the footing crew, the footing crew pointed to old Bull Dozer, and he pointed back at me. Needless to say, we did not build until the problems were resolved, and I gained some of what they call experience.

In timber-frame housebuilding, the overall high standards and unique structural considerations demand that particularly close attention be paid to both foundation design and construction. Don't assume that foundations typically used with stud construction will satisfy the requirements of a timber-frame building. Unlike a stud-framed house, in which building loads are evenly transferred through hundreds of closely spaced members, a timber frame exerts point loads on a foundation through a few principal posts—between 12 and 16 in a medium to large building. The design of the foundation and the placement of the reinforcing rod within it are geared to coping with these point loads.

In this chapter I'll discuss some basic foundation considerations, as well as the modifications to conventional foundations required by timber frames. I won't go into detail on general foundation information that may be obtained elsewhere. I'll finish by discussing stick-frame and timber-frame floor-deck framing systems.

Foundation design

Soil, climatic and geologic conditions, structural and design features of the building, and grades of the site are important factors in foundation design and are some of the reasons why foundations are not the same everywhere. Building on a delta in Louisiana suggests an entirely different approach from building on a hilltop in Vermont. If the house is to be built in California, it must be designed for earthquakes; if in Minnesota, for deep frost. As in buildings, in foundations there are no standard solutions. Instead there is a vast range of methodologies and options to be weighed against house design and site conditions.

The soil   The real foundation for all buildings is the earth. What we put between the structure and the earth is intended to transmit the load, not support it. Support, or the lack of it, comes from somewhere in the ground beneath the building. So that the sighs and groans of the earth will not destroy the foundation, the building has to be placed on terra firma, never on loose soil or new fill because settling will cause the foundation to crack. You have to dig down to fully compacted, undisturbed earth, and once you get there you have to determine what it is composed of and the best way to build on it.

The quality of the soil is critical in foundation design. Soft soils require that the foundation have a larger bearing area (which means a broader footing) than hard soils or rock would need. The chart at right lists some types of soils and their bearing values. Solid igneous rock has a

bearing capacity of 25 to 40 tons per sq. ft. or more, while soft clay or loose sand might be able to hold only a ton or less. Because they hold water, clay and silt are the bane of good foundations and have to be treated extremely carefully. The potential for excess moisture in these soils reduces their ability to compact and allows them to expand if the moisture freezes. Loose sand, which is difficult to compact, is a problem, too. A mixture of materials is best, such as a gravel having enough clay to allow it to compact well and enough sand to allow moisture to percolate through. Solid bedrock can be great under a foundation, but it, too, has some special requirements. First, a rock surface is not generally tidy and level, so its peaks and valleys have to be carefully cleaned of dirt so that the footings won't shift or slide. Second, holes have to be drilled and rebar inserted to link the foundation to the rock. Third, if you hit rock in one corner of the foundation, you should usually dig to rock for the entire excavation, so the entire foundation will be on the same type of material. (The exception to this is when compactable soils are in a rock basin, because there the soil is contained and can't shift.)

In most cases, general local soil conditions have been well studied and standard foundation specifications for various circumstances are established as part of the code. But don't fall into the trap of allowing a standard specification to fit your non-standard situation—foundations should be specific, not generic. In an urban area, you can learn about soil conditions by looking at the foundations of adjacent buildings. In the country, use the information gathered for the percolation tests done in preparation for designing the septic system. Better yet, attend the tests to see for yourself the soil the foundation will sit on. You don't have to be an engineer to use common sense. If you can make a mud ball that holds together in your hand, the soil contains quite a bit of clay. If you can wring water out of that mud ball or if water fills the test hole on a dry day, an engineer should be consulted before the foundation is designed. Designers and architects sometimes neglect the bearing capacity of the soil; if you have one involved on

Bearing Value for Some Soils	
Type of soil	**Approx. load in tons per sq. ft.**
Soft clay	1
Loose, medium sand	1
Compact, fine sand	2
Coarse gravel	4
Hardpan or partially cemented gravel over rock	10
Sedimentary rock, including sandstone and conglomerates	20
Solid bedrock: granite, slate, gneiss	25

your project, question him or her. Frank Lloyd Wright never visited the site of his house known as Fountainhead. The building was nearly torn apart by soil expansion and needed complete restructuring in a recent renovation.

Climate and geology   Most of the very early timber-frame buildings in this country had foundations that were inadequate for New England winters. Having come from a much more temperate climate, the colonists simply did not know how to deal with the deep penetration of frost that moved and heaved whole buildings. Primarily for this reason, there are few timber-frame buildings left from the first years in this country, although many examples have survived from the 14th and 15th centuries and earlier throughout Europe. Putting a building on top of the ground in harsh New England weather is almost like launching it out onto the rolling sea.

The most obvious concern is freezing, because freezing soil will heave even the heaviest buildings and crack even the most massive foundations if the footing is not designed to penetrate deeper into the ground than the frost. In other words, the footing must be on soil that will never freeze. Local building codes generally have reliable information and good regulations regarding footing depth. Some extremely cold regions demand a depth of at least 6 ft., while some warm areas require only 1 ft. or so. People from the South often wonder why so many New Englanders have full basements, thinking perhaps their breeding encourages things subterranean. Actually, it's a matter of practicality. Because they have to dig 4 ft. to 6 ft. anyway, it often makes sense to go a few extra feet and gain living or storage area.

Foundations are also designed in anticipation of certain natural calamities, such as earthquakes, tornadoes or hurricanes. Local codes in areas prone to such potential disas-

ters usually give good guidance. For example, buildings in quake zones require foundations that are heavily reinforced to resist shearing forces. The idea is that the foundation walls should act as a set of rigidly interconnected beams; in the event of an earthquake, the whole building should move as a unit rather than separating or cracking. I've never experienced a significant earthquake, but people who have been through one tell me that no amount of reinforcement seems like enough in those hair-raising moments of turbulence.

In preparation for earthquakes or high winds, foundations also need a good system for keeping the house firmly attached to the foundation. This is not an overreaction to Dorothy's trip to Oz: Every year there are stories about

Lack of concern by the excavator and foundation subcontractor caused this house to be perched unnaturally high on the ground. Hundreds of yards of fill were trucked in to correct the problem.

For the design potential of this long, low house to be fulfilled, the building needed to nestle into the ground.

buildings that are blown off their foundations. Some attachment systems are described later in this chapter.

Building design and site conditions In addition to responding to the site and climate, the foundation must also meet the design and construction requirements of the building. For example, if the house is intended to conserve energy, so should the foundation. If the house has any peculiar loading situations, they need to be directed through the foundation. The foundation is the building's roots, not just a mass of masonry beneath it. Also, how the foundation is treated can drastically change the look and feel of a building. A Victorian home perched on poles would be an absurdity, but elevated on a foundation with a brick facing,

it could appear lofty. On the other hand, a traditional design perched on a tall foundation can look unconnected to its environment.

Foundations very often are stepped to follow the contour of the land. When houses are well designed, finished grades, terraces and a landscaping scheme are all addressed at the same time as the foundation. Homes built on hillside sites are commonly designed to take advantage of the terrain by gaining living area and outside access at the lowest grade level.

Some general notes As a preface to the discussion of the various foundation systems that follows, here are a few personal prejudices.

With good siting and foundation design, this house fit nicely into a hillside. (Photo by Tafi Brown.)

I favor a system with a full perimeter wall rather than one with slabs or piers. If buildings are going to be well protected from the elements and well insulated, it is practically mandatory to begin with a good seal at the base. In addition, a perimeter foundation takes advantage of the relatively constant temperature of the earth (about 55°F), making the building much easier to heat than when cold exterior air is rushing beneath it.

When using a perimeter wall, I dislike shallow crawl spaces. They are dark, dank and forbidding. People just don't like getting down on their bellies and crawling under houses, so this area usually gets little attention and maintenance. With not enough room for good air movement, mildew is encouraged, along with the subsequent deterioration of framing members. If there is going to be a space, it should be large enough for people to move around freely, and the ceiling should be high enough to allow comfortable walking. A few whacks on the head are discouraging, and as a result a perfectly good cellar seldom gets cleaned and things get dumped but never organized. I know this for a fact.

I like wood, but for first-class homes it seems a risky choice for the foundation material. There is a rising interest in pressure-treated wood foundations, based on the arguments that wood is just as strong as concrete, offers better insulation and is quick to install. But even if all of this is true, there is insufficient data about the life expectancy of pressure-treated wood. Published figures seem to place it at between 50 and 80 years. If it were advertised to last twice that long, it still wouldn't sound right to me. Especially for timber-frame buildings, foundation life spans should not be this limited.

I like poured concrete—a mixture of portland cement (lime, silica and alumina), aggregate and water. The concrete we use today is similar to the material first used by the ancient Romans. Some of their concrete buildings and roads have survived, demonstrating the durability of the material. When the Roman Empire fell, so did this wonderful recipe. It wasn't rediscovered until the late 1700s and was seldom used until the early part of this century.

Concrete is, I think, one of the most important developments in the building field. Because it is reasonable in cost, concrete makes durable buildings possible for everyone. It can be molded to fit even the most irregular contour, it hardens to a degree we can calculate and control, and it gives strength and design flexibility with few limitations. The timber-frame buildings we construct today have an opportunity to exceed the expected lifespan of those made by our predecessors in the craft, not because of any greater skill in joinery but because of better foundations. Concrete is the key.

The richer the concrete is in cement, the stronger it will be. Density is increased by adding more cement to the mix. Common concrete for houses is rated at 2,500 psi; exotic new formulations have made 15,000 to 20,000 psi possible. For our timber-frame homes, we have established 3,000-psi concrete as the minimum standard for most situations.

Properly mixed and poured, concrete is very strong in compression. A poured concrete wall does not have the shear planes inherent in walls stacked from stone, brick or concrete block (p. 119), so it has much more resistance to lateral loads. But concrete is not an elastic material and is fairly weak in shear strength. Strength can be increased many times, however, by placing metal bars (rebar) or wire mesh as reinforcement into the forms before the concrete is poured. These bars come in sizes designated by numbers 2 through 8. Each number represents one-eighth of an inch. A #2 bar is two-eighths, or ¼ in.; a #5 bar is five-eighths, and so on. For residential construction, #4 and #5 bars are the most common. Wire mesh is employed mostly for flatwork such as slabs, walks and patios.

Obviously, I am totally in favor of improving foundation standards and making the foundations for our houses better. Better usually means more difficult and more expensive, and I offer no slick techniques for circumventing this. I'd rather talk about how to save money on the roofing material or the siding or the cabinets—items that can be more easily upgraded later. To me as a building professional, the only risk in having a first-class foundation is that it may last too long, and I know of worse gambles.

Continuous footings

Most foundations are constructed in two parts: footings first, then walls or piers. The footings allow the building load to be distributed to the earth over a larger area, as well as providing a more or less level surface for forming the rest of the foundation. A continuous footing is used for a perimeter-wall system. The footings for pier foundations are discussed with the systems they support, although many of the rules for continuous footings apply to these footings, too.

The width and thickness of the footing are determined by analyzing the weight of the building (including the concrete walls), the way loads are distributed by the structure, and the type of earth upon which the building will sit. Most codes have some general standards for footing size, concrete density and reinforcement. But these regulations should be seen for what they are—a minimum standard—and should not be applied blindly to every circumstance. Verify the situation by adding up the load that will be dis-

Continuous footing and perimeter-wall foundation

POINT LOAD SPREAD THROUGHOUT WALL

½"X10" ANCHOR BOLTS 6'-0" O.C.

#4 REBAR, TWO ROWS TOP AND BOTTOM

VERTICAL REINFORCEMENT AT POSTS

15# FELT PAPER

¾" CRUSHED STONE

DRAIN PIPE

10"X24" FOOTING REINFORCED WITH #4 REBAR

KEYWAY

10"-THICK POURED CONCRETE WALL

CONCRETE SLAB WITH 6"X6"X10-GAUGE WELDED WIRE MESH

VAPOR BARRIER

2" SAND ABOVE AND BELOW RIGID-FOAM INSULATION

tributed to each timber post. It will probably fall in the range of 3 to 5 tons at each location, including the weight of the foundation. Compare this with the bearing capacity of the soil. If the soil is soft, the footing may have to be broader and thicker to distribute the load over a larger area.

A typical continuous footing in timber-frame construction is between 8 in. and 12 in. thick and between 16 in. and 28 in. wide. Footings should have some reinforcement and a keyway (a groove along the length of the footing) to ensure a better bond with the wall. For a timber-frame building having normal loads on a site with good soil, our standard continuous footing is 10 in. thick by 24 in. wide, reinforced with two #4 bars and poured with 3,000-psi concrete. We always specify a keyway, and sometimes we even get one. Any questionable circumstances warrant a session with an engineer.

Footings must be accurately positioned and roughly level. Other than this, building the forms for them is not necessarily precise work, although it can require creativity because the rough excavation often doesn't offer an accurate base. Remember that the real foundation is the earth, and the footing must be on undisturbed ground. I once visited a project while footings were being formed and found a "professional" filling in the footing area with loose soil from the excavation to make leveling the form boards easier. His surprise and anger that I would question him about this gave me much to think about. Obviously, I was criticizing his standard practice. Such people doing some of the most important work in the house is an unnerving reality.

Footings can be poured completely in the ground, partially in the ground and partially out, or entirely on the excavation, as shown at right. If the footing is continuous, it is better to pour it on the excavation to leave room for drainage and/or insulation. The base of the footing should be fairly level across the width as well as in length—an uneven base is prone to breaking, which could reduce the bearing area of the footing to that of the wall and render the footing useless. A sloped grade could cause the footing to slip, so footings on slopes should be stepped to keep the bearing area flat. Footing forms are usually made of 2x framing stock. Wooden stakes and straps secure and stabilize the form boards.

Forming continuous footings

STRAP STABILIZES CORNER.

STRAP

STAKES DRIVEN INTO GROUND

2X FORM BOARDS

FOOTINGS CAN BE POURED ON THE EXCAVATION . . .

. . . HALF IN AND HALF OUT . . .

. . . OR FULLY TRENCHED.

Poured concrete wall

A poured concrete perimeter wall is the foundation system we use most. In timber-frame house construction, the foundation wall must distribute the point loads from the frame to the larger area of the footing. To improve the wall's capacity to withstand the weight and distribute the load, we commonly specify two lengths of #4 rebar running horizontally at the top of the wall and two running at the bottom. These parallel bars create flanges of tensile strength, and the vertical wall section transfers the forces between. In most parts of the country, the general standard is 8-in. thick walls, poured with 2,500-psi concrete. For timber-frame buildings, the minimum standards should be increased to 10 in. and 3,000-psi concrete. Soil conditions or heavy loads often demand additional reinforcement and greater concrete density.

It's possible to make your own foundation, using site-built forms of 2x4s and plywood or boards. But because of the labor and materials savings, most concrete work is done by professionals who use specialized forms that are easily assembled. Get bids from firms recommended by other professionals and hire the one who doesn't argue about your desire to improve on the generally accepted standards.

Concrete-block wall

A preference for using concrete block often reflects regional eccentricities or characteristics that make poured concrete difficult to use. For instance, in areas where aggregate material, which is essential to the concrete recipe, is scarce, the price of poured concrete is sometimes prohibitive. Good examples are parts of upper New York State and Florida, where clay and sand, respectively, predominate. Remote rural regions and islands might not have a concrete mixing plant because the economy cannot sup-

port it. Concrete can be mixed by hand but the work is obviously labor-intensive. In addition, the end product isn't as strong as a wall made with a continuous pour, because cold joints (incomplete bonds) are created in the wall between areas that cure at different times. And then there are areas where there is plenty of material for great concrete but the tradespeople demand what seem to be excessive prices. Accepting this and dealing with it can be just too much. In all these cases, concrete block becomes an attractive alternative.

Besides having an inherent shear problem, concrete block walls, unassisted, have about one-quarter the compressive strength of poured concrete walls. To increase wall strength for timber-frame construction, it is important to concentrate on the point loads. Long runs of block wall, subject to buckling from soil pressure, are commonly reinforced with wall extensions called pilasters at every principal post. Two purposes are thus served: The wall is strengthened against shear forces, and the bearing area of the wall is increased at the critical point-load positions. Also, because principal posts in a frame are usually in alignment with principal beams, including girders for the first floor, pilasters can also serve as a bearing surface for the girders. A common dimension for a pilaster is 16 in. by 24 in. so that typical 8x16 blocks can be woven into the wall without cutting. The pilasters are further reinforced by filling all the cores with concrete and running four pieces of #5 rebar vertically through the cores under the posts.

Because the pilasters are designed to take the full load of the building, the sections of wall between pilasters is essentially non-load-bearing, serving only to resist the lateral pressure of the soil. Eight-inch-wide blocks can be used, but the wall will still need horizontal and vertical rein-

Concrete-block wall

8X8 POST

TIMBER SILL

2X12 SILL

#4 REBAR APPROXIMATELY 4' O.C. HORIZONTALLY AND VERTICALLY

CONCRETE-FILLED BOND BLOCK

EACH JOINT IS A NATURAL SHEAR LINE.

PRESSURE-TREATED TIMBER-SUPPORT BLOCK

TIMBER GIRDER

STRESS-SKIN PANEL

POST MOVED IN FROM BLOCK WALL ALLOWS STRESS-SKIN PANEL TO REST ON FOUNDATION.

FLOORING

TIMBER GIRDER

2X12 PRESSURE-TREATED SILL

PRESSURE-TREATED TIMBER-SUPPORT BLOCK

½"X10" ANCHOR BOLT

16"X24" PILASTER

FOOTING AT LEAST 6" LARGER THAN PILASTER IN ALL DIRECTIONS

FOUR VERTICAL #5 REBARS AT POST LOCATIONS

forcement to increase shear strength. For vertical reinforcement, run two lengths of #4 rebar 4 ft. on center and fill the block cores with concrete. For horizontal reinforcement, use #4 rebar 4 ft. on center, substituting bond blocks (special hollow blocks) for regular blocks in that course to contain the rebar and concrete. Vertical and horizontal bars should be tied at their intersections.

The middle of the pilaster is the strongest point, and so it makes sense to push the timber post back from the edge of the foundation wall. This also allows the wall to support the stress-skin panels, rather than being overhung by them, as is the case with poured concrete walls.

Footings for concrete block walls are poured concrete and are identical to those for poured walls. But note that footings are poured for pilasters at the same time as the walls. Footings should be 6 in. larger than the proposed pilaster in each direction in normal soil, more in soft soils.

Perimeter wall and slab foundation

The two foundations I've just described are most often used in buildings having full basements or crawl spaces. These foundations can also be used for slab-on-grade construction. When there is fill on both sides of the wall, the forces are equalized and there is less need for reinforcement against lateral pressure—pilasters on a block wall would not be necessary, for example. Excavation for this type of foundation proceeds quite differently, for instead of a bulldozer to level the entire area, only a backhoe is needed to trench for the walls. As usual, footings must extend below the frost line. Although it is expensive to put this much effort into making a foundation that is almost entirely hidden from sight, it offers the surest strength and the most complete protection of any slab-on-grade system.

Grade beam and pier foundation

In this type of foundation, a reinforced concrete beam is built over a rubble trench (a trench filled with crushed stone) and supported by reinforced concrete piers. If a basement or crawl space is not required and if the area to be built upon is fairly level, this system is perfectly suitable for timber-frame structures. Although labor-intensive, it's economical of materials and can be installed without professional assistance. Probably the biggest drawback for cold climates is that this foundation is hard to insulate well. Because the beam does not extend below the frost line, a lot of heat is lost from the house at the bottom of the wall, where frozen soil is close to the heated house interior.

The entire building area is first excavated to remove the topsoil and then roughly leveled to a grade beneath the slab, allowing for insulation and drainage fill. The perimeter is then trenched another 1 ft. deep and 2 ft. wide, with the approximate center of the beam being the center of the trench. Holes are then drilled or dug around the perimeter for piers—the piers should align exactly with the principal posts in the frame and extend below the frost line. Piers are a minimum of 10 in. in diameter. Spans greater than 12 ft. require intermediate support from additional piers in cold climates to control potential heaving. Otherwise, the design of the timber frame determines the number of piers and their locations.

Perimeter wall and slab foundation

RIGID-FOAM INSULATION
½"X10" ANCHOR BOLT
SLAB
REINFORCING MESH
RIGID-FOAM INSULATION
POURED CONCRETE FOUNDATION WALL
POURED CONCRETE FOOTING
#4 REBAR

Grade beam and pier foundation

GRADE BEAM
SLAB WITH WIRE MESH REINFORCEMENT
FOUR #5 REBARS TIED IN LOOP EVERY 3'
RIGID-FOAM INSULATION
SAND BED
1½" CRUSHED STONE
MINIMUM 10" DIA. PIER ABOUT 6" BELOW FINISHED GRADE
FORMED OR FLARED FOOTING
WIRE MESH REINFORCEMENT
FOUR #5 REBARS IN EACH PIER

If the soil is good, it may be possible simply to flare the pier hole at the bottom for a larger bearing area. If not, it may be necessary to prepare a larger footing area and pour it separately. Plan for the top of the piers to be about 6 in. below finished grade. Most important, they must be level with each other. Forms for the piers could be round cardboard tubes made for this purpose or simple square forms made from framing stock and boards. One advantage of cardboard tubes is that since they can be backfilled before the pour, they do not require bracing. Each pier should have at least four lengths of #5 rebar that extend about 2 ft. above the top of the proposed concrete beam.

After the piers are completed, the perimeter trench is filled with 1½-in. crushed stone for drainage and then compacted. In poor soil, it may be advisable to put drain tile in the trench to carry away excess water. The bed of crushed stone should initially be leveled to the top of the piers to support the beam; more stone is added later. After these steps, the form is built for the grade beam. Typical dimensions are 12 in. wide by 18 in. high, but dimensions really depend on the specific site. Forms can be built with 2x framing stock for the sides and 1x3s for stakes and strapping. Although the building load will be concentrated on the piers, it's still important that the beam be well reinforced—usually, four #5 bars running in two parallel rows at top and bottom is adequate. Splice the perimeter rebar lengthwise and tie them in a loop (stirrup) 3 ft. on center with #2 rebar. Vertical bars from the piers are bent over at the top and tied to perimeter bars. Use 3,000-psi concrete for piers and 3,500 psi for the grade beam. A slab is poured, using conventional procedures, after footings for the interior posts are installed (see p. 122).

Thickened-edge slab foundation

In areas where freezing is not a concern, monolithic slabs can be poured in which the outer edge is thickened to increase strength and bearing area. Thickened-edge slabs are usually used with buildings that have evenly distributed loads; the dimensions of the thick edge tend to be constant around the perimeter. For timber-frame buildings, it is necessary to modify the design slightly to create larger pads at each post location to distribute the point loads.

If the frame will be insulated with stress-skin panels, plan for the completed foundation to be 3 in. to 4 in. larger than the timber frame in each direction. Excavate the area first by scraping to a level below the slab (including insulation and drainage soil). Trenching the perimeter for the thickened edge requires some handwork, because the transition from the slab to the trench is gently sloped—slab thickness in the middle should be about 4 in., pitching to 6 in. toward the outside of the foundation. Trench dimensions are generally about 12 in. deep and 18 in. wide before tapering to the slab. At the time of excavation a pad should be prepared for each post location. Pad size depends on building loads and soil type (often pads are 24 in. square or more). When the excavation is completed, a one-sided form is built around the outside in preparation for a continuous pour of concrete for slab, trench and pads.

Four lengths of #4 rebar are run parallel around the perimeter of the trench, two on top and two on the bottom. Linear splices are overlapped and tied. Each post pad is further reinforced with a mat of #4 rebar, crisscrossed 6 in. on center. The mat should be tied to the lower perimeter rebar to help distribute the loads. The remaining slab is reinforced with 6x6, 10-gauge wire mesh, which should be tied to the rebar intersections. Concrete should be at least 3,000 psi.

Thickened-edge slab foundation

2X12 SILL
2X8 SILL

SECTION VIEW

#4 REBAR

RIGID INSULATION

SLAB REINFORCED WITH 6"X6"X10-GAUGE WIRE MESH
TRANSITION FROM SLAB TO PAD SLIGHTLY SLOPED
SAND BED

SAND BED

CORNER OF POST PAD
PADS REINFORCED WITH MAT OF #4 REBARS, CRISS-CROSSED 6" ON CENTER.

RIGID FOAM INSULATION

THICKENED EDGE

POST PAD, 24" SQUARE OR MORE

PLAN VIEW

FOUNDATION IS 3" TO 4" LARGER ALL AROUND THAN THE TIMBER FRAME IF STRESS-SKIN PANELS WILL BE USED.

Interior post footings and supports

All the foundations described so far also need a series of footings to transmit the loads at interior post locations. These footings are generally between 10 in. and 12 in. thick and approximately 24 in. to 28 in. square, and are located under the slab. The forms are made using 2x framing stock and stakes. Reinforcement is usually wire mesh, but a mat of welded or tied rebar is better. These footings should also be poured on undisturbed soil with 3,000-psi concrete.

Either wood posts or concrete-filled steel piers are used to support the first floor (see p. 125 for more on interior posts). Capped steel piers can be set directly on top of the footing before the slab is poured. When the concrete sets, the pier is locked into position. When a wood post is used, a tapered, concrete plinth topped with a pressure-treated wood cap keeps the post off the concrete; otherwise, the post would draw moisture from the concrete and rot. Plinth dimensions are determined by the base of the post and the proposed thickness of the slab. The plinth top should be the same size as the post bottom, the taper should be about 20° outward to the base, and the top of the plinth should extend 3 in. above the slab. A ¾-in. metal pin (an anchor bolt without the nut will also work), set into the top of the plinth and protruding by about 4 in., keeps the post from moving.

Making the form for the plinth may seem a little tricky, but it's really just basic carpentry. Yet on our jobs, specifying this little oddity on plans for foundation contractors has resulted in almost every conceivable shape—from a round beauty created with the bottom of a tar bucket to a freeform job made by a person who probably flunked clay in kindergarten. (One contractor even refused to do the job unless we supplied the plinths already poured.) We now keep a few plinth forms on hand for such emergencies.

Concrete pier foundation

For buildings such as vacation homes and workshops, where energy efficiency is not a priority, a concrete pier foundation can be used. Lack of integration between the piers makes this system inherently weaker than other foundations, but some people like its easy installation and economy. Follow the guidelines for constructing piers in the section on grade beams and piers, with these changes: Increase minimum diameter to 12 in., and don't extend the rebar beyond the pier top. Even with reinforcement, these piers are weak against lateral shear, so they should not extend more than 2½ ft. above finished grade.

I don't recommend this system, but if it must be used, err on the side of strength in calculations and construction. I once advised an acquaintance about the construction of a pier foundation, but when he built it the piers extended much higher above grade than I had recommended. They were also smaller in diameter and without the necessary rebar. The way I heard the story, two piers broke when he and a friend leaned on them during a visit to the site.

A note on foundation insulation

There's no magic formula for building a house with good energy performance, and all our efforts with insulating and sealing would be misspent if we neglected the foundation level. As in the foundation itself, use the best materials. Insulation placed under a slab or outside a foundation is not likely to be replaced, so do it well the first time. For most situations, there should be 2 in. of rigid foam (R-value of 12 to 16) on the exterior of the walls and under the slab. In very cold climates, more than 2 in. may be required above grade. But wall insulation shouldn't always be installed on the outside. For instance, if the basement is unheated, I can't see how the concrete walls can be used for heat storage; worse, if the area is heated only occasionally, the cool concrete walls would have to be warmed before the room would be comfortable. Using such arguments, we often specify insulation on the inside of the foundation walls.

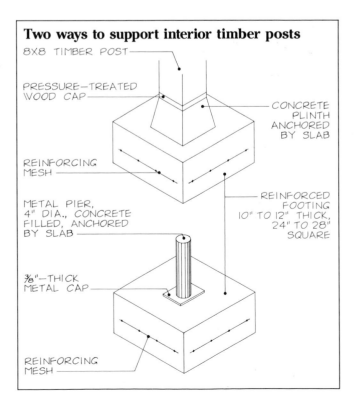

Two ways to support interior timber posts

8X8 TIMBER POST

PRESSURE-TREATED WOOD CAP

CONCRETE PLINTH ANCHORED BY SLAB

REINFORCING MESH

METAL PIER, 4" DIA., CONCRETE FILLED, ANCHORED BY SLAB

REINFORCED FOOTING 10" TO 12" THICK, 24" TO 28" SQUARE

⅜"–THICK METAL CAP

REINFORCING MESH

Concrete pier foundation

2'–6" MAXIMUM ABOVE GRADE

½"X10" ANCHOR BOLT

FOUR #4 REBARS, NOT TO EXTEND BEYOND TOP OF PIER

PIER, 12" MINIMUM DIA.

FORMED OR FLARED FOOTING

Floor decks for timber-frame houses

To cap the foundation and form the base of the timber frame, you can use either timbers or conventional stick-framing materials. Compelling arguments can be made for the latter option. Wood placed close to the ground needs to be rot-resistant, and the species with the best natural resistance, such as white oak, chestnut, cypress and redwood, are not as available in timber dimensions as they once were. Good materials for capping the foundation, including pressure-treated lumber, are much more available in stick-framing dimensions than they are in timber dimensions. For strength, it's no longer necessary to use a system made from timbers. In the heyday of timber framing, houses were usually supported with stone foundations of dubious dependability, which racked, heaved and settled, often subjecting the floor system to incredible stresses. But with sills fully supported by the best sort of modern foundation, the only force encountered by the platform is compression. A stick floor system therefore offers little compromise in strength. Also, when the basement area is not used as a living space, the workmanship of the first-floor frame does not contribute significantly to the aesthetic quality of the home. The above considerations and the realities of building costs and budgets often lead to the use of conventional construction for the floor deck of a timber-frame house.

Having said all this, we find we are slowly going back to using timbers in the floor decks of our houses for several reasons. First, we have encountered poor workmanship when relying on local carpenters to build the decks in preparation for our arrival with the frame. Too often we truck completed frames from our shop to sites and find decks that are neither square nor level, and that have the pockets for the post tenons in the wrong places. In the time it takes to fix these mistakes, we could have cut the timber deck in our shop and installed it on the site. Second, we have never been happy with the weak link at the corners of a conventionally framed deck. The outside corners have two headers butted together and nailed, but a force parallel to the direction of the nail can easily pry the two apart. Third, using a sill made from pressure-treated lumber under the timber sill reduces the potential for rot. Fourth, it makes sense to us to continue the heirloom quality of the frame right through to the deck.

Still, if a stick-frame deck is chosen for economic reasons and the area beneath it won't be a primary living area, it's not an outrageous compromise. Following is a discussion of both stick and timber systems.

Stick-frame floor deck   Only a few refinements are necessary to adapt a conventional system to a timber frame. First, the arrangement of girders should coincide with the linear arrangement of posts in the frame, either parallel or perpendicular to the bents, depending on post layout. Doing this means that the piers needed to support the girders can then also be located beneath principal posts—a system necessary to transfer the point loads to the footings. The decision regarding how girders are run in relation to frame and foundation is based on giving each interior timber post direct pier support while keeping the floor-joist spans as short as possible.

It's hard to beat the durability and the heirloom quality of a timber deck.

Stick-frame floor deck

METAL STRAPS AT CORNERS

CHIMNEY OPENING

STAIR OPENING

CORNER MORTISE

BOX BEAM

PERIMETER MORTISE

INTERIOR MORTISE

CORNER MORTISE

BLOCKING

2X8 SILL

2X12 SILL

PERIMETER MORTISE

INTERIOR MORTISE

SPLICED 2X10'S OVERLAY GIRDER.

BLOCKING FORMS SIDES OF POST MORTISE.

GIRDER

SEATING POST ON BUILT-UP MORTISE CAN RESULT IN EXCESSIVE SHRINKAGE.

SEATING POST DIRECTLY ON GIRDER MINIMIZES SHRINKAGE.

2X10 JOIST

SPLICED 2X10'S

GIRDER MADE FROM FOUR 2X10'S

4"-DIA. STEEL SUPPORT COLUMN

SHRINKAGE

SHRINKAGE

Second, the bottom sill (the 2x12 sill) must extend 4½ in. to 5½ in. beyond the outer edge of the deck to cap the insulation. Use a naturally rot-resistant wood (redwood or cedar, for instance) or pressure-treated lumber. The 2x12 sills are bolted to the foundation over a termite shield and sill seal using good standard technique. A second sill, typically a 2x8, is attached to the first with its outside edge set to a chalkline representing the outside dimensions of the timber frame. Corner joints of the 2x8 sill should overlap the 2x12 sill to lock the corners. Where sills butt together end to end, stagger the joints to prevent weak areas.

Third, the perimeter rim joist must be doubled up with blocking to form a box beam. This beam helps to distribute the load to the foundation and is designed with a built-up mortise at post locations to receive post tenons. The extra blocking is extremely important because it gives the post full bearing on the foundation. Outside corners are weak and should be reinforced with metal straps.

Fourth, at interior post locations, a mortise is created in the girder by leaving a gap in one of the laminates. In this case, as well as around the perimeter, the size of the mortise-and-tenon joint is set by the thickness of the framing stock—usually 1½ in. When subfloor sheathing has good compressive strength, the post tenon can be passed through to the box beam or girder, with the post resting on top of the sheathing. When joists overlay the girder, seat the post directly on the girder rather than making a built-up mortise in the joists on top of the girder. Since wood shrinks mostly across the grain, doing this halves the potential shrinkage (bottom drawings, facing page).

Sometimes girders are to be supported with metal piers instead of wood posts. In most situations, the piers not only bear a portion of the first-floor load, they also bear a significant load from the weight of the frame, all other floor loads above the first, and loads from the roof and all the other building materials. Many tons of weight have to be supported at that one point. Do not use hollow, telescoping jack posts; these are not strong enough. Instead use heavy-duty, concrete-filled steel piers, but do not use the small, thin caps that usually come with these posts. Have top and base caps made from ⅜-in.-thick plate metal, and increase the bearing area to about 50 sq. in. I have seen a typical 3/16-in. cap turned over like a mushroom and crushed into the girder by nearly ½ in.

When using timber posts to support the girders, use straight-grained material with few defects. In normal loading situations, posts should be at least 7 in. by 7 in. Join the posts to the girder with a mortise-and-tenon joint. The mortise is made in the same manner as for the timber-frame posts that join the girder from above.

Here timber posts are used to support a built-up girder. The posts are joined to the girder with mortise-and-tenon joints.

Building on pier foundations requires some modifications because the sills do not have continuous support. It is therefore necessary to build up a laminated perimeter beam to bear the floor load for the spans between piers. Use a 2x12 as the sill, extended to cap the insulation, and nail it to the perimeter beam. Other details and considerations in the contruction are similar to those described previously.

Slab-on-grade foundations, of course, have no interior floor framing, though there is still a need to receive the perimeter posts. A simple box beam, shown on the facing page, serves several purposes. The timber posts are locked into position and anchored to the foundation through other materials. The load from the posts is distributed more evenly to the foundation. The built-up beam running around the perimeter provides a good surface for attaching insulation. The 2x12 sill is bolted to the foundation as described previously. Before attaching the 2x8 box-beam base to the 2x12 sill, nail 2x4s to either side. And before nailing on the 2x8 cap, prepare a mortise at each post loca-

Stick-frame deck on pier foundation

LAMINATED
2X BEAM

BLOCKING FOR
POST SUPPORT

MORTISE CREATED
FOR POST TENON
BY LEAVING GAP IN
ONE OF THE LAYERS

2X12
SILL

2X JOISTS
16" O.C.

CONCRETE PIER

tion and add blocking for additional support. The cavity in the box beam can be used to run wiring, as discussed in Chapter VII.

If a house is built on a sloping site or uneven terrain, the top of the foundation might actually be on two or three levels to follow the contour of the land. You then need to build walls between the lower foundation levels and the first-floor level. There are two options. You can use a timber at each post location, insulating the wall the same way as the timber-frame walls above. Or you can frame conven-

tionally, but it might be necessary to go to extreme measures to keep the insulation value the same as that provided by the stress-skin panels (asssuming you use that system) on the rest of the house. And to support the girders and principal timber posts, you would also have to fabricate posts by laminating framing members together. Because there's so much complicated work in trying both to support the posts and match the insulation level of the rest of the house, there's no real time or money savings in this method—we've found it makes much more sense just to

Box beam for slab-on-grade foundation

SPACE FOR TENON

POST

2X8 BOX-BEAM CAP

STRESS-SKIN PANEL

CONCRETE WALL

2X8 BOX-BEAM BASE

2X8 SILL

2X12 SILL

CONCRETE SLAB

use timber posts and continue the insulation from the frame down to the sill.

If you use posts between the lower foundation levels and the first-floor level, you'll have to make some changes in the typical sill system. Eliminate the sill overhang where the post wall on the first-floor level begins, since the insulation continues to the base sill. Remember that a box-beam sill is used only where there is full bearing on the foundation. Where the foundation drops to a different level, it is necessary to use a solid laminated beam similar to that used with a pier foundation. For the lower sill, use the box beam described for the slab-on-grade foundation. The ground-level posts are cut to length with tenons on both ends to join to mortises in the box beam on slab level and in the solid beam on floor level, as shown below. Note that knee braces can be joined from the posts to the laminated

Supporting houses with stepped foundations

STRESS—SKIN PANELS RUN UNINTERRUPTED TO BASE SILL.

TIMBER GIRT

TIMBER POST

FIRST-FLOOR LEVEL

2X FLOOR JOISTS

GRADE

BOX BEAM SILL

LAMINATED CARRYING BEAM

TIMBER POST

CONCRETE FOUNDATION WALL

2X8 BOX BEAM CAP

SLAB-ON-GRADE STYLE OF BOX-BEAM SILL

CONCRETE SLAB AND INSULATION

GRADE

CONCRETE FOUNDATION WALL

beam using the same technique to join the tenon to the laminated beam. However, unless the post wall projects from the foundation as an ell or extension, knee braces serve only to stiffen the laminated beam; racking forces should be completely absorbed by the foundation walls.

Timber-frame floor deck   Using a timber floor is the surest way to maintain the integrity and strength of the rest of the frame. When the ground-floor level is used as living area (a family room, for example), the beauty of the timbers is an obvious advantage.

The system begins with a 2x12 sill and a 2x8 sill in the same manner as for a stick-frame deck. These members cap the insulation and protect the timber sill from moisture. Historically, chestnut and white oak were widely used for sills, but chestnut is now nearly extinct, and good white

Using a timber floor system gives the basement area continuity, beauty and strength. Concrete plinths protect the posts from absorbing moisture from the floor. (Photo by Gordon Cook.)

oak is hard to find. Most of the woods good for timber framing are not especially moisture resistant—redwood and cedar would be good choices for the timber sill but quality, availability and cost can be problems. Getting a suitably moisture-resistant sill in lumber dimensions is obviously much easier and less expensive. When a timber sill is used on a continuous foundation, it doesn't need to be very large because it doesn't have to carry the weight of

the floor in an open span. It need only be thick enough to allow good connections to floor joists and girders, and wide enough to transfer the weight of the posts to the foundation (a timber sill for average circumstances might be about 5 in. thick by 8 in. wide). A wire chase can be created by making the sill slightly narrower than the posts.

Stick-dimension sills are anchored easily to the foundation using typical anchor bolts, but a different technique is

Typical timber floor deck

STRESS—SKIN PANEL

POST

TIMBER SILL

TIMBER GIRDER

TIMBER JOIST

2X8 SILL

2X12 SILL

CONCRETE WALL

required for anchoring timber sills. Various scarf joints are used to make linear connections in the sills, and several types of mortise-and-tenon joints are used to join sills at the corners. In every case, except for very simple (and very inferior) scarfs, these joints need to slide together horizontally, which makes it nearly impossible to set the sills over bolts. A practical solution is to nail flat metal straps to the 2x8 sill, join and position the timber sill, then bend the straps up on the outside face and onto the top of the sill, as shown below. (The timber has to be routed at each strap location to keep materials flush.) Nail the straps to the sill using 16d galvanized nails. The straps should be of at least 16-gauge material, and usually need to be located on 4-ft. centers, but check your local code.

Floor joists and girders can be joined to the timber sill with either dovetail or mortise-and-tenon joints. The timber sill is tabled (notched) at each joint area to allow the beam to rest on the 2x8 sill. When girders require more bearing than is provided by the thickness of the timber sill, the 2x8 sill can be notched to allow the girder to rest on the 2x12 sill. If a block foundation is used, the projecting pilaster can be used to support the girders, but there should still be a protective sill under the timbers. After all the floor timbers are joined, planking or a built-up floor system is installed, as described in Chapter X.

A combination system is used by a few timber framers to reduce the expense of the deck and maintain the integrity of the floor system. Timbers are used for the sills and girders, allowing for good connections and load transfer. The joists, however, are typical 2x stock, attached to the timbers with joist hangers. The conventional joists bear only the floor loads, while the timbers are used as the primary beasts of burden. The savings is in eliminating all of the joinery involved with the floor joists.

Anchoring timber sills

VII. Wiring and Lighting

The warm colonial atmosphere of this area is achieved by using soft lighting and stained wood.

Sprawled throughout our rooms like sleeping snakes, wires are an umbilical cord to the accessories of the 20th century. In my small home office alone, there are wires for two lamps; three wires for the computer; one for the telephone; two for a radio and headset; one for a drill waiting for a job in the corner; and another dangling overhead, begging for a light fixture. Thousands of linear feet of wire course through our walls, pulsing with energy people feel they can't live without. Linking us to all the things considered necessary to a civilized lifestyle, often including heating and plumbing, the electrical system is the central nervous system of the modern home. We are hooked on electricity, and although we may occasionally begrudge the price that's paid for it and perhaps even argue philosophically that life is really not finer for it, not many people would trade it in for a life unfettered.

In timber-frame homebuilding, the issue of wiring often causes puzzlement and frustration in homeowners, builders and electricians alike. "Just how do you get wires through walls built of 6x8 and 8x8 timbers enclosed with solid stress-skin panels?" many of my clients want to know. When I explain the process we use, they are usually surprised at its straightforward logic, having expected that they would have to live amid coils of exposed wires or pay for techniques of incomprehensible complexity. Still, no matter how simple wiring a timber-frame house is in theory, there is bound to be misadventure. Many of the proce-

dures for wiring timber-frame structures fall outside conventions of the trade, and a set of new rules has yet to be formalized. Timber-frame designers and builders therefore sometimes neglect to take the time to consider the electrical system, waiting until it's too late to solve problems creatively. Caught up in the excitement of building their house, homeowners often ignore the entire question of electricity, with the result that their rooms are not illuminated in the way they would have liked and outlets and switches are inconveniently located. Confused electricians, relying on intuition rather than on systematic procedures, are often driven to poke at the timbers with their drills as if the frame were a giant voodoo doll.

The problem of wiring a timber-frame house is further complicated by the fact that there is no one right way to do the job. Instead there is a wide selection of options, some more appropriate than others, depending on the particular condition. In studying electrical systems, our goal therefore is to cultivate a way of thinking that will give us the flexibility to evaluate each situation individually and to choose the very best option possible. Only with a thorough understanding of the basic principles can we hope to have the ability to make intelligent choices.

In this chapter, I will discuss the techniques of wiring a typical timber-frame house that uses stress-skin panels as its enclosure system. I focus on stress-skins because most timber-frame houses today use them, and they require the newest methodology. (When the built-up systems are used, conventional wiring practice can be employed to a greater degree.) Bear in mind, as you proceed through this chapter, that timber frames and the systems used to enclose them do not change the theories of electrical wiring or the rules governing circuit design. Nothing about the timber-frame building system alters decisions about wire size and type, switching options, safety or any other matter related to what it takes to move electrical current properly from the generating utility to the consuming appliance in the home.

Planning the electrical system

During the design stages of the building process, it is in everyone's best interest to devote sufficient time and energy to planning the electrical system. This includes considering everything from the types of electrical devices and fixtures that will be in each room to the path of every single wire in the house. There are several strong arguments for good planning. Because running extra wires is almost impossible once the frame is enclosed, thorough planning can help guarantee that outlets and fixtures will be exactly where they're needed. Because a set of good plans makes it easier to communicate with the electrician, the job usually will run more efficiently and economically. And because good planning makes it possible for the timber framer to make the necessary cuts for the wires while the timbers are still on sawhorses, the amount of drilling the electrician has to do will be minimal—the surest way to prevent the unnecessary marring of timbers. So planning should be the rule of thumb when dealing with an electrical system.

We once dealt with a contractor who refused to plan or to follow our plans, and the results of his bullheadedness caused serious damage to the timber frame. This fellow personified the almost universal adversarial relationship between designers and contractors—he refused to acknowledge our blueprints as anything more than a rough example of what a building of the size and shape shown might look like. And the plans for the electrical system? Well, he didn't need them, because he already knew how to wire a house. We repeatedly told him that our electrical plans were critical, given that the local building code demanded that all wires be encased in conduit, but he somehow convinced the panel crew that he had a better plan, so they enclosed the house with no consideration for where the wires would go. As it turned out, his plan was simple: Eliminate all of the inaccessible lighting locations and riddle the timber frame with notches and holes large enough for a fire hose, and wiring would be a cinch. Lest you think that such matters are always properly resolved, in this case there was no cure for the damage.

Here, the feeling of expansiveness is reinforced through the brightness from the chandelier and floor lamps.

Planning begins by locating lights, outlets, appliances, stereo sets, televisions, telephones and all other wire-dependent equipment on the floor plan. The designer or architect will need a great deal of input from the owner on this, and the owner will want to anticipate alternate locations for equipment that is likely to be moved occasionally, such as televisions and stereos. Running all the wires during the construction stage will provide greater flexibility later. By code, outlets will have to be about 6 ft. on center around the perimeter of the room. This is a good regulation, but it should not dictate the exact location of the outlets. While planning the electrical system, it's smart to have as many outlets and switch boxes as possible installed on the interior walls, to minimize penetrations in the insulation. In homes with high standards of energy efficiency, even small leaks can have large significance, like a pinhole in a balloon. Doing this can be difficult, however, because timber-frame houses commonly have open floor plans and few partition walls. It is inevitable that outlets will be on exterior walls, but do your best to reduce them.

Use a copy of the floor plan to create the electrical plan. (Usually a sepia is made of the floor plan and then copies of the sepia are made with a blueprint machine. Otherwise, a copy of the floor plan should be traced from the original.) As you will see later, the position of timber posts and ceiling beams are critical in determining wire paths and the lighting scheme, so these should be indicated on the electrical plan. (To keep the plan uncluttered, draw in the beams lightly or with dotted lines.) After all the fixtures are located, the designer draws the electrical plan, including wire paths. If the electrical system is simple, a designer often will leave the circuitry to the electrician after determining the paths, but in complicated situations with few or no path options, the designer will determine the circuitry as well. In the rare instances where tradesmen are contracted early in a project, we have found it valuable to involve the electrician in planning. The electrician often has helpful input and always appreciates being a part of the decision-making process and not just a victim of it.

Plans are drawn to deliver information about how an intended result will be achieved. To be effective, all the participants need to understand the role they play in implementation; the plan won't do much good as just another blueprint in the set. The joiners need to understand what the plan means to the frame. Are there timbers to notch? Holes to drill? Panel installers should be prepared for the wires that will run through panels or panel joints. Carpenters must understand the accommodations necessary for wires or fixtures. In other words, it is critical that the construction crew, the designer and the homeowner act as a team and communicate precisely about even the small details of the electrical plan. Only in this manner can a good plan be transformed into a good electrical system.

The wiring process and prewiring

Basically, electrical wires carry currents of energy the way a pipe carries water. A single large wire brings the electricity to the house, where it is attached to a service panel, or circuit box. From the service panel, the current flows through smaller wires to various parts of the house. It does so in circuits—loops of current that flow from the service panel to the appliances and devices and back to the panel. The path for a circuit can be short and simple or long and complicated, depending on the number of devices and the distance back to the panel. Getting the main wire to the service panel, either overhead or underground, is done with standard procedure, but running the smaller wires through the house requires thought, because in timber-frame building, the wiring routes typically used in stud construction just aren't there.

The obvious difference between wiring a stud-frame house and a timber frame that will be enclosed with stress-skin panels is that in the latter there are no cavities in the exterior walls through which to run wiring. Because of this, it's necessary to do the wiring in three stages instead of in the conventional two. With a stud-frame house, the electrician comes in to rough-wire as soon as the house is enclosed by the roof, windows and exterior sheathing. Rough wiring simply means stringing the wires through the studs,

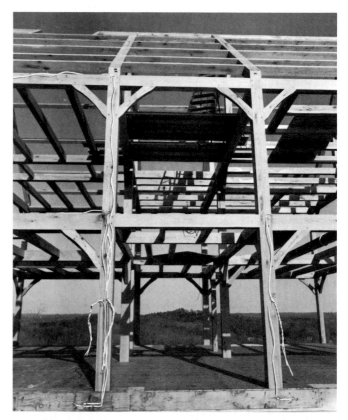

In a timber-frame house, wiring begins by stringing the wires loosely over the frame before the panels are installed.

joists and rafters to the various outlet boxes. Usually, many of the final decisions on the layout of the electrical system are left to be made during this time. The electrician then comes back to finish-wire (a matter of attaching wire ends to outlets, switches, fixtures and appliances) after the drywall is up.

But in a timber-frame house, the job starts with pre-wiring. Early in construction, just before the stress-skin panels go up, the electrician will get the wires to each general area of the house by running them loosely over the outside of the sill and frame. Where interior partitions will intersect timber posts, the electrician drills for the wires

and pulls them through. At this time the electrician also drills through rafters and purlins for track lighting, fans or chandeliers, and mounts wires and boxes for light switches.

On the first day of panel installation, the electrician will usually meet with the panel crew to review the electrical plan. It is the crew's responsibility to cut the grooves for the wires in the panels at the timber posts and to tuck the wires into place at the panel splines. When all the panels have been erected, but before the expanding foam and the 2x4 nailers have been applied, the electrician comes back to inspect the wiring and to run the wires for the switches next to exterior doors. All this is considered part of prewiring.

The panel-installation crew cuts grooves into the panels for wires and tucks the wires into spline connections. (Photo by Tafi Brown.)

After the panels have been foamed and the interior stud-wall partitions framed, the electrician will return to the house for several days to rough-wire. By this time, the carpenter will have built the extended-baseboard chases on the exterior walls, as shown on the facing page, and the electrician will be able to mount the wires and outlet boxes in them. The electrician will also mount outlet boxes on the partition-wall studs and run the wires over the floor system. After the partition walls are drywalled, finish wiring occurs in the conventional way.

It's the idea of prewiring that makes some electricians nervous about taking on a timber-frame job. But while it's true that prewiring requires a different strategy and different techniques, it's not true that different has to mean difficult or confusing. A timber-frame electrical system that is well thought out and well communicated to a responsive tradesman shouldn't be any harder to install than one for a conventional stud-frame house. In fact, electricians who have worked on several of our projects tell me that in many ways it's easier.

After the panels are installed and interior partitions are built, the electrician can complete the rough wiring.

The extended-baseboard wire chase

The primary way that wires get around the perimeter of a timber-frame structure is through horizontal wire chases. Of these, the extended-baseboard chase is the most widely used. These chases are installed on the insides of exterior walls between timber posts. Wires are mounted in the cavity between furring strips, and the outlets are mounted in the front face of the baseboard. The wires pass through the timber posts on their way around the perimeter of the house through a notch cut in the back of each post—ideally, these notches were planned and cut before the frame was erected. There are no notches in the corner posts because it's too difficult to feed the wires around corners. Instead, wires are fed down through the floor and up again on the adjacent side. While commercial surface-mounted wire chases can substitute for the extended baseboard, I don't feel they are attractive enough to be used undisguised in high-quality homes.

The extended-baseboard wire chase system actually begins at the sill. If the frame is attached to a timber sill, during prewiring the electrician will mount wires in a

Extended-baseboard wire chase

STRESS—SKIN PANEL

1½"X1½" BEADED CAP

1X6 OR 1X8 COVER

SHEET—METAL PROTECTOR

SPACE FOR WIRING

FLOORING

¾"X1½" FURRING STRIP

TOP FURRING STRIP TOE—NAILED TO POSTS

STRESS—SKIN PANEL

¾"X3½" NOTCH IN POST FOR WIRES (DIMENSIONS CAN BE INCREASED OR DECREASED AS NECESSARY.)

¾"X1½" FURRING STRIP

SCREW ALL FURRING STRIPS TO PANEL SPLINES; IN BETWEEN ATTACH STRIPS TO STRESS SKIN WITH HOLLOW WALL ANCHORS AND SCREWS EVERY 2'.

SPACE FOR WIRES

BOTTOM FURRING STRIP TOE—NAILED TO POSTS AND SUBFLOOR

chase created with furring strips on the outside of the sill. This keeps the interior of the timber floor system from being ruined visually by strings of wire running in all directions. Although simple, this system consumes a great deal of wire because all wires have to pass around the perimeter. Sometimes it is acceptable to find one place for wires to pass through the house, perhaps using a dropped ceiling between joists (similar to the plumbing chase discussed on p. 159). To feed an electric device or series of outlets in the wall, the electrician pulls a tail, or wire end, into the extended-baseboard area through a gap left in the top sill furring strip. After all the wires are mounted in the sill chase, a 1/16-in.-thick sheet-metal strip is screwed or nailed over the chase for protection. This may not be required by the building inspector, but it certainly can help prevent a problem in the event of a misplaced nail.

Timber-sill chase

TIMBER POST

FINISH FLOORING

TIMBER JOIST

5X7 TIMBER SILL

STRESS—SKIN PANEL

GAP IN TOP FURRING STRIP ALLOWS WIRE TO PASS INTO BASEBOARD AREA.

2X8 SILL

3/4X11/2" FURRING STRIP

ADD 1/16"—THICK SHEET—METAL PROTECTOR OVER WIRE CHASE.

2X12 SILL

If the timber frame is on a stick-frame floor deck, the electrician will run wires to and from the service panel in the cavities between joists during prewiring. To access the extended baseboard, the electrician drills a hole on a diagonal from the top outside corner of the subfloor toward the inside face of the perimeter box beam. One hole is drilled for each wire needed between posts. The wires are then pushed up from below at a later date, usually during rough wiring. From there the wire can be run from outlet to outlet inside the chase.

Once the frame has been prewired, it's time to assemble the extended baseboards. This is basic carpentry, although the drywall face of the typical stress-skin panel doesn't offer many opportunities for securing the furring strips. To begin, snap a line on the wall to show the top of the baseboard minus the cap. If a 1x6 or 1x8 is used for the baseboard cover, this dimension will be 5½ in. or 7½ in., respectively. Then cut the top and bottom furring strips to length, using more than one piece for each run if necessary. Apply a bead of construction adhesive to the top furring strip and fit it between posts with its top edge on the chalkline. Toe-nail it to the timber posts and screw it to the panel splines. Repeat the process with the bottom furring strip, except that you toe-nail it to the subfloor as well as to the posts. To draw the furring strips tightly to the wall, hollow wall anchors with screws are used every 2 ft. where there isn't a spline or nailer.

Using the electrical plan as a guide, next cut the holes for the outlet boxes in the baseboard cover, which is then used as a template to mark the holes on the wall. Obviously, because the space between the furring strips is narrow, duplex outlets are run horizontally. Make the cuts in the baseboard precise, because overcutting will show up as gaps around the outlet cover. Then trial-fit the baseboard between the timbers and mark the box locations on the wall between the furring strips. To keep the outlets well above the finish floor, locate the boxes directly against the bottom edge of the upper furring strip. Remove the baseboard and cut a housing in the wall for each box, keeping it as shallow as possible; you don't have to cut to the full depth of the box because of its placement in the baseboard cover. (Outlet boxes should be selected on the basis of

minimal penetration of the insulation. It's easier for the electrician if the boxes are deep, but better for the energy performance of the house if they're shallow.) Then pry the drywall and foam block loose with a flat bar or screwdriver, pulling out excess foam with a hard, sharp tool.

If the deck is stick-framed, holes are drilled between each pair of posts from the top outside corner of the subfloor to the inside of the box beam; then the wires are run through the joists.

When all this has been done, the electrician runs the wires through the chase and secures them with staples at the splines. If necessary, electric tape will corral several wires until the baseboard cover goes on. The carpenter then mounts the cover between timber posts, pulls the wires through the holes for the outlet boxes, and attaches the baseboard to the furring strips with 8d finish nails about 16 in. on center. The electrician mounts the boxes on the baseboard and attaches the outlets. For the benefit of safety (or the building inspector), a sheet-metal protector made to fit behind the baseboard cover will discourage future violation of the wire chase.

Some codes require electric outlets to be 14 in. off the finish floor, although the reasons for this have more to do with the convenience of the homeowner than with safety. If this issue is pressed, the extended baseboard can still be used for a wire chase while the outlet boxes are mounted higher in the wall. Set up the chase as usual, leaving the cover off until the outlets are installed. Mark the outlets on the wall no more than 16 in. off the floor, using a sample outlet box to scribe the lines. Cut the holes for the boxes as shallow as possible. Then ream a hole through the stress-skin panel from each box opening to the chase area with a ½-in.-dia. bar or pipe (rebar works well). Stay as close as possible to the interior sheathing. Intersect that hole with a hole drilled out from the chase. When you push a wire down from the outlet, it should be easy to pull it through from the chase. Pull the wire into the outlet box and mount it in the drywall with switch-box supports. Before closing up the box, fill any voids in the insulation with spray foam. Keep in mind that there is extra heat loss when the outlets are outside the wire chase, because more insulation is removed to accommodate the depth of the box.

Other types of horizontal wire chases

Some commercial baseboard heating systems are designed with a built-in chase for one or two wires to supply outlets in a circuit. Some brands even offer inserts that include a mounting for a duplex outlet. But if the chase needs to accommodate wires for other circuits, it will probably make more sense to use the extended baseboard behind the baseboard heating unit, as shown at right. The heating unit then caps the furring strips. In this case, you can use either the outlets in the heating unit or outlets mounted in the extended baseboard between sections of heating unit.

Other interior finish elements can also be used as wire chases without substantially altering their function or design. For example, if wainscoting is intended or if a wall is to be completely paneled, the furring strips needed to attach the wainscoting or paneling to the walls create a natural wire chase. (The furring strips are installed in the same way as the extended baseboards.) In the case of paneling, where the entire wall is set up with furring strips, the vertical wires for switches and wall lights can be run as part of the same system, but make sure all the wires are in a safe position or are protected with a sheet-metal cover.

Cabinets in kitchens and baths offer another opportunity to set up a wire chase if you mount them to furring strips. Install the furring strips on the wall about 12 in. on center, locating a strip approximately 6 in. from the top and bottom of the cabinet. Because outlets for kitchen and bath cabinets tend to be located just above the cabinet back, it's necessary to leave a gap in the furring strips so a wire can be brought up from behind the cabinet. A built-up backsplash is then constructed using the method for making extended baseboards, except that ⅜-in.-thick plywood is attached to the furring strips to back the tile. Another variation is to use tile just above the counter and a more typi-

Wires are run between furring strips attached to the wall. Holes are cut in the baseboard and wall to receive the outlet boxes.

Extended-baseboard chase with raised outlet box

STRESS—SKIN PANEL

OUTLET LOCATION NO MORE THAN 16" OFF FLOOR

HOLE FOR WIRE

1X6 OR 1X8 BASEBOARD COVER

INTERSECTING HOLE

FLOOR

cal wire chase just above that. Using tile as the backsplash is attractive and gives better moisture protection, but to prevent accidental electric shock, always use ground-fault circuit interrupters in bathrooms and in areas close to the kitchen sink.

If it is necessary to have oulets higher than the back-splash area, use the space behind the cabinets for the chase and mount the outlet in the stress-skin panel not more than 16 in. above the cabinet, as shown on the facing page. Remember to foam all the voids around the outlets.

Baseboard heating unit wire chase

STRESS—SKIN PANEL

BASEBOARD HEATING UNIT

FLOOR

¾"X1½" FURRING STRIP

Wainscoting wire chase

FURRING STRIPS

WIRE

WAINSCOTING

OUTLET BOXES LOCATED NEAR BOTTOM OF WAINSCOTING

Cabinet wire chase

STRESS—SKIN PANEL

CAP

COVER

OUTLET LOCATION

COVER

TILE BACKSPLASH CEMENTED TO ⅜" PLYWOOD

FURRING STRIPS

WIRE CHASE DRILLED THROUGH FURRING STRIPS ABOVE WIRES.

WIRES

OUTLET LOCATION

COVER

TILE

⅜" PLYWOOD

WIRE CHASE DRILLED THROUGH FURRING STRIPS

The box-beam sill used with slab-on-grade foundations, described in Chapter VI, has its own natural wire chase. Not only is there enough room for all the usual wires, there is also enough room for the outlet boxes. When the box beam is made, install 3-ft.-long pieces of 2x8 cap at the post locations. Leaving the rest of the box open until after the panels have been installed makes it possible to use it as a wire chase. At each post location, leave a 1½-in.-sq. space under the tenon for the wires to pass through. Using a scroll saw, cut rough holes within ¼ in. of the size of the outlet box on the inside face of the box beam. Run the wires through the chase, leaving adequate tails for the outlets. When all the wires are in place, finish installing the cap on the top of the box beam and add the 1x10 cover. Next, precisely cut the outlet holes in the finish baseboard, holding the baseboard over the beam to transfer the outlet locations. Feed the wires through the baseboard and nail it to the beam. For the protection of the wires, nail only to the top and bottom of the beam and not in the chase area.

In this system, exterior doorways can present a problem, because the sill is lower than the rest of the foundation wall and the box beam cannot travel around the perimeter

Box-beam wire chase

SPACE BETWEEN 2X4'S FOR POST TENON AND WIRING

STRESS—SKIN PANEL

POST

2X8 CAP

1X10 BEAM COVER

TWO—PIECE BASEBOARD

¾"X 1½" FURRING STRIP

BLOCKING TO SUPPORT POST

2X8 SILL

2X12 SILL

CONCRETE SLAB

CONCRETE WALL

of the house without interruption. The most common solution is to block up the door threshold 1 in. to 1½ in. from the slab to allow electrical conduit to pass underneath. The blocking is attached to the concrete toward the inside and outside of the threshold using concrete nails or expansion bolts, and the wires are run through conduits between. (Allow a few extra inches in the width of the concrete rough opening so wires have room to drop from the foundation wall down to threshold level.) If a wooden floor is to be laid over the concrete, this technique would not alter the typical relationship between the threshold and the finish floor.

When the house is on a slab instead of on a wooden structure, it is usually necessary to have several conduits embedded in the concrete to get wires across the building. Otherwise, all the wires would have to run around the building in the chase, wasting wire and time. It would have to be clear from the plan which wires would need to be in the conduit, and the conduit would need to have a vertical riser at the ends to bring the wires to the future wire chase. This technique is familiar to almost all electricians because the situation is commonly encountered in housebuilding.

Wiring under doorways

Interior wire chases

Except for the last method, which is specific to a particular foundation type, the wire chases described previously can be used on any exterior wall. They will work as conveniently on the second-floor or third-floor levels as on the first. But for interior walls, it makes sense to switch to more conventional wiring methods. Interior partition walls are framed with studs after the exterior walls are in place, and wires and boxes can be installed in them as usual.

Partition walls usually intersect exterior walls at timber posts, but if a partition and an exterior wall intersect between posts, the wires can be passed into the partition from the extended-baseboard chase as shown below. Where a partition is located at a post, the electrician must drill through the post to allow the wire to pass from the chase to the stud cavity. This happens during prewiring, before the stress-skin panels go on, and I'm always surprised at how many times these holes don't get drilled for lack of thorough planning. Without them, it can be quite difficult to get to the partition, requiring either passing the wires through the floor system or drilling completely through both the stress-skin panel and the post. The holes should be located in the posts at the level of the wire chase in the extended baseboard and drilled from the inside, which makes it easier to align them precisely with the center of the partition. The wire is fed through the post from the outside, and enough is left to wire the first outlet or switch box. Because partitions are usually not framed at this stage, it's necessary to notch the first stud around the wire and the hole drilled through the post. Subsequent studs are drilled in the conventional manner.

When it is necessary to bring a wire to an interior partition that does not intersect an exterior wall, bring the wire back to the floor system and drill through to the partition from the basement or crawl space. For timber floors, which are usually exposed to view, plan even further ahead and run this wire in a groove routed into the top of a timber.

Vertical wire chases

In a timber-frame house, the seams between stress-skin panels make convenient chases for vertical wires. Wires can be run either in the joints between panels over timber posts, or at the panel splines. A panel joint will not always fall conveniently on a post requiring wires, but the problem is easily solved by cutting a whole panel to make a joint at the post. No structural integrity is lost and wiring is made substantially easier. At panel splines, a cavity is created that is meant to be filled with foam, but before it is filled, it's an excellent way to bring wires to the extended baseboard between posts.

Timber-post chase Remember that during prewiring, the wires were strung loosely in position on the timber posts, their ends directed toward horizontal wire chases or run through posts toward interior partitions. During panel installation, the crew notches the inside edges of the panels meeting over posts, to make a channel for the wires. The first panel is nailed to the frame as described in Chapter V, with the wires pulled away to avoid damage. When that panel is secured, the wires are tucked into the notch to keep them out of the way while the adjacent panel is nailed. The space between the panels and the area around the wires is then filled with foam.

This technique is also used to run wires up into the roof system. Because major rafters tend to fall on major posts, the wire can go up the outside of a post and continue along the top of a rafter without interruption. A hole can be drilled through the rafter at the proper fixture location, or the wire might be directed to a purlin to feed a light or a fan. It is generally easier to deal with wires on the roof than in the walls, because there are more timbers and therefore more open panel joints for easy access. Also, because it's usually necessary to supply electricity to only a few isolated devices rather than to the complete circuits, not a lot of wire is involved.

Wiring partition walls

FURRING STRIP

SHEETROCK RUNS LONG TO COVER FURRING STRIPS AND WIRE CHASE.

STUD

DRILL THROUGH STUD.
WIRE CHASE
FURRING STRIP
STRESS—SKIN PANEL

Vertical wire chase at timber post

FILL GAP WITH FOAM AFTER WIRES ARE INSTALLED AND PANEL IS NAILED.

8" PANEL NAIL

PANEL A

PANEL B

DRYWALL

POST OR RAFTER

WIRES ARE TUCKED IN NOTCH ON PANEL A WHILE PANEL B IS BEING NAILED.

Single wires that need vertical access at posts can be pushed into the spaces left between panels after installation without the notching discussed previously. Wires to exterior floodlights or to feed a single circuit are often run this way. Make sure to push the wire deep into the seam and then fill the cavity with foam—if the wire isn't pushed in deep enough, it could prevent the foam from filling the joint. This technique should never be used for more than a couple of wires, as it could jeopardize both insulation quality and protection of the electrical line.

Panel-spline chase Wires can be run wherever two panels are splined together. After one of the pair of panels has been positioned, temporarily mount the wires on the center of its edge with a couple of light-gauge nails, as shown below. The wires must be located toward the center of the panel to protect them from possible damage by nails. From the inside and from the area of the extended-baseboard chase, drill a hole through the drywall on the installed panel and pull enough of the wire through to reach the first outlet box. Install the splines and the next panel on the frame, and then screw and nail the panels to the splines as described in Chapter V. Fill the cavity with foam, which will not only stop air infiltration but will also permanently bond the wires in place.

In a large two-story or three-story house where the path of wires from the upper areas to the service panel is unusually long and vertical access is difficult, it might make more sense to set up a sub-panel for a few of the more isolated circuits. The panel could be located in a closet or a built-in with an accessible partition. This makes it possible to run one large single line to the sub-panel and then distribute smaller wires to the circuits without having to take each line back to the main service panel.

Wiring switch boxes next to exterior doors These boxes tend to be quite large, because they are often control centers for interior and exterior lights. It is best to move these boxes to an interior wall where possible, since the air infiltration around them can be a large energy drain. If this is impossible, the electrician will need to mount the switch box in the stress-skin panel, and a chase must be created to get the necessary wires from the floor to the box. Because it is close to the switch location, try to create the space behind the nailer in the door's rough opening.

If the floor system is timber-framed, the wires for the switches are brought through the chase on the outside of the sill. For stick-framed floor systems, the wires are run through the joists, leaving enough wire to get to the switch box. With the rough opening for the door cut in the stress-skin panels and routed for stud nailers, create access for the wires by removing an additional depth of ¾ in. of foam behind the nailer location from the subfloor to switch-box height. The exact dimensions of the groove in the foam should be enough to accommodate all the wires with about 1 in. in width left over. This can easily be done by making a few kerfs with a power saw to the correct depth and then roughing the foam out with a wire brush mounted in a drill. If you have a router, use a straight bit and set it for about 2¼ in. deep. Cut the opening for the switch boxes from the inside using a keyhole saw started with a drill; because the switch location allows easy workability with power tools, a scroll saw could also be used to cut the switch-box opening. Make sure the cuts are precise and that a minimum amount of foam is removed. Now drill a hole from the door-jamb wire chase to the opening for the switch box.

In the back of the deepened groove at floor level, bring the wires into the chase by drilling a hole from the inside of the panel. Feed the wires into the chase and clip them to the center of the panel with light-gauge nails pressed in at an angle. Push the wires to the switch-box location, and the box is ready to mount with drywall clips. Install the 2x4 nailers around the door as described in Chapter V, then drill ¼-in.-dia. holes every 14 in. from the outside into the wire chase, being careful to stop drilling before the wires are endangered. Fill the cavity with expanding foam.

Next to doors, wires for switches and lights can be run behind the 2x4 door nailers.

Vertical wire chase at panel spline

FILL GAP WITH FOAM AFTER WIRES ARE INSTALLED.

WIRES ARE HELD IN PLACE BY PUSHING NAILS INTO PANEL DIAGONALLY.

SPLINE

Wiring the floor system

One of the more notable obstacles to running wires in a timber-frame building is the lack of space in the floor system. Stud-framed structures have a natural cavity of 10 in. to 12 in. between the ceiling of one story and the subfloor of the next. But because the framing is meant to be seen in timber-frame houses, the ceiling and floor are often just opposite sides of the same material.

Good planning can keep this unique quality of a timber-frame home from becoming a liability. If there is a rule of thumb, it is to follow the path of least resistance and to avoid running wires across the floor needlessly. A wire might be fed much more easily through an interior partition than through the floor, for instance, even if the path is slightly longer. Once each wire is deemed essential, the path of the wires through the floor system can be planned.

With the electrical blueprint in hand, analyze a cross section of the floor system to determine the simplest, safest method to run the wires. (A detailed description of flooring options appears in Chapter X.) If there is only a single layer of planking over the timbers, it is probably best to groove the timbers for the wires with a router or with a power saw. But if there are other layers of flooring, there are probably simpler methods, which are discussed later in this section. If grooving is necessary, locate each one in the center of the top of the timber to give maximum area for nailing the floor on either side of the wire chase. Make the cut with a router or take several passes with a power saw and clean out the waste with a chisel. Either size the groove for a steel conduit to protect the wires or make an additional few shallow passes to allow a sheet-metal plate to cover the chase. For the sake of the timbers, remove as little wood as possible.

If the ceiling is to have a drywall finish and planking is to be used for the floor above, allow space for wires between the nailers and drywall. Before the planking is nailed on, cover the wire chase with a sheet-metal cap. Be sure the building inspector approves of this procedure first.

Here, the floor timbers were routed for wires. Before the finish flooring is installed, a metal plate should be laid over the wires.

Wire chase in a drywall and plank floor

PLANKING FASTENED TO NAILER

SHEET—METAL PROTECTOR

PLANK FLOOR

DRYWALL

WIRE

FLOOR TIMBER

When there is a layer of sound-deadening board between the floor and the ceiling, it is easy to rout a wire chase in the soft material of the board. An advantage of doing this is that the wires can be run in between timbers and presumably will be in a safer environment. Still, the wires should be protected within a metal conduit or covered with a sheet-metal cap.

One floor system, shown in the drawing below, even includes a natural cavity for running wires. Here 2x4s are used as nailers over the ceiling material and the soundboard, and the finish floor is nailed to the 2x4s. The space between the nailers is a perfect wire chase, although it is not deep enough to run wires without sheet-metal covers or conduit for protection.

Most often, wires run across floors to a location for a light fixture in the ceiling below. When the fixture is to be mounted on the timber, make sure that the timber will be large enough for the box and cover—usually, a minimum of 5 in. wide. The hole from the wire chase to the fixture should be as small as possible and drilled from the finish face of the timber for accuracy. If the fixture is to be mounted between timbers (which is not possible if there is only a single layer of planking above the timbers), the junction box will have to be mounted on the ceiling surface. If there are just one or two wires, it might be worthwhile to special-order a shallow box.

Another technique for mounting fixtures between beams is to make a fixture-mounting timber from the same wood as the frame and join it to the frame between joists or beams before the flooring is laid. This special timber can be routed for the wire and the electrical box before installation.

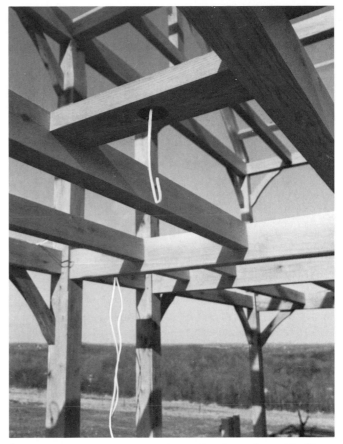

The small timber between the floor joists is used specifically to mount a light fixture.

Wire chase in sound-deadening board

FINISH FLOORING

SPACE FOR WIRES BETWEEN NAILERS

TIMBER JOIST

SOUND—DEADENING BOARD

DRYWALL

½"X3" NAILER

2X4 NAILER

Lighting and fixtures

Far too often, lighting is not even considered in the blueprint stage of a building project. It is left to be considered later, if at all. Yet lighting is a critical architectural element. Interesting spaces and unusual features are enhanced by proper and intelligent lighting, while rooms that are otherwise successful can fail if the lighting is poor. Much of lighting is subjective and much is a matter of common sense. I reject the notion that lighting needs to be left

This house uses a mixture of modern track lights and a classic iron chandelier. The chandelier hangs from a purlin in the dining area, and track lights are mounted on several timbers in the kitchen.

to the professional and can be understood only by those who have been initiated into the mysteries of the lumen. Consult books, articles and professionals, of course, but in the end permit yourself to be an expert about what is right for you. Only you know how you want a space to feel; only you know how it really will be used. If you intend to have a cozy, meditative corner, it will not need to be awash with light. On the other hand, a place where you intend to work with your hands (kitchen, sewing room or art studio) will probably require a great deal of light.

In a timber-frame home, lighting and fixtures need to co-exist with the frame, so when designing the room spaces, think about how you're going to light them, planning for the nooks and crannies as well as the soaring cathedrals. Try to avoid awkward room shapes that would be not only

hard to light, but would offer no drama or interest along with their complications. There's a difference between a dark spot in the corner of a room that creates a sense of mystery or allure, and a dark spot that is just dark. Because the flat planes of the walls and ceilings are interrupted by timbers, where you have lights you will also have shadows. Plan for them. The timber frame itself can be beautiful at night when properly illuminated, and if you think you would enjoy it, you can showcase the structure with lights.

If the floor plan includes the location of furniture and artwork, a well-conceived lighting plan will not be difficult to achieve. The first step is to determine whether it's desirable to light objects in the room, the room itself or both. Then you can consider the lighting options. For example,

It's not always necessary to use special lighting techniques or fixtures. Switched outlets connected to lamps work adequately for many situations.

when simple fixtures are mounted between the beams on a flat ceiling, the light will be focused onto the objects in the room. The beams will shade the light from the rest of the ceiling and cast shadows on the upper walls. Though this can be rather attractive in a dining room or kitchen, it might make a family room uninviting. To avoid the shadows, and to shift the emphasis from objects in the room to the room itself, use a shadeless fixture that hangs below the timbers; to accentuate the shadows, use a fixture having an upper shade, such as a billiard-room-style light fixture. To highlight the timbers and provide indirect lighting to the room, use uplights (having the shade on the bottom) mounted on perimeter walls and plan for the ceiling to be white between timbers to reflect the light.

The kitchen and dining areas feature hanging lamps mounted on the ceiling between timbers.

It is even possible to use built-in fixtures between the timber joists for subtle downlights. These lights can be either bright or muted, depending on the panel used to diffuse the light—anything from a high-intensity fiberglass diffuser to stained glass. To hold the panel, ⅝-in. rabbets are cut into the bottom of the timber headers or joists. A shallow light element (either fluorescent or tubular incandescent bulbs) is mounted to the ceiling between the joists, and then the panel is fitted into the rabbets.

Chandeliers or other fixtures hung from important beams receive added attention. But if you wish to conceal a fixture, use the timber as a valance by mounting the light on the side of a timber toward the outer perimeter of a room. Track lighting can be used creatively in this manner to wash walls with indirect light or to focus on an object.

The upper sides of roof purlins in open areas also provide good mounting for track lights. When track lights are used this way, be sure to get fixtures that can turn down past 90° or else the options for directing the light will be limited. With a full range of movement, the lights can be directed toward the ceiling to illuminate the frame or pointed down for general lighting or to highlight artwork or furniture.

Frames for large areas often have hammer beams or king-post and queen-post trusses, which can provide a mounting surface for individual fixtures or track lights. It is best in these situations if the fixtures have flexible heads, to allow the light to be focused in a number of directions. To recess tracks or boxes, dados can be cut in the timbers, but this is work best done before the frame is raised. When the tops of the timbers are not visible, it's even possible to hide a tubular light in a dado.

When houses have been well designed, the living spaces receive the natural light appropriate to their use during daylight hours. Artificial light is often intended to imitate daylight, but remember that activities and moods change during evening hours and there are new requirements involving entertainment, relaxation and romance. The easiest way to achieve the desired results while maintaining flexibility is to overlight and then use a dimmer to control the quality of light. Additional fixtures could also be installed to provide extra light when needed.

Timber-joist ceiling fixture

TIMBER JOIST
FLOORING
DRYWALL
FLUORESCENT OR TUBULAR INCANDESCENT BULBS
GLASS PANEL
TIMBER HEADER
FIXTURE
PLAN VIEW
TIMBER HEADER
TIMBER JOIST

VIII. Plumbing

Plumbing in the timber-frame house is mostly a matter of camouflage, since the building system leaves few natural cavities for pipes—especially those that run horizontally. In this case, the horizontal pipes are hidden in the platform beneath the tub.

I made a commitment to get more involved with the design of timber-frame houses one afternoon about ten years ago when I learned of a disaster caused by plumbing. A few months earlier we had completed a project in one of the local communities. We had helped with design, but on a very minimal level. When the frame was finished, we gave the clients a few words of advice, told them to call if necessary, and went to work on another frame. Later on I happened upon the plumber for the project, and asked him how things were going. He told me everything was fine, but, "Boy, I had trouble finding a 6-in. drill bit." I was puzzled. "What 6-in. drill bit?" I wondered. "Well, I had to go all the way to Boston and spend $90 to find a 6-in. drill bit to make a hole through your 8x8 timber for that waste line by the first-floor bath." I feel certain the color of my face and my open mouth said more than words could have. The plumber had acquired a new bit, and our frame had lost a timber. It was too late to argue or place blame, but I knew that from then on things would have to change. In a way, that plumber did me a favor. He helped me to understand that I would have to address the construction idiosyncrasies inherent in timber-frame building, and that I could not expect people in the various trades to solve problems foreign to their experience. As a result, I was forced to become more involved with the design of timber-frame houses and the way in which certain jobs, such as plumbing, were handled.

The problem with plumbing a timber-frame house is not so much how to do it, for the standards and techniques are essentially the same as those used in conventional construction, but how to hide it. In this respect, wiring and plumbing are similar. Much of the task is to create spaces in which to install the workings of the system and then to camouflage those spaces. This may sound simple in principle, but you'd be surprised at how often the principle is mishandled. By far the most common problem we see in completed plans for timber-frame houses is unresolved plumbing situations. It's as if in the heat of working out the floor plans and the aesthetics of the building, the designers (who are sometimes registered architects) simply forgot that plumbing fixtures must be attached to pipes to operate. When we ask how the problems will be solved, we're often told, "Oh, we'll just box the pipes in somehow." But while this may be appropriate in a laundry room or closet, it could ruin the looks of a living room, dining room or bedroom.

The secret to a successful plumbing job in the timber-frame home is early and careful planning. This is then followed by an intelligent selection of the best options for each particular situation. For the options to make sense, however, it's important to have at least a basic understanding of a few simple plumbing concepts, which we'll cover now. Then we'll look at planning and creating hidden spaces for pipes.

Some basic plumbing

The fundamental aim of every plumbing system is to pump clean water in and to drain used water out. Water usually comes from either a city supply (most often a lake or reservoir) or from a well on the site. When water leaves the house, it is directed to either a city sewage-treatment center or a septic system near the building.

Water is brought to the house through a network of pipes called the supply system, and flows out after use through a network called the drainage system or sometimes DWV (for drain, waste, vent). In the supply system, water is pumped through a main trunk line to the basement or designated utility area, where one major branch pipe connects to the hot-water heater. From there smaller branch pipes carry hot and cold water to various parts of the house, feeding into even smaller pipes for individual fixtures. Most codes require supply pipes to be copper, although PVC is gaining acceptance. Because the water in the supply pipes is under pressure from the city water main or well pump, no air is required to assist the flow. This means that the pipes can be smaller than drainage pipes (which are merely conduits for water to flow by the force of gravity)—generally no larger than 1 in. and no smaller than ⅜ in. In addition, the pipes can be run in any direction on their way from the source to the fixture.

The drainage system is more complicated than the supply system, and therefore is the focus of all our planning. When the space requirements of the drainage system have been satisfied, the requirements of the supply system will almost always automatically be satisfied as well. The drawing below shows the anatomy of a typical drainage system. Basically, it works like this: When you pull the drain plug on your bathtub, gravity pulls the water down a short vertical section of pipe to the trap, where some is captured in the loop to prevent gases in the line from rising into the living area. (Toilets don't need traps because they always contain water.) When the water passes through the trap, it drops into a pipe that is slightly pitched, called a branch drain. The branch drain directs the water to a larger verti-

---

Typical drainage system

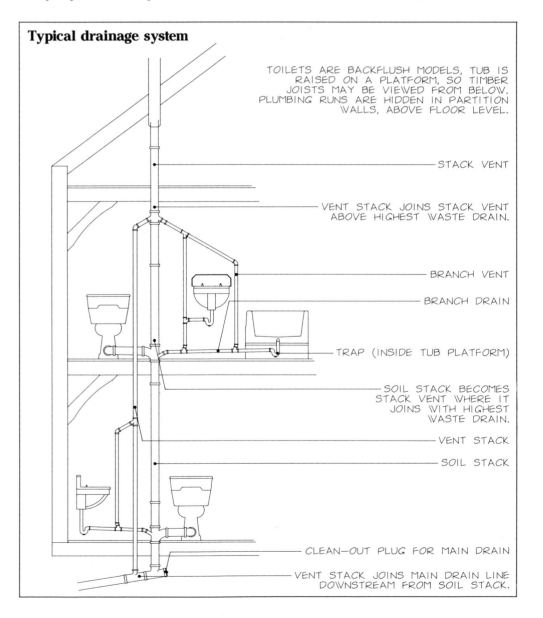

TOILETS ARE BACKFLUSH MODELS, TUB IS RAISED ON A PLATFORM, SO TIMBER JOISTS MAY BE VIEWED FROM BELOW. PLUMBING RUNS ARE HIDDEN IN PARTITION WALLS, ABOVE FLOOR LEVEL.

— STACK VENT

— VENT STACK JOINS STACK VENT ABOVE HIGHEST WASTE DRAIN.

— BRANCH VENT

— BRANCH DRAIN

— TRAP (INSIDE TUB PLATFORM)

— SOIL STACK BECOMES STACK VENT WHERE IT JOINS WITH HIGHEST WASTE DRAIN.

— VENT STACK

— SOIL STACK

— CLEAN-OUT PLUG FOR MAIN DRAIN

— VENT STACK JOINS MAIN DRAIN LINE DOWNSTREAM FROM SOIL STACK.

cal pipe, the soil stack. A pipe connected to the branch drain just beyond the trap allows air into the branch drain and releases the sewage gases. This branch vent rises vertically to a point above the fixtures and then pitches upward toward the upper part of the soil stack, which is called the stack vent. Essentially, drainage occurs in the lower portion of the stack while the upper part brings air to the branch vents and allows the sewage gases to escape. Meanwhile, the bath water drops through the soil stack until it reaches the main building drain, which carries all of the household waste water and sewage to the septic tank or town sewer.

Because the water in the drain pipes is not pressurized, the pipes must be oversize to allow air in the lines. The smallest drain for an individual fixture would have a 1½-in. diameter and the largest pipe, the soil stack, would have a 4½-in. diameter. (This pipe won't even fit within a typical stud wall.) Drainage pipes are commonly made of ABS plastic, although cast iron is often a better choice for the stack because it helps muffle the sound of the water as it cascades downward. Branch drains must be pitched all the way to their stacks; codes require a minimum pitch of ¼ in. per foot. Tubs, showers and toilets require the most planning because their drains are usually underneath the fixture, requiring space in the floor system. For most situations, the minimum space required beneath fixtures for drains is 6 in., but it can be much more if the run from the drain to the stack is long. For instance, if a pipe were pitched ¼ in. per foot and had to run 12 ft., an additional 3 in. would be required from the point of connection to the branch drain. Sinks are simpler to deal with because their traps and drains are above the floor. If the stack is not too far away, sink drains can be run to it without a special cavity.

Designing the plumbing system

Plumbing design should begin at the earliest stages of house design, when there is only blank paper and a full bank account: You will want to know that everything has been done to avoid unnecessary complications. No doubt, even after careful planning there will still be situations calling for imaginative thinking, but keep these several rules of thumb in mind.

1. The most important rule is to consolidate plumbing areas wherever possible. Primary plumbing facilities (bath, laundry and kitchen) should be clustered in one section of the house, with plumbing areas on different floors stacked atop one another. The benefits are that pipe runs will be kept short, and there will be more opportunities for shared drains and stacks. Fewer feet of pipe minimize potential problems with the plumbing system; fewer vents passing through the roof reduce potential for heat loss and present less of a visual disturbance. Consolidation of plumbing areas also saves money. Hotel designers have this down to a science, and always place bathrooms back to back and stack them one over another.

2. After the plumbing areas are clustered, consolidate further by trying to get supply and drain lines to share a single chase in a common wet wall. If this isn't possible, use more than one wet wall for supply and drains, but attach the drains to only one stack. Keep working toward the simplest and most compact arrangement until the number of plumbing walls and the lengths of pipe required have been reduced to a minimum.

3. To reduce noise, avoid locating wet walls adjacent to major living areas. Wherever possible, run the plumbing through secondary partitions, such as those that enclose a bathtub or shower stall, or the partition between a bathroom and laundry.

Likewise, when plumbing areas can't be stacked floor to floor, avoid locating wet walls over or under open areas or primary rooms. Remember that drains go down and vents go up. When a bathroom on the second floor falls over a dining room on the first floor, the problem of hiding pipes immediately becomes difficult. Creative solutions, even design innovations, can arise from such situations, but much more often the result is disappointment. I know of a house with a hollow fake post, a camouflaged mastery that gurgles from time to time. And I've heard a story about an eccentric with an interest in the details of his household plumbing—he required Plexiglas pipes that would be revealed to the living room. When the suggestion came, my bet is that the designer wished he had located the second-floor plumbing somewhere else. I suppose exposed pipes are an option, and recently there has been a movement among some avant-garde architects to reveal all the mechanics of a building, but so far this "warehouse architecture" hasn't gained much momentum. Most of us are happiest with the more old-fashioned practices.

4. Partition walls that align with beams cannot be used as wet walls, because it would then be necessary to drill through the timbers. (This principle conflicts with the one established in Chapter IV, which says timbers should be used to define rooms, but supports the idea that plumbing walls should not be adjacent to primary living areas.) Instead, try to use secondary partitions, such as closet and bathroom walls, for wet walls. These secondary walls seldom have interference from timbers and are separate enough from the rest of the house so that their treatment need not match the decor of the primary living areas (see the discussion in this chapter on vertical pipe chases). Wet walls should align on each level so that pipes can run uninterrupted from the first floor to the roof.

5. In any plumbing area, position the fixtures as close as possible to the soil stack. When there are several fixtures, try to arrange them so that those with the most critical drainage requirements (usually the toilet first, then the tub) are closer to the stack. It would not make sense to back the sink up to the soil stack and locate the toilet in the far corner of the room, because then its drain would have to travel a long distance to the stack. Draining water from the sink is much less difficult than draining waste

from the toilet, and the branch drain from the sink can be run to the stack without interaction with the floor.

6. Don't plan to run plumbing through exterior walls. It would compromise insulation and allow pipes to freeze.

These guidelines may sound like a lot to keep in mind, but they actually dovetail nicely with good house design; therefore, many of them come rather naturally. Consider the following example of plumbing layout in the three-bay timber-frame house we used as an example in Chapter IV. The major living areas are gathered in one end of the house (for the sun or the view) and the secondary areas are pushed to the opposite end, toward the north. The kitchen is located near the utility entrance for convenience when bringing groceries into the house—part of the plumbing has therefore automatically been located. People doing household chores shouldn't have to run from one

Plumbing layout in simple three-bay house

end of the house to the other, so we try to keep the laundry (if it is to be located on this level) near the kitchen. Next, we attempt to back up the bathroom to the laundry. In the best possible arrangement, the wall that contains pipes for the laundry is shared by the bath. This not only makes plumbing easier, but also removes the wet wall from the living areas. So, by following some natural design inclinations, all of the plumbing is in one bay. The rest of the house is open and unencumbered by partitions, and yet the bathroom is convenient, especially since the middle bay typically provides central access to the outer bays.

The second floor would follow the pattern of the first. Bedrooms would be located toward the view or the sun, with closets and bathrooms pushed toward the opposite end. Take the further step of stacking the second-floor bath over the first-floor plumbing area, and the difficulty of creating spaces for pipes will be minimal.

In residential construction, the set of plumbing plans itself is not usually very complicated or precise. Plan views are drawn as overlays on the floor plan. The plan views show the location of wet walls in relation to fixtures and depict pipe routes, but do not necessarily show pipe connections, elbows, etc. Typical building sections and sections specific to the plumbing area give the plumber and the carpenter an exact description of each plumbing chase. These plans and elevations should show hot and cold supply lines, drains, stacks and vents, but again it's not usually necessary to be specific about pipe connections. The plans should be drawn by the designer and reviewed carefully with both the plumber and the carpenter before work commences. This is one of the places where it's critical that the separate trades work together. The designer plans the spaces, the carpenter builds the spaces and the plumber uses the spaces. Together they can accomplish near miracles of deception. As separate forces, they can touch off a small war.

It would take a large budget, and a very skilled carpenter and plumber, to rescue a project if the design criteria I've listed are neglected. Yet even if you give planning the plumbing system your best shot, house design includes a consideration of many factors and often it will not be possible to adhere to each guideline. Final decisions on frame design and room layout will inevitably include compromises that will affect the complexity of the plumbing system. To be properly prepared for planning, it is therefore necessary to have a small arsenal of solutions for the various problems that may arise. Although vent pipes often angle diagonally upward and drain pipes always pitch toward the stack, pipe chases are always oriented either vertically or horizontally. We'll look at some typical solutions in terms of these requirements.

Vertical pipe chases

The most obvious and common vertical chase is an interior partition. But as I've mentioned, the difficulty is that in a timber-frame house there should be a deliberate alignment of partitions and beams—a goal that conflicts with creating pipe chases. To allow the unimpeded passage of pipes, it is necessary to design wet walls to stand away from beams. This idea needs to be conceived in the planning stage; if it is, execution is easy.

When framing wet walls, remember that partitions in a timber-frame house exist only to separate rooms. They have no load-bearing function, so there need be only enough structure within the walls for stiffness and to support the finish surfaces. Therefore, try to anticipate where pipes will fall within wet walls and eliminate or reduce structure as much as possible. For instance, if the wall is being built in sections anyway, consider constructing it so there will be no obstruction to the soil stack. There certainly isn't any reason to have top and bottom plates in the wall when the hole for the stack will eliminate any structural usefulness the plates might otherwise have had.

When wet walls fall by necessity at beam locations, there are three choices, none of which calls for drilling through the timber. The first choice is to build two parallel walls between which to hide the plumbing—one wall between timbers, the other in the plumbing area. In this case, each wall supports sheathing on only one side, and the structural requirements are almost nil. To reduce the cost of lum-

This bathroom employs parallel walls to allow pipes to pass between them. Two-by-three studs for each wall would have worked as well as wider boards.

ber, frame each wall with 2x3s. Hold the inside wall away from the beam far enough to contain the pipes. The advantage of this method is that the reveal of timber to the living area is kept consistent throughout the house. The disadvantage is that the aesthetic value of the timber is lost to the room with the wet wall. In a bathroom or laundry area, this may be a worthwhile compromise.

The second choice is to build only one wall and to locate it completely on the plumbing-area side of the timbers. The timbers are then concealed from the plumbing area, and their full depth is completely exposed to the living area in the same manner as those on the exterior walls. This is most acceptable in a house having no other first-floor partitions besides those surrounding the plumbing areas (as in the floor plan on p. 155). Otherwise, the relationship of timbers to walls will be noticeably inconsistent. The walls can be created the same way as built-up exterior walls (p. 94), by applying the drywall first and the framing members afterward. Because nothing has to be fitted between timbers, this technique is easy.

The third choice is to box the pipes in a corner or in a specially designed chase, which allows the timbers to be revealed to the plumbing area as well as the living area. This works well if the plumbing can be run in the wall at the end of a shower stall or in the back of a cabinet. The partition wall is then built between timbers as usual, with a chase for drains, stacks and supply located on the inside of

This plumbing wall is built on the bathroom side of the timbers to allow pipes to be run without compromising the frame.

The partition between this sink and tub conceals a plumbing chase. It falls to the side of the timber, so that pipes can be installed easily.

the wall. Bathrooms and kitchens are sometimes especially dense with cabinets and closets, and it is occasionally possible to camouflage pipes on the inside of a room.

Despite the best intentions, it is not always possible to prevent plumbing from falling over or under living areas without convenient wet walls. The first order of business is to look for an opportunity to make an unobtrusive vertical chase from some other design element in the house, and then to use horizontal runs, described in the next section, to get the pipes to the chase. The chase can be a closet or built-in cabinet or even a chimney. (See the photo on p. 65—the built-in cabinet in the dining room conceals plumbing.) In the latter case, all that is usually necessary is to make a masonry partition within the chimney to isolate the pipes from the flues. (Check local code before proceeding.) If no enclosure is available, it may be necessary to design a built-in cabinet or shelving unit to serve the purpose. The trick, of course, is to make the built-in look natural while still providing adequate space for pipes.

To keep noise from the drain pipes from disturbing the living area, make the chase large enough to leave room for packing the pipes with fiberglass insulation. Using cast iron instead of plastic for vertical drains can also cut sound transmission.

Horizontal pipe chases

The basic issue with horizontal pipe chases is to find a way to run pipes in the floor, given the absence of a cavity. In a timber-frame house, the floor material is usually the ceiling for the living area below, consisting either of planks over beams or a thin, built-up membrane of flooring and ceiling materials (see Chapter X). These floor systems provide aesthetic and economic benefits, but the lack of space for plumbing is a significant obstacle. With good planning, however, the problem (and the pipes) can disappear.

Assume that through careful design, the plumbing areas have been consolidated, and convenient vertical chases for supply pipes and stacks have been provided. The next step is to arrange the fixtures so they have an efficient relationship with the plumbing walls. As I mentioned earlier, by far the most difficult fixtures to accommodate are toilets, tubs and showers. The drains for these are usually in the floor and, in the case of the toilet, there is both solid waste and water. Obviously, if these fixtures are located a great distance away from the plumbing walls, the required length and slope of the pipes create difficulties. If at all possible, the toilet should be the closest fixture to the soil stack, the tub or shower next, and the sink farthest away. Furthermore, all fixtures should be as close as possible to the plumbing wall and stack. The natural extension of this rule is that vertical and horizontal chases are designed simultaneously and for the benefit of each other.

After wet walls have been determined and fixtures arranged, you must devise a way to get the horizontal pipes to connect with the vertical pipes. In most cases the horizontal pipes run in a chase built either above floor level or below it. In a few lucky situations, no chase will be required, such as when supply and drain pipes can be passed directly from the fixture to the wet wall. This is

Raising the floor for plumbing need not inhibit the proper functioning of household systems. In this bathroom, the sink (not shown) is on the same level as the hallway, while the toilet and shower are a step up.

quite possible with all sinks and with backflush toilets. A backflush toilet has an outlet in the rear instead of underneath. It's more expensive but worth the expense if it eliminates the carpentry involved in creating a chase. In the basement, it just might make sense to let the pipes run through the floor and under the timbers in the typical helter-skelter manner. If this area is not used for living, it is impractical to spend money and effort to hide what will seldom be seen. Anyway, it's often helpful to have the pipes exposed in the basement for maintenance, especially at the points where water enters and leaves the house.

But, more likely than not, there still will be a need for a horizontal chase. The simplest, least compromising solution is to place some of the fixtures on a raised platform while leaving most of the floor level undisturbed. Doing this separates the bathroom into distinct areas, making it a design device as well as a way to conceal pipes. If the sink is close to the entrance and the tub and toilet farthest away, the sink would remain on the common-floor level and the other fixtures would be raised. A raised tub is considered something of a luxury, and a raised toilet doesn't necessarily affect comfort or convenience. Or the sink and a backflush toilet could be hooked directly to branch drains in the wall, with just the tub elevated. Often, it will be necessary to build a chase that continues around most of the perimeter of the room, with a platform only for the fixtures. Technically, the chase for the sink plumbing has to be just large enough for its pipes, while the tub and toilet chase has to be large enough for both the fixtures and pipes. But after fulfilling this requirement, we can increase the chase area to whatever size benefits room design.

The structure of the platform is simple, since it has little load-bearing responsibility. Construct it using conventional floor-framing standards. Joists are typically 2x6s placed 16 in. on center, but if the plumbing run is long, wider joists (and therefore a deeper chase) may be required to allow the proper pitch from the fixture to the stack. The finished ceiling for the room below is installed first, whether it is planking or drywall, and then the joists are laid on top, perpendicular to the timber joists and attached by toenailing. Before beginning, check the manufacturer's specifications and be sure that the fixture will have adequate support.

If raising the floor is awkward or not desirable, the plumbing can be run in a cavity between timber joists. But because this system has severe limitations, we usually don't recommend it. Since plumbing can fall only between joists, the direction of travel is restricted, and the distance of travel is limited by the next intersecting beam; this means that the branch drains running between a pair of timber joists must connect with a vertical chase before they meet up with the next perpendicular beam. The distance of travel for a branch drain that runs between timber joists is also limited by the relationship between the depth of the joists and the drop of the drain as it pitches toward the stack. If it goes too low, the timber ceiling will be lost. Yet another problem is that it is unlikely that all of the fixtures will be located over the same joist bay, causing multiple branch drains where they wouldn't normally be necessary. Of course, this sort of chase has an impact on the room below. It is usually desirable to finish

the entire ceiling in the same manner as the area with the plumbing chase, in order to keep the look consistent. This does not necessarily present a problem, but it does cause extra expense.

When plumbing is consolidated, as discussed earlier, optimally there will be a bathroom or two on the second floor located directly above the plumbing on the first floor. With such dense plumbing, it is often prudent to allow these areas to have different aesthetics from the rest of the house. The most practical solution might be to drop a ceiling completely beneath the timbers, as shown in the drawing below, but this is desirable only if all the plumbing is localized and if the area is properly isolated. It is also only possible if the timber ceiling is high enough to allow a finish ceiling to be up to 6 in. below the bottom of the timber joists.

Dropped-ceiling plumbing chase

BATHROOM SUBFLOOR

SMALLER JOISTS, CLOSER TOGETHER

2X'S FORM CHASE AND SUPPORT DRYWALL.

DRYWALL CEILING

Plumbing run between timber joists

CHASE WIDTH AND DIRECTION RESTRICTED BY INTERSECTING TIMBERS

BATHROOM SUBFLOOR

DRYWALL CEILING

5X7 JOIST

When it's important to maintain the timber ceiling and the floor above can't be raised (for instance, if there are height restrictions imposed by the roofline), you can design the frame with the timber joists dropped in the area of the plumbing. The idea is to keep the timbers revealed below and the floor level consistent above by laying a built-up floor over a lowered timber ceiling—the cavity above the timber joists is the plumbing chase. This works particularly well if the area below benefits from the coziness a lowered ceiling produces: The only division between a living room and study might be the point at which the ceiling becomes lower. (The ceiling must meet code requirements for height, and usually can't be any lower than 7 ft.) To keep the perimeter timbers exposed as they would be in other parts of the frame, use deep beams (typically 12 in. to 14 in.) to receive the joists. Join the joists far enough below the tops of the timbers to leave room for the chase. A common height for the chase is 5½ in., to fit a standard 2x6 (or 2x4, if no accommodation need be made for the 4-in.-dia. waste line from a toilet). Make sure the drain pipes have an escapement from the timber-floor system at the point where they will be directed toward the vertical chase; the timber adjacent to the vertical chase should be dropped to allow the pipes to pass through. Include the finish ceiling material when considering the depth of the chase. Whether drywall or planking, it should run over the top of the joists as it does in the rest of the house.

If the frame is designed with this feature, creating the plumbing chase is easy. First install the ceiling material over the timbers as discussed in Chapter X. The built-up floor and plumbing chase is then constructed with conventional materials and techniques, with the finish floor level maintained from the timber floor to the plumbing chase area. I like to think of this system as an example of how a problem can be transformed into a design asset. It is also an example of how good planning can reward.

Dropped-floor plumbing chase

CEILING PLANKS AT NORMAL HEIGHT

SUBFLOOR

FLOORING DADO

2X'S SUPPORT SUBFLOOR

DROPPED CEILING PLANKS

The floor joists have been lowered in this oversize bent girt to make room for a false floor above the joists. The routed groove in the girt will receive the floor planks.

Sink vents

Kitchen plumbing often poses a problem in timber-frame houses because the kitchen is the one space that is not easily isolated from the primary living areas. In addition, during design an attempt is usually made to make the kitchen spacious and open, which further reduces the opportunities for convenient plumbing walls.

In the kitchen, the items of concern are usually the sink and the dishwasher. Supply and drainage pipes aren't often a problem for these, because the kitchen is usually located on the first floor and plumbing can run between joists directly to the basement. Because the sink and dishwasher are almost always side by side, they can share a

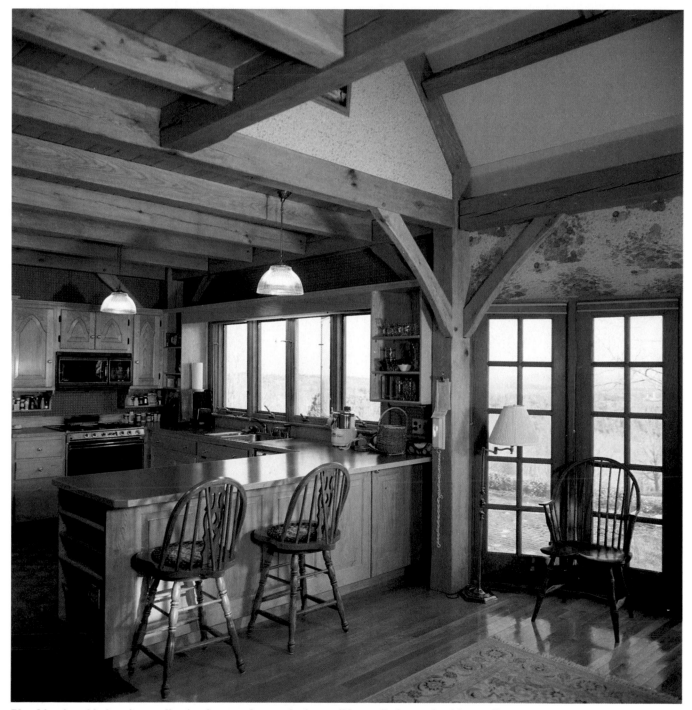

Plumbing in a kitchen is usually simple enough to make it possible to eliminate plumbing walls.

drain and vent, which reduces the plumbing to a single hot and cold supply line and a single branch drain and vent. But when the sink is on an exterior wall or in an island, a problem arises in determining where to put the branch vent. You don't want to run a vertical pipe chase in an exterior wall because this would compromise the insulation, and you certainly don't want to run pipes directly up from an island through the room.

There are two common solutions to this problem—the loop vent and the mechanical vent—but before choosing either, check local code. With the loop vent (also called a dry vent), the pipes form a long upside-down *U* up to just under the top of the counter and then go back down to an air-intake line, as shown below. The loop vent must rise at least 6 in. above the drain to prevent siphoning waste water. The system is simple to install, uses normal plumbing fittings and usually works well, but the vent does take up space in the cabinet and some codes don't allow it.

The mechanical vent is a device that is installed into the top of a pipe that extends 6 in. above the sink drain. It works by using water pressure to open and close a valve that lets air into the line when water is draining and reseals when the drain is not operating. The disadvantage here is that the device can wear out; many codes don't allow it anyway. The advantage is that it's easy to install and easily replaced if there's a problem.

If neither of these options can be used, a vertical plumbing chase may be fabricated in a kitchen cabinet. This solution is often used but seldom successful, because the normal arrangement of kitchens and cabinets makes it difficult to hide a vertical pipe chase. The cabinet that will house the chase should reach to the ceiling and be as close as possible to the sink—examples would be a cabinet pantry or an extension of the cabinet next to the refrigerator. Modifications to the cabinet would need to be made to make room for the pipe.

Two sink vents

LOOP VENT

MECHANICAL VENT

6" MINIMUM

SINK

SLOPE UP TO VENT

SLOPE DOWN TO DRAIN

6"

SINK

SLOPE DOWN TO DRAIN

Notes on heating and cooling

Installing heating and cooling systems in timber-frame homes is somewhat troublesome, because there aren't many hidden spaces and people are usually reluctant to commit space to ductwork. In addition, cutting into a space for a heating or cooling duct spoils the definition and balance provided to the room by the timber frame. The solution in large part is to minimize equipment (and fuel consumption) by making energy efficiency a top priority in house design.

Basically, heating and cooling options will be described when the floor plan, insulation levels, and location and number of windows have been determined. The energy audit we commission on each of our houses (see p. 90), gives us a computerized series of "what ifs" that allow us to see the relative heat performance of various combinations of insulation and glazing. Before committing to any plan, we can determine with some certainty the point of diminishing returns—when money spent doesn't mean appreciably

The open area in the middle bay allows heat to rise naturally to the upper regions of the house without the use of heating ducts.

better performance. When a strategy has been determined, the same heating engineer designs the complete system, keeping it as simple and small as possible. A problem with the conventional method of allowing the installer's supplier to lay out the system is that the result is typically three or four times larger than necessary. Let's face it, the guy pushing furnaces has little incentive to worry about future heating bills. We have found it's better to hire a person who is trained to think, not sell, and to address the problem while there is still design flexibility.

A simple, well-insulated, three-bay timber-frame house with an open area in the middle usually requires only one small, central heat source. It could be the sun, a woodstove or a small furnace. A little heat (about 30,000 to 40,000 BTUs for about 2,500 sq. ft.) emanating from the central core should keep the whole house warm. If a hot-air furnace is used, the ducts run under the first floor to strategically located registers (perhaps as few as five), which bring warm air to the first level. It is usually not necessary to run the heating system to the second or third levels, since the rooms on these floors use the open area as a plenum and receive heat through conduction and convection. The same thing can be done with hot-water or electric-baseboard heat. And that, for most houses we build, is the solution to the problem of the heating system.

Should it become necessary to run heat to various parts of the house, hot-air systems, which require extensive ductwork to move air, are not generally the first choice for timber-frame houses because of the lack of spaces. Unless a convenient cavity can be found for each duct, it is too difficult to be worthwhile. Sometimes we'll choose to use a combination of hot-air heat to the first floor with a few electric-baseboard heaters where necessary on the second floor. Considering the difference in cost between running the ducts and installing the baseboards and how rarely the electric units would actually operate, this alternative can be quite successful.

To bring air to the furnace, a return air duct made from sheet metal is often housed in the masonry chimney. The duct must be completely isolated from flues with a solid-brick partition, and is sized according to the specifications of the heating system. The duct should be packed around the outside with fiberglass insulation to keep it from contacting masonry and to isolate it from stray smoke and flue gases. Even if the furnace does not require return air, it might make sense to put a duct into the chimney for recycling the air. The duct can be used like a fan to even out the temperature between the upper and lower levels of the house. Obviously, sheet-metal ducts, unlike flues, are capped at the peak, inside the house.

Hydronic (hot water) and electric systems are certainly easier to accommodate in the crannies of a timber-frame house than hot air. Because the pipes for hydronic systems are rarely larger than ¾-in. dia., they can be run through partitions and in some of the floor systems, using the guidelines in this chapter. For instance, avoid situations that require drilling holes through timbers. When the pipes need to pass around the outside walls, have the posts notched before the insulation is installed over the frame.

The grill near the top of the wall covers an opening to the return air duct, which brings air down to the basement for the furnace. This duct can also be used for an air-to-air heat exchanger, or simply to circulate the house air.

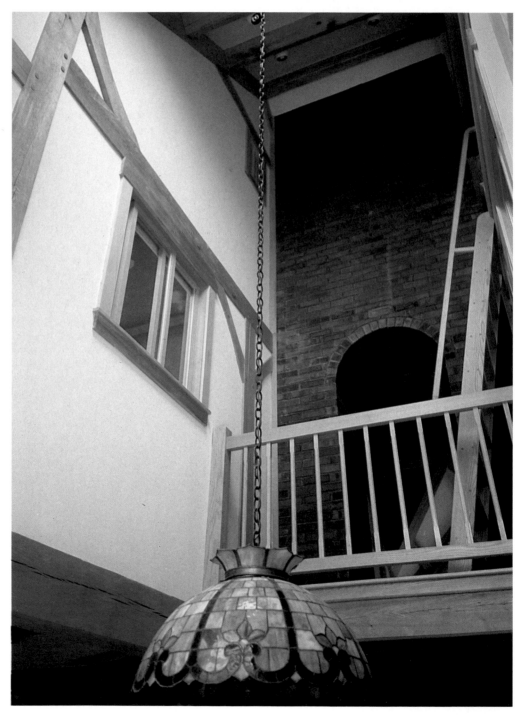

Electric heat is by far the easiest to install because all the wires can be run along with the rest of the house wiring. But unfortunately for most of the country, electric heat is also the most expensive per BTU. As I mentioned before, we often use electric heat as a backup for other systems, such as in houses having good passive-solar systems and a woodstove. A few of our clients with electric backup systems have never actually used them. But bankers who finance construction still usually like to see big, impressive heating systems, even though the most successful heating systems are quite unimpressive.

Cooling systems are hard to disguise, but the same design concepts that keep a heating system small can make a cooling system superfluous. There are many parts of the country, however, where it is almost a necessity, no matter how well the house is conceived and built. While heating systems should be placed at the bottom of the house because warm air rises, cooling systems should be placed at the top to let the cool air drop. Air conditioners require quite a bit of room, and it is almost inevitable that space for these units and their ducts will have to be designed into the plan. One of our houses uses just one supply, located close to the peak (immediately above the collar ties) in the central bay. The cool air falls through the central area and cools the outer perimeter enough to keep the house comfortable. If it is necessary to feed other areas, keep the unit high in the house and run the ducts down to the rooms. Closets, knee walls and other secondary or inaccessible areas are the best places for ducts.

The preceding paragraph probably sounds like a quick dismissal of the problem of installing cooling systems. It's not, really—there just isn't much to say. Air-conditioning ducts and equipment potentially can consume large quantities of space, so the first step is to design a well-insulated house that rejects heat. This way, only a small system will be necessary, one that does not need much space. Then, you specifically locate the places for equipment and ducts, knowing that design flexibility inevitably will be sacrificed to the necessities of the system. The theories and techniques described throughout this chapter for finding and creating cavities and avoiding timbers should apply to the cooling system, too.

Return air duct in chimney

RETURN
AIR DUCT

FIREPLACE
FLUE

AIR RECIRCULATES
TO FURNACE
WITH FAN OR
AIR-TO-AIR
HEAT EXCHANGER.

ASH DOOR

CHIMNEY PAD

IX. Frame Details

Pendants embellish the bottoms of the second-story posts in the framed overhang.

In any house there are many thousands of design and construction details. Most are taken for granted; if they go unnoticed, they are successful. These are the details that keep treads and risers at a consistent dimension so people don't trip, that keep wooden posts from rotting on concrete floors and that prevent drywall from cracking at the seams. Failure to pay attention to such detail is the definition of poor construction. It causes the need for constant repair and makes the house more of an annoyance than a joy. Other kinds of details can become highlights of the decor. These are the "frivolous" details which, although technically unnecessary, are undeniably important to good house construction—the frosting on the cake. Embellishing the edges of timbers is not essential, but it can change the feeling of a living space from rustic to elegant. Designing an alcove window seat might seem to be an extra expense and bother, but could result in providing the most inviting place in the house. Inevitably, what anyone in house construction learns is this simple lesson: Everything matters. Good house construction requires attention to details both large and small.

In this chapter and the next (which is devoted to exterior and interior finish details), we will take a look at both the frosting and the cake, exploring some points that were not discussed in other chapters. Here I cover frame embellishments, roof windows, chimney and fireplace openings, exterior timbers (roof overhangs and porches), roofline

changes and solariums. It is not my intention to explicate every possible circumstance; rather, I offer a smattering of ideas in a few critical categories associated with timber-frame construction. Don't look at any of these discussions as prescriptions to be used without thought of revision or modification. Instead, it is my hope that they will provide an outline for a way to think about details, and become a springboard to discovering the solutions best suited to your own home.

Frame embellishments

Embellishments are refinements made to the edges and ends of a timber. They may be as simple as quarter-rounds or bevels to soften hard timber edges, or as complex as elaborately carved pendants at the ends of posts. Whatever the case, determining the level, type and location of embellishments is an important part of the design process that should occur during the development of the frame and floor plans. Even the decision to use no embellishment at all ought to be well considered. Timbers are milled to a severe rectilinear shape, and leaving them that way will affect frame design as surely as carving gargoyles on the rafter ends.

Edge treatments   For their origins, edge treatments probably owe more to practicality than decoration. Ceilings in ancient timber frames were sometimes so low that they were a problem even for our shorter ancestors. Beveling those hard timber edges was a safety precaution that grew into a design feature. In those days the work was done with a drawknife and plane, but today typical edge treatments are executed with a single router pass that is stopped before the timber end. The drawing below shows some styles, but the most popular are the quarter-round and the straight chamfer, because the end of the cut is naturally symmetrical to the timber edge. More complicated edge treatments can be done by building up a molded appearance with several passes of the router, or by using hand tools to make deeper and wider cuts than those possible by machining. Working an edge by hand also produces a less regular surface, which can be made to appear rustic or rich, depending on the desired effect.

How edges are treated has enormous influence on the look of a home. One of our recent houses was intended to have the shape and feel of a barn, and we hoped to create an atmosphere that might be described as "elegant rusticity." Because of their unrefined character, hemlock timbers were used for the frame; we planed them just enough to remove the saw marks and left the edges completely un-

This chamfered edge treatment was done with a combination of power and hand tools, as described for the complex chamfer shown in the bottom drawing below. (Photo by Tafi Brown.)

Types of chamfers

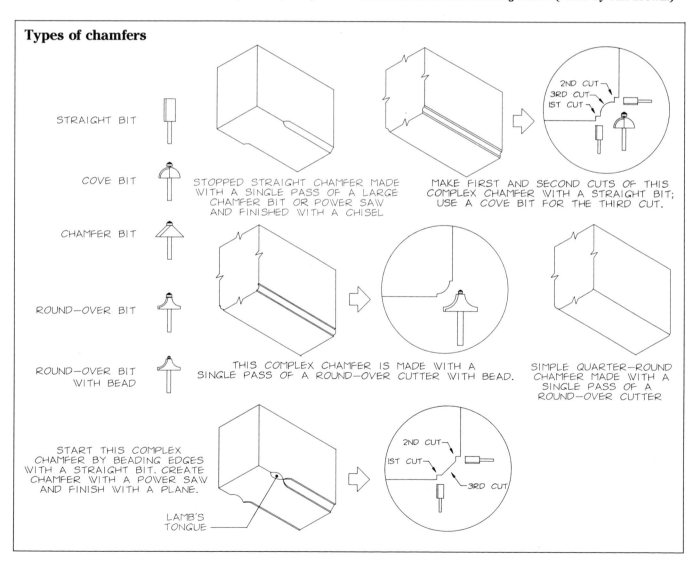

STRAIGHT BIT

COVE BIT

CHAMFER BIT

ROUND-OVER BIT

ROUND-OVER BIT WITH BEAD

STOPPED STRAIGHT CHAMFER MADE WITH A SINGLE PASS OF A LARGE CHAMFER BIT OR POWER SAW AND FINISHED WITH A CHISEL

2ND CUT
3RD CUT
1ST CUT

MAKE FIRST AND SECOND CUTS OF THIS COMPLEX CHAMFER WITH A STRAIGHT BIT; USE A COVE BIT FOR THE THIRD CUT.

THIS COMPLEX CHAMFER IS MADE WITH A SINGLE PASS OF A ROUND-OVER CUTTER WITH BEAD.

SIMPLE QUARTER-ROUND CHAMFER MADE WITH A SINGLE PASS OF A ROUND-OVER CUTTER

START THIS COMPLEX CHAMFER BY BEADING EDGES WITH A STRAIGHT BIT. CREATE CHAMFER WITH A POWER SAW AND FINISH WITH A PLANE.

LAMB'S TONGUE

2ND CUT
1ST CUT
3RD CUT

changed. Any kind of edge embellishment would not have been true to the barn idiom, and the lack of it keeps the eye moving past the frame to the volumes and shapes of the house. By contrast, we designed another house to have some very formal rooms, which would contain chandeliers, cherry woodwork and fine furniture. To make the timbers complement this formality, we decorated them with large, beaded-edge chamfers and cut them entirely with hand tools. We also created the illusion of an arch in the summer beam by beveling the entire timber from the bottom, making the center less deep than the edges. Although these details are not overly complicated, they are sufficient to impart an elegant air. We gave the less formal rooms of this house, such as the country kitchen, a light edge treatment on the primary timbers and left the secondary timbers alone except for typical planing and oiling.

Most often we choose the middle road on edge embellishments. We frequently opt for small chamfers on all exposed edges of the secondary timbers, just enough to soften them without creating a design statement. Proportionally larger versions of the same treatment would then appear on the principal timbers. One of my favorite refinements is a simple broken edge created by whisking off the hard timber edges with a hand plane. The timbers are left looking crisp, but they feel smooth to the touch instead of splintery. (With natural edges, splinters and tears can be a real problem as the wood dries.) Another device I like for formal situations is a decorative stop called a lamb's tongue, which we usually use with quarter-rounds and chamfers (see drawing, p. 167). This is a traditional timber-framing technique but it comes to us with a history of infinite variations; modern timber framers have added their own interpretations. Lamb's tongues are always executed by hand, using a chisel, drawknife and scoop-bottom plane. We usually confine their use to hand-worked, rather than machined, edges, simply because it's difficult to rout a chamfer that is wider than 1 in., and this is insufficient room to exercise the lamb's tongue's decorative potential.

The timbers receive their edge embellishments while still on the ground, so when deciding on the subtlety or grandeur of each, it's critical to visualize the relationship of the frame to the floor plan and future partitions. A simple

Hemlock timbers without edge embellishments were used for a house intended to have a barn-like atmosphere.

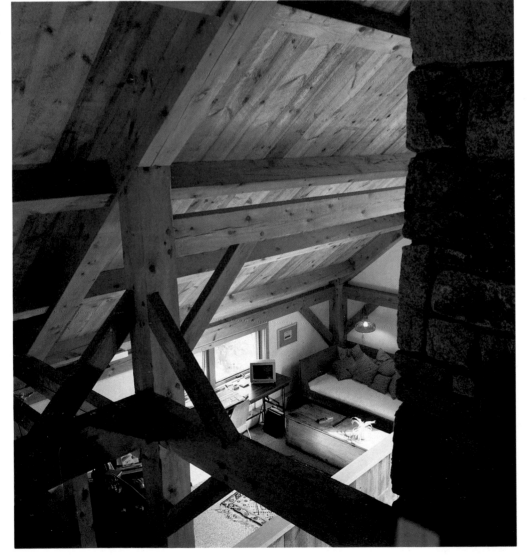

way to generate an edge-treatment plan is to develop a color code for each type of embellishment and then indicate it in that color on copies of the frame plans (both elevations and plan views). To help in planning, we usually adhere to a few general rules. The first is that partition walls should never encroach on edge treatments. Imagine for a moment a beam divided by a partition that separates the living room and dining room. If the timber edge exposed to the living room has a large, elaborate chamfer, the partition wall will automatically be pushed toward the dining room. If the beam is a 6x8, on the edge exposed to the dining room there will be either no room for an edge treatment or room for only a very small one. Failure to consider this during design can result in a partition that overlaps the treatment on one or both edges—a mistake made obvious as the drywall climbs into the embellishment.

Another rule of good embellishment is that timbers defining the perimeter of a room should all be treated in a similar way; using a molded edge on a corner post suggests that other posts in the room should be molded, too. Large summer beams invariably dominate other timbers and therefore often receive larger, more elaborate edge treatments. The size and style of embellishments used on major beams should duplicate those used on major posts.

Edge treatments rarely continue to the timber end. Instead they stop (often with a lamb's tongue), at a prescribed distance from the intersection with other timbers in the frame. Stopping the embellishments this way is attractive and accentuates the joinery, but it also helps the joiner avoid complications. As an example, if the embellishments weren't stopped, housings to receive timbers would have to be carved to the contour of the edge treatment at the corners. Timber joinery is hard enough with square corners and right angles, so we keep edge treat-

Edge embellishments usually stop before the intersection of other timbers.

Deeply embellished timbers lend a sense of formality to this house.

The end embellishment on this hammer post was roughed out with a series of power-saw cuts and finished with a chisel and hand plane.

ments away from all timber intersections. The stops should also be noted on the edge-treatment plan.

As a last note, choose embellishments that reflect the overall ambitions of the individual house design; far too frequently, edge treatments become standardized. And make sure that they are within the abilities and time constraints of the joiner. Attempting to do too much is more likely to be in error than doing too little. One rarely goes wrong with subtlety and simplicity.

End embellishments   Embellishments at timber ends are actually a type of carving. They typically occur where a timber passes 6 in. to 1 ft. through a joinery intersection—leaving wood beyond the joint increases strength, but the exposed end grain is unattractive and demands further attention. When the exposed end is at the bottom of a post, it is called a pendant. The most common situations calling for a pendant are at framed overhangs, where the upper-story post passes through the second-floor girt, and where a hammer post passes by the hammer beam. When the exposed end occurs at the top of a post, especially in framing around a stairway, it is called a finial. The ends of projecting beams, such as where a plate passes by the last bent post, are also usually carved, as are rafter ends that pass through the frame and support the roof overhang. Timber framers usually cut away the bulk of the waste on end embellishments with a power saw, and then finish the work with a chisel, slick and hand plane. Work time can be reduced by simplifying the design so that it can be mostly finished with a series of power-saw cuts. Unless a portable

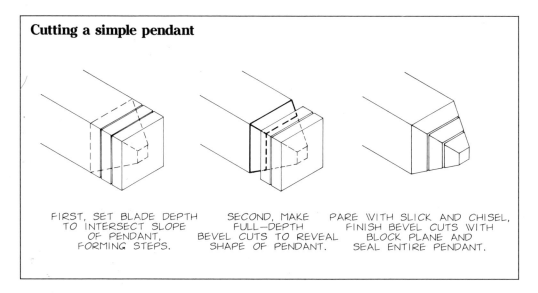

Cutting a simple pendant

FIRST, SET BLADE DEPTH
TO INTERSECT SLOPE
OF PENDANT,
FORMING STEPS.

SECOND, MAKE
FULL-DEPTH
BEVEL CUTS TO REVEAL
SHAPE OF PENDANT.

PARE WITH SLICK AND CHISEL,
FINISH BEVEL CUTS WITH
BLOCK PLANE AND
SEAL ENTIRE PENDANT.

bandsaw is available, carvings with lots of curves are time-consuming, although enjoyable, to make.

Design end embellishments to set the tone for other details of the interior finish. A highly molded design would be out of place if every other aspect of the finish were based on square edges or flat chamfers. Repeating elements of the end embellishments in the trim, stair parts or even in the furniture further integrates the frame with the rest of the house.

Traditionally, and especially during the Middle Ages, an incredible range of designs has been used for end embellishments, including meticulously detailed human and animal figures. A story I've heard a few times tells of a building in which the heads of saints is carved on the ends of the hammer beams, and each is identified with an inscription. One of the carvings did not have an inscription and could not be identified as a saint, but is now believed to be a likeness of the master carpenter on the job.

Here the hammer-post pendant detail is repeated in the stair newel for continuity.

Roof windows

In the building lexicon, "roof window" seems to be replacing "skylight," probably because almost all of the new models operate like windows. Most can be outfitted with shades and screens and can be cleaned from the inside—a valued convenience. But perhaps the most important advance in roof windows is that flashing systems are now sophisticated enough that they almost never leak. In a timber-frame house, the beauty of the timberwork between the rafters encourages designers to use the space under the roofline for living rather than for storage, and roof windows are an inexpensive way to bring light and ventilation into these areas. The other alternative for bringing in light—dormer windows—adds considerably to the cost of construction.

Roof windows should be located for visibility (so you can see through them from a designated position) and for illumination of appropriate areas. In a bathroom, for example, you might want to locate a roof window over the jacuzzi, or in a bedroom over a work area. Because of their lack of horizontal members, common-rafter roofs naturally offer more choices in window placement than do rafter systems containing purlins. But most of the time, roof windows can be incorporated without changing the timber frame, since for the benefit of other building materials and roof loading, timber purlins or rafters tend to be spaced on 48-in. centers. This allows plenty of space for several standard sizes of roof windows.

If you want to trim out the roof window with wood all around, choose a size that will give you 4 in. to 6 in. between the roof-window rough opening and the timbers. Try to center the window horizontally between rafters and vertically between purlins. I prefer to choose a roof window size that will fit as tightly as possible between the timbers. The timbers then do double duty as trim, while the other two sides are trimmed with wood or, better yet, left trimless by making a drywall corner return to the roof-window sash. Remember that, like wall windows and doors, roof windows are not actually mounted in the timber frame, but instead are fastened to the stress-skin panels above the frame with nailers (see Chapter V).

Since roof windows are on a slope, it is best if the top of the opening can be trimmed level with the glass and the bottom of the opening vertical to the glass, so that maximum light can enter the living area. Purlins falling at the top or bottom of an opening have the disadvantage of slightly restricting the admission of light, but in most situations it's not worthwhile to change the framing system just to avoid this problem.

In this bedroom, the roof window is mounted between headers that break a purlin span to make a large vertical opening in the roof. Drywall finish extends to the sash instead of to wood trim to allow the timbers to define the opening.

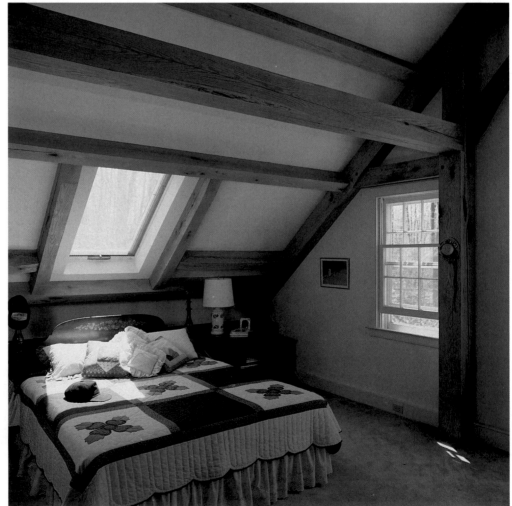

Sometimes it's necessary to create an opening for a roof window by interrupting a purlin or rafter with headers, which span between two perpendicular framing members as shown below. In a purlin-roof system, headers are used to locate a roof window where there would otherwise be a purlin, or to make an opening larger than the span between purlins. Conversely, in a common-rafter roof, headers are used either to locate the roof window where there would otherwise be a rafter, or to accommodate a window that is too wide for the opening between rafters. When headers are used, they increase the roof load on the members they span, which must be considered in sizing those pieces.

Roof window and chimney headers for common-rafter roof systems

CRIPPLE RAFTERS PAIR INTO CHIMNEY HEADER

CHIMNEY HEADER

HEADER

HEADER WITH SIDE FRAMING FOR ROOF WINDOW

HEADER INTERRUPTS COMMON RAFTER.

COMMON RAFTER

RAFTER WITHOUT HEADERS

PLATE

COMMON RAFTER

Chimney and fireplace openings

Fire has always been an essential design consideration for houses. In the earliest timber-frame buildings, a hole was usually left in the roof to allow smoke to escape from the open fire that burned in the middle of the house. As I pointed out in Chapter I, usually there was no second floor in these buildings because it would have been too smoky. So the first buildings were more like elaborate tents or caves. They began to resemble our notion of a home only after chimneys were designed to exhaust the smoke.

The first thing to say about chimneys is that they must be completely independent of the timber frame; if you were to strip away the house, the chimney should stand entirely on its own. I don't know why this is, but in the preliminary plans we review, a common mistake is locating the chimney where it would pass through a bent or an exterior timber-frame wall. Wooden structures move a bit and masonry structures should not. Never use the masonry to support the frame or the frame to support the masonry. Like so many other things in a timber-frame house, it is important to plan the chimney in some detail before the frame is cut. You must know the size and location of the chimney at each floor level and where it passes through the roof. If there are fireplaces attached to the chimney, it is necessary to know how they will affect the size of the chimney opening. It's not possible to explain every detail of masonry construction here, but allow me to provide a few tips.

1. Know enough about typical masonry details to communicate with the professional you hire. *Audel's Guide to Masonry Construction* (see bibliography, p. 229) is a particularly good reference. Then, rely heavily on the advice of a mason you trust. If you can retain this person to help you in the design phase, you'll be a lot more confident when the timbers are being cut. After you have described all the things affecting chimney dimensions, the mason will be able to provide precise measurements based on personal construction techniques. And believe me, every mason is different. Two masons setting out to make a chimney with exactly the same specifications and using the same materials could wind up with completely different measurements, and each would tell you it was done exactly the right way. I don't pretend to understand this.

The frame and the chimney should be designed to be completely independent of each other. Diagonal headers outline the opening on the second floor of this house, while the chimney passes behind the valley rafters.

2. Despite your confusion and lack of knowledge, speak up. On one of our jobs, I argued weakly with a mason who was putting in the flues without brick partitions between them. I told him it didn't look right. He argued eloquently and persuasively that "the latest befaddle on counterflow air currents and retroactive heat flow has it that the weight of the mass is inversely proportional to the ability of the flues to do headstands," or some such gibberish. I looked at the four wobbly flues standing in his brick cavern, shook my head and just walked away. Recently, when a chimney sweep attempted to clean one of the flues, it collapsed under the mighty weight of the chimney brush. I learned that there's no sense in compounding ignorance with timidity.

3. Make sure every possible flue has been included in the chimney. If in doubt about a possible furnace or woodstove, put in the extra flue. Retrofitting a chimney would be a mess.

4. Make sure the mason is aware of the need for exterior combustion air for all fireplaces and woodstoves. Accommodation for such air passages should be considered a part of the construction of all chimneys and hearths in well-insulated houses. It is accomplished by passing a 4-in.-dia. or 5-in.-dia. galvanized pipe to the outside in the basement. The pipe brings the air to one or several openings in the hearth near the woodstove intake or just in front of the hearth for the fireplace. The air intakes for the fireplace can be hidden by dropping the base of the fire-box below finish floor level by about 5 in.; the air enters just below finish floor level in the drop.

5. Beware of the use of stone for interior masonry because of the possibility of bringing radon into the house.

Framing for the chimney For fire safety, the usual code requirement is that the chimney should be at least 2 in. away from framing materials on all sides. This means that the chimney opening in the frame will have to be a total of 4 in. larger than the proposed chimney in width and length. (This rule also ensures that the chimney will be far enough away from the frame so that it won't be damaged by wood movement.) The finish flooring should be held back by ¼ in., but the trim can be cut to fit tightly to the chimney.

Often the chimney imposes no special framing requirements on the floor system, for the spacing between joists is frequently as much as 32 in., which allows more than enough room for the width of a typical chimney. It is sometimes the case, however, that the flooring requires support around the chimney. A small timber header on either side of the chimney, perpendicular to the joists, will keep the flooring stiff. If necessary, frame between these two headers with a third header to bridge the gap between the adjacent joist and the chimney, as shown below. Try to use as few timbers as possible to keep the opening uncluttered.

Where the chimney has to interrupt the joists, use headers to create an opening in the floor. Particularly if the

Supporting flooring around chimneys

THIRD HEADER PROVIDES NAILING SURFACE.

JOIST

TIMBER HEADERS ON EITHER SIDE OF CHIMNEY, PERPENDICULAR TO JOISTS, STIFFEN THE FLOORING.

opening is large, it may be smart to plan the joist layout around the chimney. If it can be done symmetrically, start by designing a joist on two sides of the chimney and then put headers between those joists on the other two sides of the chimney. Then divide the headered space equally, putting a joist in the middle. Remember that half the load borne by the headers will be transferred to the joists on either side of the chimney, so they will have to be sized to handle the increased load.

The chimney also needs to pass through the roof timbers, but this can be a little more difficult to resolve than passing it through the floor timbers. First, good geometry is critical. The opening in the roof has to fall directly above the opening in the floor and be the same size horizontally, even though it must be calculated along the roof slope. It's pretty simple math (remember Pythagoras?). I'm urging that somebody do it, with the hope that it might save wholesale embarrassment when looking up through the chimney opening on raising day. Whether the roof system is framed horizontally with purlins or vertically with rafters, there is always the possibility that no special framing will be needed. With luck, the chimney will just slide through the timbers. We always check to see if we can help luck along by changing the layout slightly. If it's close, it's worth a try. For instance, if a rafter or purlin needs to be moved only an inch or two, the change probably won't upset the bearing for materials or compromise symmetry.

When the chimney falls on one side or the other of the roof peak, the header has to span between purlins or common rafters (but never through a principal rafter, which is part of the bent) to create a larger opening. I prefer to see

the chimney pass through at the ridge because it leaves less masonry above the roofline and solves some flashing problems. (When a chimney falls below the peak, it needs a roof-shaped water diverter, called a cricket, on the upper side to prevent snow, ice and water from getting trapped behind the chimney.) When the chimney passes through the peak, the framing is a little more difficult because the header has to be a small duplicate of the top portion of the rafters (see drawing on p. 173). This small truss then frames to purlins or rafter headers on either side of the roof peak.

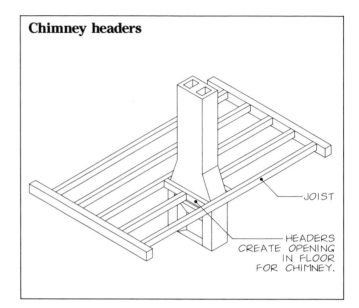

Chimney headers

An opening for the chimney is framed into the peak of this building. Two small rafters between the upper two purlins act as the headers. King-post trusses frame and decorate the area to the left, used as a music room. (Photo by Tafi Brown.)

Exterior timbers

In modern timber-frame construction, it's perfectly possible to protect the frame completely from the pernicious effects of weather and condensation. With the timbers snug inside the cocoon of warmth and protection offered by the exterior insulation system, the frame (and the building) should last as long as people care enough to keep the roof tight. In our designs we therefore strive to keep all the timbers inside the insulating system, but situations continually arise in which exterior porches and long roof overhangs are important, even critical, to the design of a house.

Roof overhangs In warm climates, long roof overhangs are used to keep the house cool; in wet climates they help protect the siding and windows from excessive moisture. A roof with a long overhang is like a hat with a decent brim. When the roof overhang is created within the enclosure system rather than by passing the timbers through it, the limit is about 2 ft., based on using structural, or double-chip, stress-skin panels (p. 103). If one of the alternate insulation systems is employed instead, especially the foam-and-nailer system (p. 98), the length of the overhang would be based on the relative strength of the framing members. For instance, 2x6s cantilevered beyond the frame could probably create an overhang of about 3 ft., depending on the roof load.

What happens when the timbers of the frame have to fall outside the protection of the insulation system? Essentially, there are three hazards. First, where timbers pass through the insulation, wood movement can cause a sizable gap to develop between the timber and the skin. Even if the gap is only ⅛ in. on both sides of a 6x8 timber, its effect on air infiltration would be comparable to bashing a 1½-in. by 1½-in. hole in the side of the house. In addition to compromising the insulation, the gaps offer a place for condensation to collect, which could cause rot in the frame. These gaps must be caulked at least once a year while the timbers are drying and stabilizing. So important is this detail that I have only half-jokingly considered carving the maintenance instructions into the timbers.

The second problem with timbers passing through the insulation is that the part of the timber that lives on the inside of the house will stabilize, while the part that lives outside will seasonally swell and shrink with changes in moisture content. Even if the joint looks tight on the inside, it should be checked on the outside—there's no way to know if there's a problem unless you climb 25 ft. up a ladder once a year.

The third problem is that the life span of the whole frame is potentially shortened by the life span of that part exposed to the elements.

Having pointed out these drawbacks, I can say that I am well aware that there is no substitute for timbers when it comes to creating a strong, beautiful roof overhang. If, after carefully weighing the options, this detail wins out, here are some things to do to minimize negative effects.

1. I would be much more reluctant to use a framed overhang in New Hampshire than in Arizona. Hot and dry climates are the most benign to exposed timbers, and houses in these areas suffer the least from air infiltration. Even in my native Colorado, which is sometimes cold but always dry, timbers can be left exposed for a long time without significant damage. But here in New England, where everything is either frozen solid or supporting fungal growth, it is wise to consider every other alternative before exposing the timbers to the weather.

2. Our modern timber frames are more protected now than at any time in history, and because of this we can use almost any kind of wood that is structurally sound. But our forefathers in the craft, who infilled between the timbers rather than cladding from the outside (thus exposing them to the elements), chose white oak as the standard in Europe and cypress and cedar in Japan. Think like the Europeans and the Japanese if you are making a frame overhang, and use a rot-resistant wood.

3. Detail the roof system to protect the frame members in the overhang. Extend the roofing beyond the timber ends as much as possible to keep moisture out.

4. The most protected overhang is one whose timbers cantilever beyond the frame without the need for support from plates or braces. When horizontal timbers support the overhang, they have a tendency to hold moisture; diagonal braces can pull moisture back to the frame through surface tension. But if the overhang is too great, some form of bracing for the rafters will have to be used.

Principal rafter and purlin roofs are the easiest to protect at the eave for two reasons. First, only a few pieces pass through the skin. For example, in a 36-ft.-long, four-

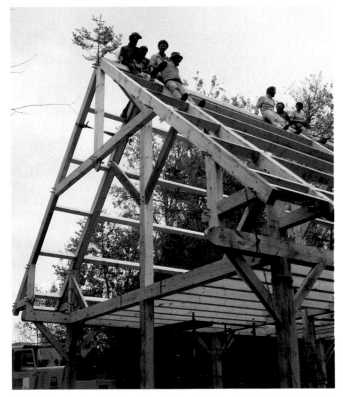

In this frame, a plate overhangs the gable-end wall to support a truss that will be roofed, but unprotected by a wall. The problem is that the cantilevered plates, their supporting braces, the exterior truss and all the short purlins are not only exposed to the weather, but also cause numerous penetrations in the insulation. (Photo by Tafi Brown.)

bent building, there would be eight penetrations at the eaves, whereas a common-rafter system would probably require twenty. Second, at the gable end, the common rafter system requires that a plate be extended from the walls to support the last rafter pair, which causes several more penetrations and a horizontal timber. (This detail was often used on old Swiss chalets. The top of the extended plate would be protected with a little shingled roof.) In the principal rafter and purlin roof, however, the end rafters can be lowered to allow the purlins to pass over the top. We ordered extra-deep rafters for one of our projects so they could be notched across the top. No wood could be removed from the purlins because the complete cross section was needed for shear strength.

5. Protect all exterior-exposed wood with oil or varnish. Homeowners should remember that they will have to make a commitment to caulking the gaps between the timbers and the insulation. This should be done at least once a year for as long as the wood continues to dry and shrink.

Porches   Porches are a different situation entirely from roofs because they must be supported by posts, and there isn't a good way to protect exposed posts to the same degree that exposed rafters or purlins can be protected. Therefore, the porch (or at least the posts that support it) simply can't last as long as the rest of the frame. Thus the best solution is to separate the porch completely from the house by isolating it on the other side of the insulation. This also makes it possible to construct the porch with a wood chosen exclusively for its weather-resistance. To make it easy to attach the roof framing to the exterior sheathing, use timbers for the front wall of the porch to support the roof, but build the roof itself with conventional framing members.

The most difficult part of the porch to protect is the base of the posts. If posts are to be attached to a concrete floor, use the plinth detail on p. 122. When the posts will rest on a wooden deck, allow water to drain by cutting any mortises to pass through the sill. (This is not a good situation for a timber sill because it is so difficult to prevent the surface from retaining moisture.) If circumstances demand the use of a timber sill, use the most water-resistant wood available and bevel the exposed top surfaces to ensure that water will run off.

The porches in this house are supported with posts and beams, but these exterior timbers are not attached to the rest of the frame for fear they will deteriorate prematurely.

Changes in building height and width

For structural reasons, a change in roofline or building dimension almost always has to occur at a bent; for design purposes, the change has to be aesthetically, as well as technically, satisfactory, since the timber frame is an important part of the interior space. When one building has two or more roofline heights or any change in width, there should be a structural decision about how to support the upper and lower rafters at the break, and design decisions about which timbers will be visible and how to apply the finish and insulation.

An illustration will clarify the problem. In the floor plan below, the change in building dimension between the living room and the rest of the house results in a complete change in volume and feeling. When you take those two steps down to the living room, you move from an area with an 8-ft. ceiling to one with a ceiling that soars to about 20 ft. The three bents in the living room were designed with dramatic hammer beams, while the bents for the rest of the house had function at their core. During design, we were concerned about how the structure would look from both areas and about the transition from the grand cathedral space to the rest of the house.

As it turned out, the most practical solution was to build two independent frames—one for the living room and one for the rest of the house. If we had tried to use a single

When you step down to the living room in this timber-frame house, you move from a low, flat ceiling to the drama of a soaring cathedral space.

Bent and floor plans for house designed with two widths

bent instead of two side-by-side, we would have needed rafters to support purlins, and posts would have been necessary for the inside corners. Each bent would have lost some distinctiveness. But by creating two separate frames, we were able to define each area completely with timbers—a design decision that was particularly important in the living room, which had a nice sense of symmetry and unity from the three hammer beams. We left a 5-in. space between the two bents at the building break for insulation and for the finish wall surface of both areas (4½ in. for the typical stress-skin panel with drywall on one side, and

½ in. for a layer of drywall to be applied to the nail-base sheathing on the other side.)

In this example, our biggest concern was to make sure the two frames were securely fastened together. While designed to be structurally independent, they also had to act as a unit. We made the tie in the insulation. The panels between the two bents are attached to the main house, and the panels on the living-room wing are routed and fitted over a nailer attached to the outside of the main-house panels. The living-room panels are screwed to the nailer and nailed to the main-house timbers.

Attaching two separate frames

A 5" SPACE BETWEEN BENTS ALLOWS INSULATION AND DRYWALL.

NAILER, NAILED TO SHEATHING.

SCREWS HOLD LIVING ROOM PANEL TO NAILER.

SHEATHING

DRYWALL

The best structural solution is to integrate elements of both bents within a single bent at the point of transition, because it ensures that everything will work as a single unit. But especially when there are internal rafters, building math and bent assembly become pretty tricky. (For that reason, these are referred to as "infernal rafters" in our shop.) There is also a finishing and insulating problem where the wall and the lower roof intersect. In the case of the house shown at right, we put the lower roof panel on first with the bottom edge held back ½ in. and routed for a nailer. After the nailer was secured, a base plate for the wall panel was precisely located and nailed to the roof panels. The wall panels were cut and routed to fit over the base plate, allowing the wall panel to be secured where there wasn't any nailing area in the frame. Finally, a drywall strip was attached from the inside to the end of the roof panel. In this frame, the internal rafter is in the same plane as the rest of the bent. It would have been better to have the internal rafter project at least a few inches toward the lower roof, to receive the panels, as shown below.

Here, an internal rafter was framed into the mid-bents to receive the purlins from the outer bents. Internal rafters solve a connection problem but involve tricky mathematical calculations.

Detail of internal rafter and panel connection

MAIN HOUSE POST

GABLE-WALL PANEL

2X4 BASE PLATE ATTACHED TO ROOF PANEL BEFORE VERTICAL PANEL

2X4 NAILER

ROOF PANEL, HELD BACK FROM POST ½" FOR DRYWALL STRIP AND NOTCHED TO CLEAR GABLE-WALL PANELS

2" EXTENSION ON INTERNAL RAFTER

Another way to solve the finishing problem at the roof break is to tie the frames together at the wall level, but hold the rafter for the lower roof away from the wall, allowing the insulation to be fitted between. This requires that the first rafter be framed to a plate, which wouldn't be a problem in a common-rafter system. In the frame shown below, the bent girt for the larger structure has to support a very large load. It carries a portion of the floor load, a point load from the upper part of the gambrel roof, and the weight of the plate and the roof system for the gable wing. Even though it is a short span, it would probably be better to have a post at the inside corner.

The bent girt of the main house not only supports a major roof load transferred through the post, but it also must support the plate and roof system for the gable wing. Luckily, the bent girt is short and well braced.

Timbers and glass

In my years as a designer and builder of timber-frame houses, I have talked to at least a thousand people about their dream homes. Only one of them did not list the admission of sunlight as a priority. A shady spot on the north side of a hill would have suited this man just fine; the house would have let in only enough light to cause shadows. I admitted to being concerned about his dim lifestyle, and he confessed to being a Hobbit. We didn't build for this client, and I can only hope that somewhere he was able to find the dark home of his desires.

This fellow would have been perfectly content in the typical home built prior to the early-to-mid-1800s, when the use of sheet glass for windows had not yet become widespread. During that time, glass window panes were individually made by craftsmen who would blow a glass bubble and then spin it into a sheet, leaving a crown in the middle. These same glassblowers also created vases and goblets, and the window panes were likewise small and precious. While they admitted light, they did nothing for visibility, for anything viewed through the bubbles would appear distorted. Only the very wealthy could afford much glass. Most houses had a few small penetrations to allow a little light, supplemented by candles, lanterns and even the fireplace. By day and night, homes were like above-ground caves. The average modern house is a crystal palace by comparison.

There is no doubt we have come a long way, and within the last 15 years alone, significant improvements have practically revolutionized the way we think about glass. For example, by sealing air between two or three panes, windows today can have unheard-of insulating qualities; using argon gas instead of plain air in the cavity can provide an even greater R-value. Large panes can be strengthened to allow spans once requiring structural materials. Low-emissivity (low-E) coating, an infrared reflecting surface, is transparent but limits the passage of heat. Ultimate performance is achieved through a combination of technological developments, such as when argon gas is sealed between two layers of tempered, low-E glass. A recent test demonstrated that even with an exterior temperature of 0°F, the interior glass felt warm to the touch. Glazing materials and hardware have also improved over the last few years, and an array of new caulking and gaskets can give site-mounted glass reliable performance.

As a result of this technology, the creative use of glass has become a force in modern architecture. Designers have to balance the aesthetic qualities of expanses of glass against the concomitant heat loss; glass giving better energy performance means the balance shifts toward glass. By using top-shelf, low-E glass and carefully calculating optimum glazing area, significant amounts of glass can now be used without compromising energy performance. These calculations (usually computer-generated), consider solar gain, surface area of exterior walls and the roof, house volume and glass type, among many other factors. The goal is to find the point at which the heat gain from sunny days exceeds the loss from cloudy days and from the nights. Predictably, the results show that most of the glass should be concentrated on the south side of the building, with modest amounts on the east and west sides to receive light, and as little as possible on the north. Often a solarium is recommended for heat collection.

Glass and timber frames are perfect mates. The spaces between frame members can be filled in with any kind of rigid sheathing material, and glass is such a material. Because the posts carry the entire building load, windows and doors can be mounted just about anywhere in the insulating system. In this section, we'll explore a few aspects of the glass-and-timber relationship, starting with a few notes on integrating manufactured windows and doors into a timber-frame house. Then we'll cover solarium design. We'll conclude with several flashing and glazing details associated with mounting glass on timbers.

Integrating manufactured units Window and door units are mounted in the insulation (as discussed in Chapter V), which is in turn secured to the frame. The only relationship between the frame and these units is therefore an aesthetic one, but it is by no means unimportant. In fact, it is critical that the frame and fenestration interact with symmetry and balance (see p. 68).

Design goals can be achieved either by altering fenestration to fit the frame or by changing the frame to suit the fenestration. In several of the houses we have designed, clients have decided that they wanted to see the frame from both the inside and the outside. Instead of mounting the windows between timbers, we located them over the timbers so visitors would meet the frame before entering the house. We have also mounted large windows between posts so that the diagonal braces could be seen from both sides. The brace pair can actually enhance the window opening, and it does not interfere with the operation of the window since it is mounted in the insulation outside the frame.

Because the glass is mounted in the insulation outside the frame, windows can be designed to allow timber members to be visible from the outside as well as from the inside.

Usually it is best that window and door design coincide with frame design. Fanlight windows, for instance, can be made to fit nicely between the curved arches of knee braces. Another technique is to use timbers to frame window or door openings. The unit is still mounted in the insulation, but the timbers act as the trim. For one of our projects, an architect designed almost every window and door in the house to be trimmed completely with timbers. The jambs of the units were received into rabbets cut into the perimeter of the timber opening. The timbers were dry, which allowed us to make a firm attachment between the jambs and the timbers. If they hadn't been dry, there would have been big problems.

Solariums A solarium is typically thought of as a separate space used to collect heat for distribution to the house. The distribution can be accomplished through opening doors and windows, through fans and ducts, or through a masonry mass. But better glass and more intelligent sizing of glazed areas make it possible to build solariums that do not have so much heat loss that they need to be separated from other living areas. The solarium then becomes an inviting place for sitting, reading and gathering—a place of heat and light, not unlike the hearth in early homes. This is the type of solarium I am most enthusiastic about, even if it sometimes means accepting the compromise that occasionally heat loss will exceed gain.

I came to this preference the hard way. Quite a few years ago we designed a modest-sized house for a site with good solar exposure, and correctly judged that we would be able to heat with the sun on days that weren't cloudy. We added a detached solarium to the design, so that we would not lose heat through the glass when sunlight was unavailable. When the solarium was warm and the house cold, a French door and an awning window would be opened to let heat into the house. A fine idea, but we weren't prepared for the fact that since the solarium would not benefit from the house heat, it would get very cold during long cloudy periods. Also, by the time the solarium had been warmed by the sun, the house had also been warmed by solar gain through other windows and heat conducted through the solarium. Because there was no reason to open it to the house, the solarium seriously overheated in sunny periods. (The owner told me the thermometer registered over 140°F right before the mercury popped.) This solarium was either too cold or too hot for use. The solution was to reduce the amount of glass in the solarium, take out the back wall and incorporate the space into the house.

If a solarium is to be detached and useful, it must have a huge amount of mass to store the heat for night and cloudy periods. This type of solarium is usually complicated to build, always expensive and will still sometimes get too cold. Window insulation (there are many types) is a good idea, but too often it is only an idea. If people don't take the time to operate the insulation, it won't work. One of our clients figured it required five minutes in the morning and five in the evening to pull the insulation over each window. While this doesn't seem that long theoretically, it takes more time than the garbage and less than the dishes; just long enough to become another daily chore.

In this gable-end wall, white-cedar framing was designed to coincide with custom window units. The windows will be mounted to the outside of the frame along with the panels, and the timbers will serve as interior trim.

Solariums that are incorporated into the main living space of the house can take many forms, from a simple large window to the common three-sided addition with a large expanse of south-facing fixed glass. Operable window units are mounted on the east and west sides and often on the roof as well, making it easy to vent the solarium when there is too much heat. Since the long side of the building tends to face south anyway, the simplest way to create a solarium is to extend the roofline on the eave side. In essence, the solarium becomes an extension of a bay and is framed by passing the principal rafters over the outside posts of adjacent bays to the shorter posts at the solarium corners. From a construction standpoint, it is not important that the solarium be in the middle bay; but its placement there is usually more beneficial to heat distribution.

Using fixed glass on the south wall is also not a requirement of solariums. If you plan carefully and use stock glass sizes, it is an Inexpensive way to develop a large glass area. (Stock glass is generally about one-quarter the cost per square foot of custom Thermopane glass.) We use a few different sizes that are commonly available as replacement panels for sliding glass doors. Unfortunately, the dimensions of the panels of stock glass will probably not add up to the width of the bay, so unless the bay was designed to accommodate available glass or luck prevailed, there is likely to be some insulated wall on each side of the glass.

The edges of the glass are mounted on the outside faces of the timbers, so any wood that will contact the glass must be dry, even if the rest of the frame is built from green material. Otherwise, you risk disturbing the seal between the glass and the frame or even breaking the glass as the drying wood shrinks, twists, warps or bows. Since the principal posts carry most of the building load, wood with less structural value, such as cedar and white pine, can be used to receive the glass. The solarium shown in the photo below, which has insulated walls extending past the glass to fill out to bay width, uses a few pieces of dry old-growth southern pine to accept the glass. For details on mounting glass, see p. 188.

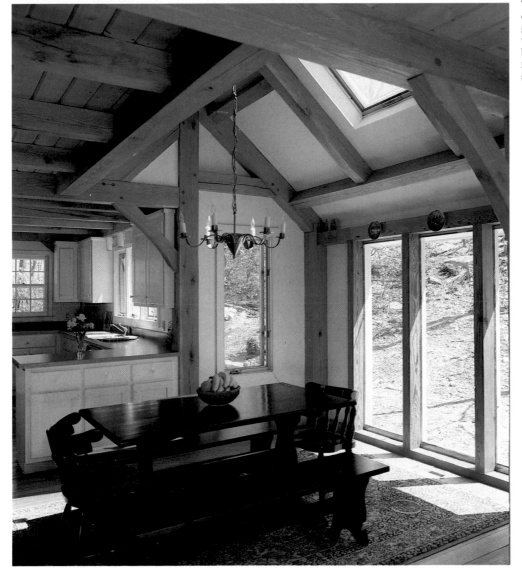

The solarium is often just an extension of the eave. Stock glass size helps determine wall height; dry timbers must be used where glass will be mounted. The roof window assists ventilation.

The fixed glass area is framed below the roofline break with a plate (or connecting girt) between principal posts; the vertical members of the solarium are mortise-and-tenoned to the plate. But if fixed glass is intended for the roof slope as well as for the wall, the position of the plate becomes a problem in that it creates an awkward transition between the sloped and the vertical glazing. There are two solutions. One is to eliminate the plate entirely, connecting short rafters to the solarium posts, as shown at right. A purlin joined to the frame receives the solarium rafters at a point determined by the glass size. The roof glass meets the wall glass at a horizontal 2x2 turned round on a lathe between rafters and left square in section where it meets the rafters. When the eave is low and a plate would obstruct the view, this is a nice alternative. The other solution (if a slightly obstructed view is not a problem), is to frame common rafters from a purlin to a plate that rests on top of the solarium posts. The plate is ripped to the roof slope on the top outside edge to serve as bearing for the roof glass.

The plate system is also useful when the solarium spans more than one bay. Using a plate to connect from one corner of the solarium to the other eliminates concern about the location of the bent post, which would otherwise probably interrupt the layout of the glass panels. Solarium posts are framed into the plate at intervals determined by the glass size, and the plate also supports the bent rafters.

There are many ways to design a solarium under an eave. For example, in one contemporary-style house, we increased wall height in the solarium bay to frame a dramatic three-story window (photo facing page). Two rows of fixed glass were mounted on fir timbers and topped with a custom fanlight. Light penetrates deeply into the house, and the view is visible from a third-floor study. Roof windows operated with electric switches increase light and assist ventilation.

Where the sloped roof glass and the vertical glass come together, a special flashing detail is used instead of a timber. Here, a plant hanger is screwed to each timber and helps keep the framing rigid.

A plate sits on these solarium posts, providing a good connection between members. The plate is ripped on the top outside edge to make a bearing surface for the glass.

Increasing the height of this wall provided room for the framing of a three-story window. Two layers of fixed glass were attached to fir timbers, and a custom fan unit, placed on top, was designed to match.

Solariums with gable roofs can also bring sunlight deep into a building and provide a dramatic focal point. But because the compound joinery required is difficult, they are also quite expensive. Gable solariums work best when they are extensions of a single bay, if only to keep the valley framing from bisecting principal rafters. You can bet I learned about this the hard way. A building we did quite a few years ago had a gable-roofed solarium that was accessible from three levels. It began at the base with a layer of fixed glass mounted on fir timbers. Then there was a layer of operable manufactured units, reached by walkways on the second floor. Finally there was a fixed custom fanlight, through which a person on the third-floor balcony could view the outside. The only problem was that the width of the solarium extended past the middle bay into the two adjacent bays, so the valley rafters crossed two bent rafters. It is quite difficult to pre-fit this kind of joinery, so we generally make careful cuts to mathematical and geometric calculations and then just put it together. Try to imagine the situation. The valley rafter frames into the

principal rafter and then picks up on the other side, continuing to the eave where it frames into the outside wall. The math drove us silly, the cutting made us dizzy and the assembly was nearly impossible physically. But we did it like that . . . once.

Shed-roof solariums can also be designed at a gable end. The bent that connects to the shed has to have an additional horizontal member to receive the shed rafters, and there should be posts in the bent to align with the corner posts of the solarium. Otherwise, the framing is no different from an eave solarium. In fact, a shed solarium on the gable end is probably a little easier because the restrictions of bay width do not apply. Stock glass dimensions usually determine solarium width.

Mounting glass on timbers   The first thing to know is that it is not necessary to rabbet the timbers for the glass. Everyone seems to want to do this but it doesn't really help anything. Along with the insulation, it is better to keep the glass, flashing and any potential condensation

This gable-roofed solarium is left open to the peak, but is also accessible from three levels. Walkways on either side of the second floor provide a nice overlook from the bedrooms and also allow access to the double-hung windows. A cantilevered balcony from a third-floor studio looks out through the round-top window.

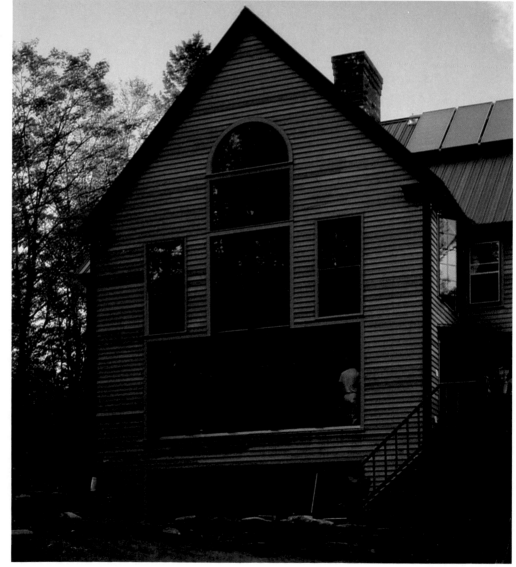

outside the frame. So rabbets are created by nailing plywood spacers to the sides, tops and bottoms of the solarium timbers just prior to installing the glass. This method is also easier than rabbeting the timbers. After all, you can't exactly pick up a timber and run it through a shaper.

Before getting into the various glazing details, let's quickly review how glass is normally installed. Basically, the glass sits in the rabbets created by the plywood spacers between two layers of glazing tape, and is capped by a metal or wood trim piece. The plywood spacers are usually built up of two layers, but if you can't find a combination that works, use a piece of plywood plus a piece of dry lumber. To calculate the correct thickness of the spacers, subtract $\frac{1}{16}$ in. from the thickness of the glass (to ensure a snug fit between the trim and the glazing tape), and add in the two pieces of $\frac{1}{8}$-in.-thick tape. In other words, if the glass is 1 in. thick, the thickness of the spacer would be $1\frac{3}{16}$ in. At least $\frac{5}{8}$ in. of glass should bear on the timber and there should be an extra $\frac{1}{4}$ in. allowed for expansion, making the depth of the rabbet $\frac{7}{8}$ in. In the plan view of a typical solarium post below, the 4x6 has nominal dimensions of $3\frac{1}{2}$ in. by $5\frac{1}{2}$ in. Because this is a middle post, receiving glass on both edges, you would subtract the $\frac{7}{8}$-in. depth of each rabbet to calculate a spacer width of $1\frac{3}{4}$ in.

After the spacers are nailed to the solarium timbers with galvanized ring-shank nails, the setting blocks, which act to level the glass and cushion it from expansion and contraction, are placed in the bottom rabbets. Each glass panel sits on two $\frac{1}{4}$-in.-thick neoprene setting blocks posi-tioned at what are called "quarter points." To calculate these, simply divide half the width of the glass by two and measure in that far from each edge; for a 4-ft.-wide panel, the quarter points would be 1 ft. in from each edge. If further leveling is required, small strips of aluminum under one of the setting blocks make good shims.

Once the setting blocks are in, the first layer of glazing tape is carefully applied to the timbers around the perimeter of the opening. The glazing tape is $\frac{1}{8}$ in. thick by $\frac{1}{2}$ in. wide and pre-shimmed, which means there are wires embedded in it to keep it from compressing and deforming in hot weather. The tape is applied so that its edges will be flush with the edges of the $\frac{1}{2}$-in.-wide dessicant band between glass panes. It is held back $\frac{1}{8}$ in. to $\frac{3}{16}$ in. from the timber edges to receive a bead of silicone sealant. After the sealant is applied, the glass is then set in the opening, and the second layer of glazing tape is positioned so it also aligns with the edges of the dessicant band. Another bead of silicone sealant is applied. Wood or metal trim is positioned over the plywood spacers and the glass edges, applying pressure to the glazing tape and thus to the dessicant bands—it is important that no pressure be put on the glass where it is unsupported by a dessicant band. When the trim is installed, it will force excess sealant to ooze out of the glazing tape. Peel this off later.

That's the general scheme. Before proceeding, check with your supplier to ensure that the sealant is compatible with the glazing tape. There are many stories about chemical reactions causing a break in the glass seal. Now let's look at some specific details.

Installing solarium glass (plan view)

WOOD OR METAL TRIM

BEAD OF SILICONE SEALANT

$\frac{1}{2}$"-WIDE DESSICANT BAND

1"-THICK INSULATING GLASS PANEL

BUILT-UP PLYWOOD SPACER, $1\frac{3}{16}$" THICK X $1\frac{3}{4}$" WIDE

$\frac{1}{8}$"X$\frac{1}{2}$" WIDE GLAZING TAPE ALIGNS WITH EDGE OF DESSICANT BAND.

$\frac{1}{4}$" FOR EXPANSION

4X6 TIMBER POST (NOMINAL DIMENSIONS $3\frac{1}{2}$"X$5\frac{1}{2}$")

The basic theory on treating the bottoms of the glass panes comes from the people who make roof windows. They use battens on the top and sides to hold the glass in place, but generally do not cap the bottom, allowing water to run off freely. On solariums we use trim at the sides and top to hold the glass to the timbers, but at the bottom we use two different details, depending on whether or not there will be insulation beneath the glass. If there will be insulation, it is necessary to make the transition from the thickness of the glass to the thickness of the insulation. The panel (this is assuming the use of stress-skin panels) would be held beneath the top edge of the bottom solarium beam by about 3 in. This beam is often at or near floor level. A 2-in.-wide plywood spacer is then nailed to the bottom beam, then a block of wood is ripped to slope from the top edge of the spacer to the outside edge of the panel.

Bottom glazing detail, insulated below (side view)

BEAD OF SILICONE SEALANT
⅛"X½" GLAZING TAPE
PLYWOOD SPACER

1"
2"

BOTTOM SOLARIUM TIMBER
2X4 NAILER
STRESS-SKIN PANEL

1" INSULATING GLASS PANEL
BEAD OF SILICONE SEALANT
¼" SETTING BLOCK
TAPERED WOOD BLOCK
FLASHING

FASTEN FLASHING WITH COPPER TACKS, 6" O.C.
1X2 RABBETED FOR SIDING

FLASHING DETAILS

U-SHAPED CAP FLASHING; WEEP HOLES DRILLED EVERY 8"
EXTERIOR SILL FLASHING

1"
1"
1"
1⅛"
30°
4¾"
5/16"
4⅛"
5¼"
60°

ALL FLASHING FROM .032" ANODIZED ALUMINUM STOCK

This block must be accurately cut and shimmed to fit precisely, because it describes the finished surface. After it is installed, some tricky flashing, generally custom-made by a sheet-metal company, goes down. The exterior sill flashing is installed first, then the *U*-shaped cap flashing accepts the neoprene setting blocks and the glass. As shown on the facing page, beads of silicone sealant prevent water from entering the assembly.

If the bottom beam of the solarium is on a slab foundation, there is usually no need for insulation below the glass. Thus the glass may rest on a trim board built out to the proper thickness for the glass plus glazing tape. A simple piece of flashing caps the top of the board and runs down about ¾ in., as shown in the drawing below. Then the *U*-shaped cap flashing is installed as specified previously.

Bottom glazing detail, uninsulated below (side view)

1" INSULATING GLASS PANEL

BEAD OF SILICONE SEALANT

⅛"X½" GLAZING TAPE

BEAD OF SILICONE SEALANT REDUCES LEAKING BEHIND FLASHING.

¼" SETTING BLOCK

TRIM BOARD

6X8 BOTTOM TIMBER

FLASHING DETAILS

¾"

U—SHAPED CAP FLASHING

WEEP HOLES DRILLED 8" O.C. ALONG OUTSIDE BOTTOM EDGE

1"

1"

ALL FLASHING FROM .032" STOCK ANODIZED ALUMINUM

1"

EXTERIOR TRIM FLASHING

¾"

On the corners of the solarium, there are usually two detail options. In one situation (below), the insulation is mounted to the side of the post because there is no need for it on the front. In the other situation (facing page), the insulation is mounted to the front of the post because the wall surface surrounding the glass needs to be insulated. In the side detail, the trim board must cap not only the corner post but also the insulation. In the front detail, the stress-skin panel should be held back on the timber enough to allow for a plywood spacer, as shown. Three pieces of trim then cap the glass and cover the exposed panel edges. The face trim goes on first, side trim is installed second and the end trim is last. This detail might also occur at the top of the glazing when the glass does not extend all the way to the eave, as in a gable-roofed solarium. The only necessary alteration would be to add window-header flashing to the top of the end-trim board. In point of fact, a solarium is a big site-made window; when completely surrounded by the insulating system, the flashing and sealing details are the same as those on commercial windows.

As I mentioned earlier, we often create solariums by extending the roofline on the eave side. We have found that the most consistently available stock glass is 76 in. long, so we commonly design the roof extension to conclude at a height that allows for framing, flashing and trim of 76-in.-long glass. The solarium on p. 185 was designed on this basis. The roof was insulated with a typical panel overhang and trimmed as described in Chapter X. Under these circumstances, the friezeboard at the top of the wall also becomes the top batten for securing the glass, no matter whether the roof trim is based on a flat or sloped soffit. Flashing is not necessary under the eave because the roof overhang solves the moisture problem.

Roof glass   There is justifiable argument over the wisdom of using sloped roof glass in solariums. There is more air

Outside solarium corner with insulation on side (plan view)

#12 X 2½" STAINLESS STEEL SCREW, WITH WASHER, 12" O.C.

BEAD OF SILICONE SEALANT

1" INSULATING GLASS

⅛" X ½" GLAZING TAPE

¼" FOR EXPANSION

4X6 SOLARIUM CORNER POST

STRESS—SKIN PANEL

1 ³/₁₆"X2½" PLYWOOD SPACER

2X4 NAILER

1X CEDAR TRIM BOARDS

movement next to glass than next to an insulated wall, so there are likely to be more convection currents in a solarium than in the rest of the house. These currents carry lots of warm air to the solarium roof. If the roof is glass, expect the heat loss in this area to be significantly greater than if the roof were insulated. Add this to the fact that the heat gain through roof glass in summer is unnecessarily high, and it becomes hard to argue the case in practical terms. So when the design of a house suggests roof glass, I get emotional instead. I talk about a view where horizon and sky come together, a place to stargaze on a cold winter's night. I mention the effect of warm washes of sun penetrating deeply into the living area. With this out of the way, I should point out that we have used roof glass only about a dozen times on more than ten score houses. Roof glass makes the most sense when there is a relatively small solarium attached to a large living space. Roof windows are much more practical because they limit the glass

area, provide much-needed ventilation in summer and are easy to install.

If roof glass will be used, try to reduce its area by keeping the individual panes short. A strategy we commonly employ is to use pieces of full-length stock glass (usually 76 in.) for the vertical glazing, and half-sheets of the same width for the roof. Keeping width consistent is important to the design, and using a stock size for the vertical glass keeps cost down, even though the half-size glass is a custom order.

Following are several details for the application of roof glass. The first thing you might notice is that there aren't any wooden members capping the glass as there are on the wall. Using wood in an area that gets so much heat and moisture is simply an invitation to trouble. Also notice that all solarium roof glass is mounted on rafters instead of purlins. This keeps the glass size manageable and encourages water runoff.

Outside solarium corner with insulation on front (plan view)

END TRIM
SIDE TRIM
FACE TRIM
1" INSULATING GLASS
⅛"X½" GLAZING TAPE
¼" FOR EXPANSION

15# FELT PAPER
STRESS—SKIN PANEL
2X4 NAILER
1³⁄₁₆"X1" PLYWOOD SPACER
4X6 SOLARIUM CORNER POST

Using a plate to make the transition between the wall and the roof simplifies and strengthens framing and flashing. The plate serves as a good stiffener and connects the entire assembly. It is angled to correspond with the roof slope and creates a bearing surface for both the roof glass and the vertical glass. Give the top and outside face of the plate extra moisture protection with an elastomeric membrane, positioned as shown below. These membranes have become popular for a number of different roofing applications because they remain elastic despite temperature fluctuations and tend to seal holes that might develop, even around nails and screws. Install the plywood spacers using the method to calculate thickness described on p. 189. Always use a good grade of plywood—it's important that it not absorb moisture and expand. Cut the spacer for the roof glass to fit from the outside edge of the vertical-glass spacer to about 1 in. from the top edge of the plate.

A piece of cap flashing is placed into the rabbet, with its lip bent over the top edge of the timber and securely fastened with ¾-in., #6 galvanized nails every 10 in. Flashing is a bad place to save money, so use as a minimum standard 20-oz. copper or .032 anodized aluminum. All the roof flashing should be custom-formed in a shop. The glass is laid into the channel using neoprene setting blocks, pre-

Wall and roof-glass connection at plate

BEAD OF SILICONE SEALANT

⅛"X½" GLAZING TAPE

PLYWOOD SPACER

COVER FLASHING

DRIP EDGE

TRIM BOARD FOR VERTICAL FRIEZEBOARD

PLYWOOD SPACER

BEAD OF SILICONE SEALANT

INSULATING GLASS

INSULATING GLASS

BEAD OF SILICONE SEALANT

¼" SETTING BLOCK

CAP FLASHING FASTENED WITH COPPER NAILS

20-MIL ELASTOMERIC MEMBRANE

4X6 TIMBER PLATE

¼" FOR EXPANSION

GLAZING TAPE

shimmed glazing tape and sealant as described on p. 189, but here the procedure differs. It's a little tricky to lift the flashing enough to allow the glass to sit on the glazing tape and sealant. The problem can be solved by sticking the glazing tape to both the top and bottom edges of the glass that will sit in the rabbet. A couple of small wedges on both sides of the glass keep the tape separate from the flashing while it enters the rabbet. After the glass is seated on the setting blocks and before the wedges are pulled out, apply sealant liberally between the flashing and the glass. Install the drip edge next, which is the small piece bent to the roof angle attached to the friezeboard at the top of the

wall. The cover flashing is bent at the ends to slip over the top of the cap flashing and over the top edge of the drip. With the drip edge, cap flashing and glass in place, fit the cover flashing over the drip edge, push it forward so that it can engage the cap flashing, then pull it back down the roof slope, locking it in place. Obviously, it is quite important that the cover flashing be tight to the glass, and there should be no ridges to trap water. Add more sealant to the drip edge and finish the sealant by beveling the excess with a putty knife to encourage runoff.

Another way to make the transition between roof and wall glass is to frame short rafters to connect with the so-

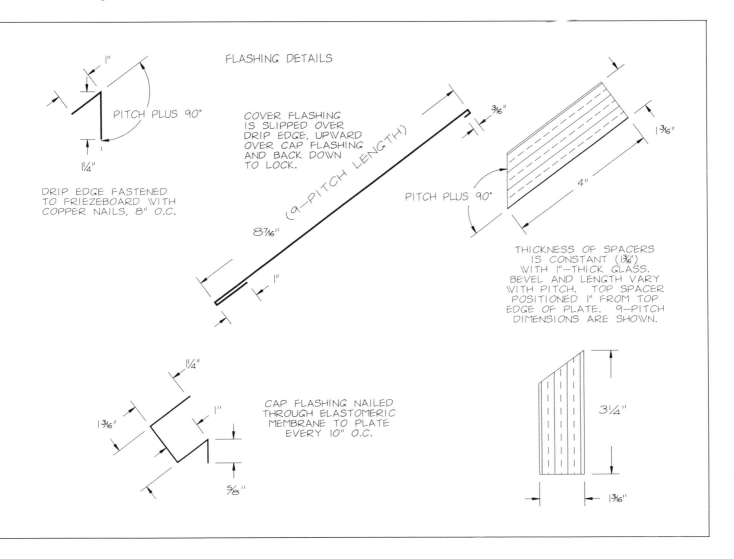

FLASHING DETAILS

1"
PITCH PLUS 90°
1 1/4"

DRIP EDGE FASTENED TO FRIEZEBOARD WITH COPPER NAILS, 8" O.C.

COVER FLASHING IS SLIPPED OVER DRIP EDGE, UPWARD OVER CAP FLASHING AND BACK DOWN TO LOCK.

(9-PITCH LENGTH)
8 7/16"
1"
3/16"

PITCH PLUS 90°
1 3/16"
4"

THICKNESS OF SPACERS IS CONSTANT (1 3/16") WITH 1"-THICK GLASS. BEVEL AND LENGTH VARY WITH PITCH. TOP SPACER POSITIONED 1" FROM TOP EDGE OF PLATE. 9-PITCH DIMENSIONS ARE SHOWN.

1 1/4"
1 3/16"
1"
5/8"

CAP FLASHING NAILED THROUGH ELASTOMERIC MEMBRANE TO PLATE EVERY 10" O.C.

3 1/4"
1 3/16"

larium posts, as shown in the top photo on p. 186. The roof glass meets the wall glass with no horizontal framing at the transition; flashing makes the joint leakproof. A 2x2 plant hanger mortised into each rafter serves as the horizontal connection. It is placed about 10 in. from each rafter end and 1½ in. from the inside face. The 2x2 is screwed and plugged to the rafter from the inside.

This detail is more prone to heat loss than the previous one. Because the flashing passes through to the inside, you get condensation in cold weather and ice on the inside of the glass in extreme conditions. Two pieces of flashing are needed, both of which should be made from heavy-gauge material. The vertical glass is installed to stop at a point ¼ in. below the roofline as extended from the timber rafter, to leave room for flashing and keep the roof glass from contacting the vertical glass. A piece of U-shaped flashing with ⅛-in. neoprene setting blocks at the top caps the vertical glass. The setting blocks, again placed at quarter points, create a cushion should there be any pressure from the roof glass. No glazing tape is needed with this detail. The second piece of flashing is tricky and should be precisely shop-formed. The general dimensions are shown below, but the angle would change depending on the roof pitch. The weep holes are extremely important. Before the roof glass is installed, setting blocks are positioned to create space for expansion and for any water that might leak into the cavity; a bead of sealant along the top edge inhibits water entry.

Wall and roof-glass connection at 2x2

Setting the roof glass over the rafters is identical to the procedure for vertical glazing installation, with two exceptions. First, cover the top face of the rafters with elastomeric membrane, and second, use metal for the top cap instead of wood. On the middle rafters, use ¼-in. aluminum bar stock as a stiff batten for the glass, screwing and counter-sinking it to the rafters on 8-in. centers. Take every precaution when installing the glazing tape and sealant—the potential for leakage is great. Then, for a more attractive finish, use anodized aluminum or copper to cap the bar stock. Attach the cap with #6 stainless-steel sheet-metal screws and rubber washers 2 ft. on center.

Solarium-rafter glazing detail (exploded section perpendicular to pitch)

#6X2½" STAINLESS SHEET—METAL SCREW, 2' O.C.

COPPER CAP FLASHING

4⅜"

³⁄₁₆

⅛"X½" GLAZING TAPE (SEALANT NOT SHOWN)

¼"X4¼" ALUMINUM BAR STOCK

INSULATING GLASS

⅛"X½" GLAZING TAPE (SEALANT NOT SHOWN)

20—MIL ELASTOMERIC MEMBRANE

PLYWOOD SPACER

SOLARIUM RAFTER

The detail on the outside edge of the solarium is basically the same as that described previously. It is necessary to cap both the timber and the top edge of the insulation. The plywood spacer extends to the outside edge of the exterior panel sheathing; a ¼-in.-thick plywood strip has to be added after the ¼-in.-thick aluminum batten to keep the top face flush. The flashing must span from the glass to the rake edge, and should be custom-formed as shown. Sheet-metal screws are fastened about ¾ in. from the plywood edge on the glass end. Another attachment for the flashing is made by nailing the rake edge of the flashing to the wall. Use 1-in. nails, 12 in. on center, to attach the rake flashing to the wall. Copper nails are best for copper and aluminum for aluminum.

Solarium-rake glazing (section perpendicular to rafter path)

#6X2½" COUNTERSUNK STAINLESS SHEET—METAL SCREW, 12" O.C.

.032" CUSTOM COPPER FLASHING AND DRIP EDGE

GLAZING TAPE AND SILICONE SEALANT

INSULATING GLASS

¼" AIR SPACE

ELASTOMERIC MEMBRANE

SOLARIUM RAFTER

¼"X4" ALUMINUM BATTEN

PLYWOOD SPACER

¼" PLYWOOD

IX3 SPACER

RAKE BOARD

TUCK SIDING BEHIND RAKE

STRESS—SKIN PANEL

1"   3"

FLASHING DETAIL

11½"

9¹⁵⁄₁₆"   1⁹⁄₁₆"

¼"   ¾"   2½"

One of the easiest solarium details is at the top of the roof glass, where glass and insulation intersect on the purlin that receives the solarium rafters. Moisture coming off the roof falls away from the intersection, so leaks are prevented. The bottom edge of the insulation stops about 1 in. from the edge of the purlin to leave a bearing surface for the glass. A 20-mil elastomeric membrane strip is first laid into the corner, positioned between the top edge of the timber and the spacer as shown in the drawing below. The rest of the installation follows the guidelines discussed earlier; roof trim on the face of the insulation holds the glass in place. Because it is not subjected to as much weather and moisture as it might be elsewhere on the roof, wood trim works fine here.

Purlin detail

ROOF SHINGLES

COMMERCIAL DRIP EDGE

WOOD TRIM

20-OZ. COPPER FLASHING

INSULATING GLASS

¼" AIR SPACE

⅛" GLAZING TAPE AND A BEAD OF SILICONE SEALANT

20-MIL ELASTOMERIC MEMBRANE

STRESS—SKIN PANEL

SOLARIUM PURLIN

1"

X. Finish Details

The interior detailing should match the high quality of the frame.

As we head into another chapter dense with design details, I would like to remind readers that the following information is not as rigidly prescribed as it might appear. These are not precise instructions for how to do; look at this chapter instead as a series of guidelines for how to think about how to do. Let it steer you along a relatively safe path, but do not let it stand in the way of individuality and creativity. The chapter starts with trim, both inside and out; flooring systems are next, followed by interior partitions. Finally, we'll end with a discussion of the treatment of interior surfaces.

Window, door and baseboard trim

The process of timber framing is more likely to defy mass-production than to embrace it—the timbers are large and unwieldy, their sizes must change to suit structural conditions in the frame, and the joints are numerous and varied. In addition, timber framers themselves tend to be an independent lot. They often do what they do for reasons that are other than monetary, preferring the joy of creativity to the boredom of repetition. As a result, each timber frame takes on an individuality that becomes an important part of the character of the house. It is precisely this individuality that makes the use of stock trim materials one of my pet peeves. For if you go to just about any lumberyard in the United States for trim, you will probably be faced with many racks of trim types, but few real choices. They really boil down to two or three types that are used all the time. I have nothing against these designs, just against their incessant and automatic use, which has brought a stifling sameness to houses all over the country. The economics of using stock trim also bothers me, because you wind up paying a lot more money for a lot less wood than if you were to buy unmachined stock. For instance, a flat 1x4 purchased from a lumberyard is typically ¾ in. by 3½ in.; when it becomes casing stock, it is further reduced to ⁹⁄₁₆ in. by 3¼ in. The skinny little rounded-over piece of wood sold at about twice the cost of the "full-sized" material it came from is an abuse of wood and, to my mind, an insult to otherwise good construction.

Using plain, flat board stock for casing is less expensive and already more appealing than stock trim, but with surprisingly little effort, flat stock can become distinctive. Start by varying the width and thickness of the pieces. I like to make the head casing for windows and doors heavier than the side casing—the heavier board refers to a structural lintel, and the different dimensions create depth and define each piece. Play around with proportions to fit the circumstances. Consider the species, the intended color and finish of all adjacent surfaces, and the architectural and decorative style. Painted casing will look very different from wood left natural. Large, molded casing imparts a completely different feeling than small, flat casings would. Edges can be refined by molding with a router, shaper or hand plane.

My favorite trim detail is based on using 5/4 stock for the head casing and ¾-in.-thick stock for the side casing, as shown below. On windows, the stool is made from 5/4 stock and the apron from ¾-in. stock. Widths are variable. The head casing extends past the outside edge of the side casing by about ½ in. to reinforce the idea of a lintel. They meet with a simple butt joint, which can be improved with a lap on the back of the head casing. The window stool is rabbeted to fit the sash and also extends past the side casing by ½ in. Below the stool, the ¾-in. flat-stock apron is held back from the stool ends by ½ in. It's a simple scheme and easy to install. Even left unadorned, this type of trim stands apart from standard trim because it is rather raw and honest. But it can be made more elegant by adding chamfers to the inside edges of the side and head casings, to the top edge of the stool and to the bottom edge of the apron. Stop each chamfer 1½ in. before the end or, for the head casing, before it meets the side casing. When the chamfers repeat the embellishment of the timber edges, they can be especially unifying. Beads can also be routed into the face of the casing, stopped usually at the same point as the chamfers. Add a crown molding to the top edge of the header and the casing takes on more formality. The variations are endless, and that's the very point of using this type of trim. Almost anything you do will be better than the lumberyard offerings, but for less money and not a great deal of work it's possible to create a truly grand alternative.

The frame eliminates the need for crown moldings at the intersection of ceilings and walls, so in addition to window and door trim, we are primarily concerned with baseboards. These should match the material and style of the other trim, and also match each other where partitions meet exterior insulated walls. If the extended baseboard detail described on p. 137 and shown below is used, make sure the partition-wall baseboards are the same height as the extended baseboard plus the cap, and add a bead to match the bead on the extended-baseboard cap. Make the same kind of bead on window and door-trim edges for unity.

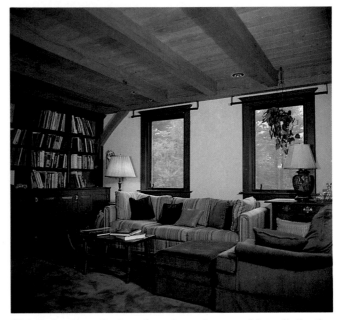

With little effort, flat board stock can be turned into distinctive trim. In this house, standard molding was added to side and head trim to add character and depth. The homeowner developed the idea for the curtain-rod attachment at the windows.

Simple interior window trim

- 5/4"—THICK HEAD CASING
- BUTT OR LAP JOINT
- STOPPED CHAMFERS
- ¾"—THICK SIDE CASING
- ⅜" RABBET FOR SASH
- 5/4"—THICK STOOL
- ¾"—THICK APRON
- STOPPED CHAMFER

Extended-baseboard trim

- ¾" CAP WITH ROUNDED NOSING
- ¾" FURRING STRIP
- SPACE FOR WIRES
- BASEBOARD COVER

Stairs and rails

During design and construction, seize every opportunity to make the details and material of stairs and rails compatible with the timber frame. Perhaps an existing frame post could act as a newel to receive rails and stringers, or a post could be added for this purpose. At the very least, the edge and end embellishments of the frame can be repeated in the stairs.

Careful planning of stairways is absolutely necessary in timber-frame houses because their openings have to be created in the timber-floor system when the frame is being constructed. Stairs usually fall between bents, with the normal joist span broken with timber headers. They can also be designed to pass through a bent if necessary, by raising the bent girt in the area of the stair to allow headroom. The plan should detail the exact layout of risers

and treads so that the frame openings will fit the stairway. Check the local building code on all stair requirements. Since stairs are a principal means of egress, the codes tend to be quite specific, although not the same from state to state.

As I have often described, in simple three-bay timber-frame homes the stair frequently falls in the middle bay. This area is commonly used for passage and transition, and so is seldom divided with partitions; sometimes it is open to the roof. To preserve this spaciousness, we often design open-riser stairs, housing the treads in the stringer and dadoing the balusters into its top edge. At the base and top of the stair, the stringer and the rail mortise into a newel post, which in turn is mortised into the stair header. The newel post has to be projected out of plane toward the stringer so that there will be enough material for a good

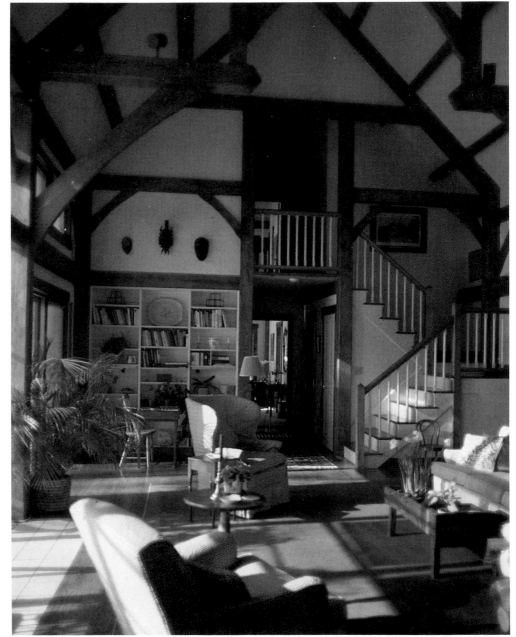

In this frame, the bent girt is raised in the area of the stair to allow head room. Newel posts and stair details are designed to match frame details. Note the simple flat-stock trim around the doors.

Two ways to frame open-riser stairs

STRINGER ATTACHED TO NEWEL, WHICH IN TURN IS TENONED INTO HEADER

NEWEL POST

FINISH FLOOR

JOIST

STAIR HEADER

NEWEL RUNS PAST HEADER.

BALUSTERS DADOED INTO TOP EDGE OF STRINGER

TREAD

STRINGER

STRINGER AND NEWEL ATTACHED TO HEADER SEPARATELY

NEWEL POST

FINISH FLOOR

JOIST

STAIR HEADER

BALUSTERS DADOED INTO TOP EDGE OF STRINGER

TREAD

STRINGER

connection with the stringer. The projected portion of the newel extends below the stair header and is embellished much like a timber pendant. One great advantage of this system is that the stringer, newels, rails and balusters all can be shop-made and installed as a unit.

Another option is to attach the newel to the stair header separately. The newel is designed to align with the edges of the stair header and still receives the tenoned end of the stringer, but the bottom surface of the stringer bears on the face of the stair header. Do not drop the stringer so low that its end grain would be visible from below. Newel-post tenons should be at least 4 in. long to maintain rigidity.

Railings for catwalks or balconies also can be built into the frame. All that is required is that the railings align with timbers and their components (upper rail, lower rail and balusters) be designed into the frame plan. The railing can then be installed when the frame is built, making it stronger and, more important, taking full advantage of the frame as a finish element. Completely house (by at least ⅜ in.) the entire contour of rails that join to timbers, to allow for shrinkage.

Balcony railings were built into this frame when it was raised. A housed mortise-and-tenon joint is used between rails and timbers to hide potential shrinkage.

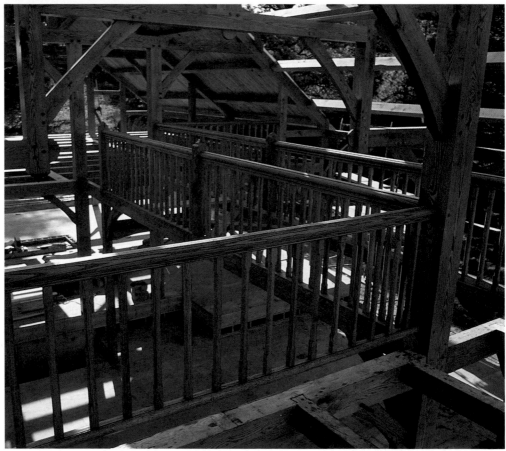

Exterior trim on stress-skin panels

Exterior trim makes a statement about the significance and style of a house. It is a critical design feature, too often ignored or undervalued. If you look at old houses, you will notice that more often than not great attention was paid to the details of exterior trim, especially in the roof. Frequently, the finest woodworking was reserved for elaborate cornices and eaves with multilayered moldings. Contrast this with the modern ranch house, on which any kind of roof trim at all has been practically eliminated. I think lack of attention to this kind of detail is one reason why modern houses frequently look nondescript.

In Chapter V we discussed the stress-skin panel insulating system in detail and several alternatives in general. I didn't go into detail on the alternatives because they are based on conventional building systems and, as such, don't require much more than an explanation of procedure. The stress-skin panel system, however, is quite different from normal building practice in both theory and execution. This section will therefore touch on a few more details that relate to panels—things we didn't explore in Chapter V. Most of what follows is a direct result of the fact that typically the panels have less structure for the application of other materials than do standard insulating systems. I should note here that carpenters are by necessity creative people and often are able to deal with the following situations without advice. Indeed, most of the information in this section is comprised of things I have learned from the many carpenters who have worked on our houses over the years.

Trim boards Depending entirely on architectural style and siding, there potentially are quite a few different types of trim boards that might be on the walls of a house. Corner boards are the vertical trim pieces that reach from the base of the siding to the cornice work on the outside building corners. Skirt boards, used only on elaborate trim styles, run around the perimeter of the house at the base. Exterior door and window trim is just like the interior casing except that it gets much more abuse. There are usually a few other miscellaneous trim boards used for mounting such things as light fixtures and electric meters. Despite the relative lack of surfaces to nail to, mounting all these boards can become quite routine once a procedure has been established.

To secure trim boards to a panel where there is not a 2x4 edge nailer, use galvanized self-tapping screws or galvanized ring-shank nails. (Galvanized screws are used frequently for exterior decks and are available at most lumberyards.) Screws should be long enough to pass through the panel sheathing by at least ⅜ in.; nails need to pass through by about ⅝ in. Edges of boards that are 2½ in. or more away from a 2x4 nailer should be secured with screws to prevent cupping. If the board edge is less than 2½ in. away, use ring-shank nails. For instance, there is typically 1½ in. of nailing around a typical window or door opening. The trim is mounted onto the unit by at least ½ in., spans the gap between the rough opening and the nailer, and then is nailed to the nailer. Under these circumstances, unless the trim for the door or window is at least 4 in. to 4½ in. wide, no screws would be required. Near the ends of boards, always predrill for screws to prevent splitting. I see no reason why the visible head of a screw should be considered less attractive than the head of a nail, but if you disagree, take the trouble to countersink the screws and plug the holes.

Roof trim Of course there is no standard roof-trim detail that is appropriate for all houses. Trim is designed to fit the style, proportions and, yes, the budget. We have used numerous roof-trim details, but they fall into two basic

Attaching trim to panels

SKIRT BOARDS OR FRIEZEBOARDS

CORNER BOARDS

CORNER POSTS

2X4 NAILER

TRIM IS SCREWED TO EXTERIOR SKIN WHERE IT EXTENDS MORE THAN 2½" BEYOND A NAILER, TO PREVENT CUPPING. OTHERWISE USE GALVANIZED RING-SHANK NAILS.

categories. One has a sloped soffit at the eave, the other has a flat soffit.

Applying roof trim to stress-skin panels need not be any more difficult than trimming conventional rough framing, but it does require good planning. The easiest way to achieve the roof overhang is to extend the roof panels beyond the wall panels; the trim is attached to nailers let in to the perimeter of the roof panels. The problem is that the roof panels are then cantilevered beyond the wall panels and have limited load-bearing capacity. Generally, the overhang for the standard panel (drywall on one side) should be held to between 8 in. and 12 in. Structural panels (doublechips, p. 100), usually can extend beyond the wall panel by 16 in. to 24 in. Applying 2-in.-thick tongue-and-groove planking to the roof as the finish ceiling and extending it beyond the wall panel allows the overhang to be increased to 16 in. to 24 in. even when standard panels are used. Before making a decision about the length of the overhang, however, check the roof-load requirements in your area and ask for the panel manufacturer's recommendations about supporting the load.

Sloped-soffit trim The simplest trim style uses a sloped soffit made of a solid ¾-in.-thick board or, at the very least, ⅝-in.-thick AC exterior plywood. One edge of the soffit is ripped to fit against the wall panels, and then the soffit is pushed into place—if the fit between the top of the soffit and the panels is snug, the soffit will hold itself in place temporarily while the bottom is being secured to the nail-

ers in the panel edges. (When standard panels are used, there is no way to screw or nail the top edge of the soffit to the drywall underside of the panel.) The bottom edge of the soffit must fit tightly into the fascia dado. Assuming the nailers in the panel edges are straight, simply use a combination square as a depth gauge to set dado depth; if they aren't straight, set up a string line for each run of trim and plan on shimming behind the fascia at the low points. Special nails are not needed to attach the trim to the nailer in the panel edge. Galvanized nails or galvanized ring-shank nails are usually appropriate for exterior applications.

The friezeboard, which performs the critical function of holding the top edge of the soffit in place, goes on next. The top edge of the friezeboard is ripped to the roof slope, then pushed up until it forces the soffit tightly against the panel, as shown below. Usually the bottom edge of the friezeboard is rabbeted to hold the last cut of shingles or clapboards. A built-up rabbet is sometimes used, as shown on p. 208. It will probably be necessary to use some screws (as described in the section on trim boards) to attach the friezeboard to the wall panel, since there is not likely to be good nailing between panel seams.

When installing the rake trim, the lack of an acute angle between the wall and the roof means there is nothing to hold the soffit in place before the friezeboard goes on. Solve this problem by installing the friezeboard first, using an appropriately sized spacer to set the dimension for the soffit. Remove the spacer, push the soffit into place and nail it to the nailers in the panel edges.

Types of sloped-soffit trim

SPLIT FASCIA
FASCIA
NAILER
FLAT SOFFIT
FRIEZEBOARD
RAKE VIEW

ROOF PANEL
NAILER
SPLIT FASCIA
FASCIA
SLOPED SOFFIT
FRIEZEBOARD
RABBET HOLDS SHINGLES OR CLAPBOARDS.
EAVE VIEW

The deep overhang, not the trim, is the focus of this house. Using doublechip (structural) panels made it possible to extend the overhang. Cedar 1x6s nailed to the panels form the soffit. Gable-end glass is fixed directly to the timbers of the end bent. Using dry wood is critical where glass will be attached.

When tongue-and-groove (or shiplap) planking is installed as an interior finish before the panels go on, it can be used to create the soffit. On purlin roofs, lay the planking perpendicular to the purlins, running from the eave to the peak. For expediency and accuracy, extend the planking a few inches past the end of the overhang and cut an entire roofside of planking to a chalkline. If you're going to do this, there's the potential for an awkard transition between the eave soffit and the rake soffit, because there is a lack of nailing surface on the rake side. Plan the rake soffit so that a single plank spans from the wall panel to the roof nailer, since there won't be a nailing surface between. To do this, extend the next-to-last plank beyond the last wall panel (which is the last nailing surface) far enough so that you wind up with your last plank at the outside edge of the rake. After the roof panels are installed, the last rake plank can be attached from below.

On common-rafter roofs, the planking is laid perpendicular to the rafters (parallel to the eave). In this case, extend the planking over the gable ends to form the rake soffit. Cut the plank ends all at once after they are in place, as you would at the eaves. Plan the soffit at the eave to be a single plank. Extend the first plank that is applied to the roof surface over the wall panel, as before, so that the matching can continue from the eave to the wall.

An overhang of more than 12 in. implies the use of structural panels, and since structural panels have a nail base on both sides, the problem with soffit attachment is automatically solved. Remember that codes require a fire barrier over the foam, so even if the roof will be sheathed first with planks, it will be necessary to use a material with a 15-minute fire rating (probably drywall) between the planks and the panels.

With the friezeboard and soffit in place, the fascia boards can be installed. Cut and nail the fascia boards directly to the panel nailers—the tablesawn dado in the fascia, which receives the soffit, helps with alignment. In a high-quality job, linear splices and corner joints are mitered. When the fascia boards are over 1 in. thick, we like to use finger joints or dovetails at the corners for decoration and strength. After the fascia has been attached, cut and nail the split fascia to it. The split fascia gives the trim more depth and a molded appearance.

What makes this type of sloped soffit so easy is that the trim at the eave and rake meet at right angles, resulting in relatively simple cutting and fitting. Changing species, size and treatment of the components allows the trim to be customized to suit the house. We have used everything from a single, heavy, cedar plank to small boards painted in soft colors for both the fascia and the split fascia.

Planking soffit on purlin roof

ROOF PANEL

NAILER

FASCIA

SPLIT FASCIA

FRIEZEBOARD

½" PLYWOOD SPACER BEHIND FRIEZEBOARD CREATES RABBET TO HOLD SIDING.

SIDING

TIMBER RAFTER

ROOF PLANKING FORMS SOFFIT

TIMBER POST

Now we'll look at another variety of sloped-soffit trim, used when it is important to design to have a vertical eave fascia rather than one perpendicular to the roof slope—for instance, to accept gutter brackets when gutters are to be used. To give the fascia a vertical orientation, it is necessary to create an additional nailing surface after the panels have been installed. This can be accomplished either with individual wedge blocks attached to the panel nailers or a single, continuous piece ripped to the correct wedge shape. The problem with the latter method is that a fairly large piece of wood could be required, depending on the roof slope. For example, if the roof pitch were 10/12, the smallest leg of the wedge would be about 2½ in. Making individual wedge blocks takes more time, but the pieces can probably be made from scrap. When the fascia is plumb, housing the soffit in a fascia dado is much too complicated, so instead carefully rip the soffit to the plumb line and hold it about 1/16 in. beyond the wedge block to improve the odds of a good fit. Rake soffits can still be dadoed as described previously.

When a gutter is mounted on the fascia, it adds lines to the detail similar to a crown molding. To keep all of the trim consistent, a crown added to the rake trim is usually desirable. Simply add a wedge strip to the fascia (already fixed to the panel nailer) and nail on a crown.

Sloped-soffit roof trim is easy and simple, but can still display nice detail. The rake boards on this house are 2-in.-wide cedar, dovetailed at all outside corners. The soffit material is 2-in.-thick tongue-and-groove planking.

Another type of sloped soffit and trim

CROWN

WEDGE BLOCKS SCREWED TO FASCIA

FASCIA

NAILER

SOFFIT

FRIEZEBOARD

NAILER

RAKE VIEW

EAVE VIEW

ROOF PANEL

NAILER

PLUMB FASCIA

GUTTER

WEDGE BLOCK

SOFFIT

FRIEZEBOARD

RABBET HIDES TOP OF SIDING.

Flat-soffit trim In addition to having some aesthetic advantages, flat-soffit trim also provides support for the panel on the eave where the loads are likely to be the greatest. While there are too many possible variations to cover here, they all spring from a few basic procedures. The drawing on the facing page shows a built-up system that over the years has become one of our favorite details. Just as in sloped-soffit trim, the eave and rake overhangs are determined by the overhang of the roof panels. For best effect, try to design the detail to include a crown molding that follows the plane of the panel nailer and a soffit located approximately 2 in. to 4 in. below the bottom edge of the overhanging eave panel.

Start by installing the blocking, soffit and fascia. In most cases, the blocking can be cut from 2x4s; a wider fascia might require a 2x6. Each block is angled to fit against the underside of the roof slope and has a square front edge to serve as vertical nailing for the fascia. Installation is simplified by nailing a number of blocks onto a ⅝-in. plywood strip on the ground and installing the assembly as a unit. This also helps ensure a straight line at the fascia, because inconsistencies in the wall surface can be corrected by shimming between the wall panel and the plywood—it is hard to shim one block at a time. Position the plywood along a chalkline snapped on the wall panel, and screw it to the panel with galvanized self-tapping screws. Then toenail the blocking at its angled surface to the panel nailer. Shim as necessary between these two pieces to keep the front edge of the soffit level.

The next step is to provide the framing for the corner return, as shown at the left of the drawing. The corner return is optional, but I think it really enhances the richness of the roof trim by creating a visual base for the roof. When the trim is completed, the corner board should fall in the middle of the corner return, giving the whole unit the feeling of a column and capital. Because the corner return allows the eave line to continue at the gable end, the rake can finish to the top of the return instead of being mitered to the fascia—a procedure which is usually difficult, with results that are not always attractive. Set up the corner return by putting together a small assembly of plywood and blocking. It would fit against the gable end of the building, from the last eave block to the end of the return. This small assembly would be screwed to the eave block, to the panel nailer on the building corner, and to the outside sheathing of the panel beyond the corner. Then the soffit and the fascia are installed along with the eave trim. A solid 2x cap is put on the return, followed by the sloped plywood cap, which has a 15° slope to shed water. Use shims or a nailing strip on the building surface to create the slope. The 2x cap should be ripped to receive a crown at the same angle created by the roof slope on the eave side. The entire top of the corner return should be covered with flashing. It's easiest to make up a pattern and have all of the returns made by a sheet-metal shop.

For the crown to continue on the rake trim, it will be necessary to cut a beveled wedge strip to repeat the roof angle at the eave. If at all possible, this piece should be ripped from a solid piece of wood. If not, plan on installing blocks for nailing at least every 24 in.

Begin the rake trim with the soffit and freizeboard. The rake soffit would be attached using the same method described in the sloped-soffit system because of the lack of nailing on the rake overhangs. Fascias are installed after the soffits. The beveled wedge strip is next and the crown trim is last. Shim to correct alignment, especially on the fascia and crown. Good preparation when installing panels and soffit blocking saves time when the trim is attached. It is not necessary to vent the soffit because there is no air movement through the insulation.

The dimensions of this type of roof trim can be altered according to taste and circumstances. For added depth in the crown, for instance, nail a ½-in.-thick by 1½-in.-wide strip to the fascia before the crown. Generally, gutters need a flat vertical face for attachment; if they are required, make the fascia wider by using a larger block and dropping the soffit down to accommodate it. The crown usually remains on the corner return and rake when a gutter is used on the eave.

Using only flat boards, this trim detail has a rather molded appearance in a colonial style. The corner return is centered over the corner board for balance. The extra strips on the corner board reinforce the idea of a column.

Elements of flat-soffit trim at corner

FASCIA

BEVELED WEDGE STRIP

CROWN

ROOF PANELS

WALL PANEL

PLYWOOD

SOFFIT

RAKE FRIEZE

SLOPED PLYWOOD CAP

CROWN

FASCIA

2X CAP

BLOCK

PLYWOOD BACKING

FRIEZEBOARD

CLAPBOARDS

CROWN

FASCIA

BLOCK

SOFFIT

FRIEZEBOARD

CLAPBOARDS

CORNER BOARDS

ROOF PANEL

AT EAVE

CROWN

FASCIA

FRIEZEBOARD

BLOCK

SOFFIT

PLYWOOD

WALL PANEL

Roofing over stress-skin panels The typical stress-skin roof application is technically a "warm roof," meaning that one side of the panel is exposed to the heated interior and the other to the outside. When warm roofs are used in cold climates, the heat passing through the insulation can cause the snow to melt on the surface of the shingles, flow down the roof and form an ice dam at the eave; water then backs up behind the dam and leaks through the shingles. A good panel allows very little heat loss, making this problem minimal, but we still like to use 50-lb. felt or an elastomeric membrane for the first 5 ft. at the eave and for 2 ft. on either side of valleys.

Since stress-skin panels are an effective moisture barrier in both directions, it is possible for moisture to collect on the exterior surface of the panel, under the shingles. This is most likely to occur during extremes of high humidity and heat, or high humidity and cold, and while leakage is improbable, certain kinds of roofing materials might be damaged. The following types of roofing should therefore be laid over furring strips to allow air flow: wood shingles and shakes, slate, tile and standing-seam metal. (Corrugated metal can be laid directly on the panels.) The air flow keeps the roofing material away from the warmth of the panel, creating a "cold roof."

Shrinkage and movement of the timber frame cause a certain amount of movement in the panels, and even if it is slight, this movement can cause shingles to wrinkle slightly at the panel seams. For this reason I don't recommend applying lightweight asphalt or fiberglass-based shingles directly to the panels. (If you're going to use these, first nail and glue an additional sheathing membrane, such as ⅜-in.-thick plywood, to the panels to prevent movement. Of course, this extra cost would greatly exceed the cost of buying heavier shingles to begin with.) Shingles should be the heavily textured architectural type or the heaviest available weight, generally about 310 pounds per square in fiberglass and 350 pounds per square in asphalt. Asphalt shingles are becoming hard to get and are being replaced by those with a fiberglass base.

Furring strips are being attached to this roof surface in preparation for wood shingles. Since the shingles will be laid with a close exposure, the furring strips have to be quite close as well.

Application of felt or elastomeric membrane on warm roofs

2' BOTH SIDES OF VALLEYS

5' AT EAVE

Flooring

The issue of flooring in a timber-frame house is a classic case of good news and bad news. The good news is that the floor of one story becomes the ceiling for the story below, making construction efficient and reducing costs. The bad news is that a floor with sound-deadening characteristics is not automatic, as it is when using conventional construction techniques. It is harder to deaden noise transmission through floors than walls in any event, because floors are subjected to both airborne and impact sound. The design and installation of floors and ceilings are therefore crucial not only to aesthetics, but also to comfort and privacy.

It is a very simple, but too often overlooked, observation that proximity to noise is the crux of the sound-transmission problem. In other words, if you expect to find privacy in the library, don't put it underneath your teenager's rock-and-roll headquarters. Such oversights are nearly impossible to rectify during construction. As much as possible, stack rooms that require privacy and those that are public. Let the teenager compete with the blender instead of with Mozart. It is thus sometimes possible to solve problems of sound transmission entirely during the development of the floor plans, by isolating critical areas. But such houses are necessarily large and spread out (read expensive). House plans intended to use space and volume efficiently are the most difficult to insulate against sound. I give special emphasis to this issue because, frankly, it is not one we have always dealt with well. We didn't forget about noise, we just assumed it wouldn't be a problem. Very often the house was being built for a couple not yet with children—people absolutely ignorant about the meaning of the word noise. So here is one more suggestion I offer, having learned the lesson the hard way: For the benefit of yourselves or future inhabitants, assume that someday your house will also be home to a tumbling gymnasium and a rock concert, sometimes simultaneously.

In timber-frame construction, it makes sense to install the finish floor and ceiling materials over the timber floor—applying the finish floor to one side and the ceiling to the other excludes the possibility of using the frame as finish work. The other alternative, fitting materials between timbers, turns the frame into an obstacle to efficient construction. There's a huge difference between installing flooring over timbers with 5-in. or 6-in. surfaces for fudge factors, and attempting to scribe materials to fit precisely between timbers on 30-in. to 36-in. centers. So, except to solve a few plumbing problems, we always apply flooring on top of the timber structure.

As a general guideline, it's wise to try to design timber-floor systems for nominal 2-in.-thick tongue-and-groove planks. The most commonly available planking species are pine and spruce, followed by fir and hemlock. Planking usually comes in an "adequate" grade, but hardly ever "good." It will be called something like "#2 common," which sounds pretty good by the grading book; however, every piece is likely to be as bad as is allowable and probably a little worse. Unless there is a clear demand from the client for a rustic appearance, I prefer to pay the difference for a higher grade of material, or I purchase planking from one of our small, local mills. Small mills are great. I like to sit down and have a discussion with the owner (who is also usually the sawyer) about the qualities of good wood, and then we go outside and identify what we both think is good wood. Finally, I ask how much this good wood we've been talking about will cost. From that day forward, I can throw out the grading rules and just order "good wood."

Assuming the use of planks or a system with equivalent strength, timber joists ideally should be located about 30 in. on center to keep the flooring stiff. This is about the right spacing for pine planking (good wood); it is a little conservative for fir, hemlock or spruce. (This is not a political discussion. "Conservative" as a structural reference is a good thing for even the most liberal.) Of course, joists ought to be evenly spaced between major beams, so the trick is to find the on-center number closest to 30 in. All timbers still have to be sized to support the floor loads as suggested by the local building codes.

Planks on timbers The simplest floor is a single layer of planks over timbers. Although it does nothing to deaden sound, planking is useful in such open spaces as lofts and walkways (photo below). People who wish to build their homes in affordable stages often choose to start with a layer of planks over timbers, adding other materials when they can afford them.

Tongue-and-groove planks usually come with a *V*-groove on the visible face, which helps to mask shrinkage or an uneven surface by creating a shadow line. For a straight match without the *V*-groove, just expose the opposite face. Widths of 6 in. or less are easiest to lay and cause the fewest problems.

Because this loft is open to the rest of the house, sound-deadening insulation would not have been useful. Therefore, a single layer of planks is both the ceiling below and the flooring above.

Wide planks (8 in. or more) are hard to straighten when they are bowed, and because there are fewer joints to absorb movement, seasonal expansion and contraction of the wood will be more noticeable. I know of a building where wide, very dry hardwood planks were laid over timbers late in the winter. When the planks took on some moisture in the summer and expanded, they pushed the walls of the building out as much as 2 in. in some places. This story gave me new respect for narrow softwood planks, and reasonable (but not extreme) seasoning. Narrow planks can also be secured by blind-nailing (angling the nail through the plank from just above the tongue), which is much easier than screwing and plugging, and much more attractive than face-nailing.

Installation begins by laying the planks perpendicular to the joists at one end of the floor system, using construction adhesive to glue the planks to the timbers. (This helps prevent squeaking and makes the floor stiffer and stronger.) Nails for blind-nailing should be 16d common; if the timbers are oak, they should be galvanized to prevent corrosion from tannic acid. When blind-nailing, use two nails directly next to each other on each timber. A good trick is to hold both nails in your hand and drive them at once; they tend to spiral around each other and provide further locking. Where posts pass through the frame, a notch made about ½-in. deep receives the plank. By simply pushing the plank into the notch, scribing is eliminated, and any gaps that might develop when the timbers shrink will be hid-

Plank floor

POST

⅝" BETWEEN FLOORING AND WALL FOR EXPANSION AND CONTRACTION

½" DEEP NOTCH TO ACCEPT PLANK

T&G FLOORING, GLUED AND BLIND—NAILED

CONSTRUCTION ADHESIVE

CONNECTING GIRT

JOIST

CONNECTING GIRT

den. Leave at least ⅝ in. between the planking and the wall for expansion and contraction. This space will be hidden behind the baseboard and can also be used for running electrical wire.

The ceiling side of the planks can be finished with stain, oil or both before installation. The floor side can be sanded and finished later in construction. Wall-to-wall carpeting over the planks helps absorb noise, especially that caused by impact—kids playing with blocks on a plank floor can make a deafening clatter. If you plan to use carpeting, shop as carefully for the pad as you do for the carpet, and ask for the one that would be the best sound barrier.

Drywall over timbers The timber frame itself brings a great amount of wood into the living environment, and adding more exposed wood on the ceiling is often detrimental to design. The alternative is usually a light-colored drywall ceiling, which makes the room brighter by reflecting light and gives the frame more distinction by avoiding wood on wood. My tendency is to use wood planks over timbers for high ceilings and cathedral ceilings, and to use drywall on low ceilings. Wood can make a large volume seem warmer and cozier. A painted ceiling in a light color makes a small volume feel larger.

To apply drywall over timbers, start by gluing and nailing a 2-in.-wide strip of plywood over the center of each

Drywall ceilings laid over the timbers help to make small rooms feel brighter and larger by reflecting light. A painted background also gives contrast to the frame.

Large, open rooms often benefit from wood ceilings. The boards absorb light and make the large space feel warmer and more comfortable.

joist, leaving approximately 1 in. of timber on each edge toward the joist bay. Use ½-in.-thick plywood for ½-in. drywall (which is what we commonly use), or ⅝-in.-thick plywood for ⅝-in. drywall. When the strips are in place, cut sheets of drywall lengthwise to fit between the plywood strips in the joist bays. Since the timbers are on approximately 30-in. centers and drywall comes in 48-in. widths, this will mean a large amount of waste. However, by using drywall that is the same length as the joist bay, seams between joists can be completely avoided, and the money saved by not having to tape and spackle seams is greater than the cost of the waste. You can eliminate yet another finishing step by prepainting the drywall before installing it over the joists.

After the drywall is down, glue and nail all the planking to the plywood strips as if they were the timbers. Finally, screw the drywall to the planking from below midway be-tween the joists on 16-in. centers. Even if the drywall has been painted, it isn't difficult to spackle and touch up the screw heads.

It's possible to use plaster-base drywall or rock lath in-stead of standard drywall, with the intention of plastering between the timbers. We don't generally recommend this because it is so much more work and shrinkage eventually pulls the timbers away from the plaster edges, creating a gap. Still, there's nothing like plaster, and it's hard to argue against the warm feeling and natural texture of a good plas-ter job. If clients choose this option, I encourage them to wait one year before applying the plaster. The problem is that it's hard to wait if you're building on a time-limiting construction loan, or if you are simply anxious to move into a finished house. When using plaster-base drywall, don't worry about the seams, because the entire surface will be coated with plaster; try instead to reduce waste.

Drywall and plank floor

T&G FLOORING, GLUED AND BLIND-NAILED

1" OF TIMBER EXPOSED ON BOTH SIDES

½"X2" PLYWOOD SPACER

CONSTRUCTION ADHESIVE

JOIST

½" DRYWALL

POST

½"X4" PLYWOOD SPACER

CONNECTING GIRT

Sound-deadening floors Adding drywall to the flooring system does almost nothing for soundproofing. The interconnected posts and beams of a well-built timber frame are designed for stiffness and assembled under tension, like strings on a guitar; great strength is achieved but so is a great ability to transmit sound. To reduce sound transmission significantly, you must absorb the sound with a material of less density than the framing members.

We often use a rigid sound-deadening board such as that manufactured by the Homasote Company. Soundboard comes in 4-ft. by 8-ft. sheets and several thicknesses, of which ½ in. is the most commonly used. It has enough compressive strength to support floor loads and enough resilience to absorb some sound. To be effective, it should be installed in an unbroken layer between other materials; for instance, between the drywall and the planking in the system previously discussed. It goes over everything with no regard for joints. (It is not necessary to join the soundboard seams to timbers—just tack where possible to secure temporarily.) The soundboard is followed with blind-nailed planking, but since the nails now must pass through ½-in.-thick soundboard to get to the plywood strips, use 20d nails instead of 16d. The drywall still has to be secured to the planking through the soundboard; use 1¾-in. drywall screws. Probably the biggest problem with installation is to get the soundboard down without stepping through the ceiling. Keep yourself on a solid floor by laying the soundboard and the planking at the same time.

What's lost in this system is the structural advantage of gluing the planking to the framing. But you might want to glue the planking to the soundboard to prevent squeaking.

When soundboard is used in this way, the ceiling does not need to be drywall. Instead, the finished ceiling could be ¾ in.-thick boards (as shown in the next flooring solution, p. 218). Soundboard and planking would then be installed as described previously. In either case, the planking must span from joist to joist. Remember that it is a good idea to notch the entire thickness of the floor assembly into any posts that pass through the floor level to avoid gaps when the timbers shrink.

Floor using soundboard

T&G FLOORING, GLUED AND BLIND-NAILED

½" SOUNDBOARD

½"X2" PLYWOOD SPACER

CONSTRUCTION ADHESIVE

JOIST

½" DRYWALL

POST

½"X4" PLYWOOD SPACER

CONNECTING GIRT

A floor system with even better sound-deadening characteristics uses the first two steps described on pages 216 and 217 (ceiling material of drywall or planking plus sound-deadening board), but then incorporates an additional step. After the ceiling material and the soundboard are in place, 2x3s are nailed or screwed 16 in. on center perpendicular to the joists. The 2x3s span the joists and

are a nail base for the flooring. Both the air space between the soundboard and the finish floor and the reduced area of contact over the joists help to increase sound-deadening. If the finish floor will be either carpet or tile, a ¾-in.-thick plywood subfloor is first attached to the 2x3s. One advantage of this system is that it creates plenty of space to run wires and is even useful for some plumbing runs.

Excellent sound-deadening floor

T&G FLOORING, GLUED AND BLIND—NAILED

2X3'S, 16" O.C.

CONSTRUCTION ADHESIVE

JOIST

¾" CEILING BOARDS OR ½" DRYWALL

POST

½" SOUNDBOARD

SPACE FOR WIRING

CONNECTING GIRT

Interior partition walls

In timber-frame construction, all interior partitions are superfluous as structure. Even partitions as delicate as *shoji* (light Japanese screens made of a wooden grid overlaid with rice paper) would work. In fact *shoji* would be perfect for a timber-frame house—light, thin and movable, offering the ultimate design flexibility. But in most cases, partitions must be of sturdier construction to perform the important duties of providing privacy and blocking sound. As I pointed out in Chapter IV, the design of the timber frame should coincide with the design of the floor plan; rooms should be defined by timbers as well as walls, and therefore most walls will be aligned with timbers. In this section, I will talk a little more specifically about the relationship of walls to timbers and the various ways to install partitions.

For partitions to be integrated successfully with the frame, the designer needs to determine precisely where they will fall in relation to the timbers. Partitions usually consume a total of between 3½ in. and 4½ in., and with this in mind a decision must be made on how much of the timber will be revealed on each side of the wall. To simplify construction, try to hold partitions to one side or the other of the knee braces whenever possible, revealing the frame to the more public area and concealing it on the opposite side. The alternative—revealing the frame on both sides of a partition wall—requires that individual pieces of framing

and drywall be fitted around knee braces—a laborious job. When knee braces are not an obstacle, partition walls can be constructed on the floor and installed as a unit. To the carpenter, the difference between these two methods is extreme. Note that when walls are to be constructed on one side or the other of the knee braces, the designer must specify to the framer that the knee braces be pushed toward the opposite edge of the timber to allow room for the partitions. Edge embellishments must also be considered when planning partitions (p. 169).

Timbers will shrink, which is a problem for interior partitions because it is likely that shrinkage will occur after the partitions are in place. It's not just aesthetics at stake here, for even small cracks greatly reduce the ability of the partition to deaden sound. There are only a few solutions to the shrinking-timber dilemma.

1. Construct the partitions and sheathe both sides, but don't finish the walls until the timbers have stabilized. If the timbers are almost dry or just in need of acclimating to the environment, this might be a reasonable wait of only a few months. However, if the frame was made of green hardwood, the wait could be up to three years.

2. Finish the interior walls immediately and plan on filling the spaces with paintable caulking when the cracks appear. As you can imagine, even if this does not seem like

Partitions in a timber-frame house are not essential for the structure. Therefore, they should be built in a way that enhances the beauty of the frame, yet also provides privacy. In this house under construction, most of the partitions are built with 2x3s and will be insulated with soundboard. The framing is fitted around the knee braces, exposing the timbers to both sides of the wall.

the best solution, it is the one most often used. The pleasure of the finished product is not deferred, and caulking the cracks is put off until the next time the walls need painting. Wallpaper should not be put on until the timbers dry because cracks around the edges are unsightly.

3. Make the shrinkage a design detail by installing *L*-bead where drywall meets timber. *L*-bead is basically a hard metal edge that is attached to the partition before the drywall. The drywall is cut so it roughly meets the *L*-bead and is finished after the joint is taped and spackled. When the timber shrinks, a distinct gap (usually not more than ¼ in.) is left between the edge of the *L*-bead and the timber—it shows up as a dark space. This works well in situations that will not have to be caulked, such as closet partitions. But on one of our projects an architect specified that *L*-bead be used on almost every wall and that a deliberate gap be created from the beginning, which would be filled with dark caulking.

Defining living areas with timbers instead of partitions results in an open floor plan and a feeling of spaciousness that is really a part of the definition of a timber-frame home. But this freedom of movement and of view also allows sound to travel freely. If privacy is a requisite, compensate by adding sound-deadening to all partitions in private areas.

The easiest solution is to use 2x3s to build the entire partition, and then apply sound board as the first layer of sheathing on both sides. After the sound board, attach the drywall. The only potential problem with this system is that the electrician may need to change to wide, flat switch and outlet boxes to have enough area for wires—standard electrical boxes are too deep for a 2x3 partition.

For even better performance use a standard 2x4 for top and bottom plates, but use staggered 2x3s as studs. The 2x3s, on 8-in. centers, are alternately aligned with either plate edge, giving 16-in.-on-center nailing for each side. The advantage is that no stud touches the drywall on both sides, greatly reducing sound conduction through the wall. Half-inch soundboard is then applied to the partition on both sides before ½-in. drywall is installed. Obviously, no sound-deadening system will work effectively without a good seal between the surrounding timbers and the partition. Apply acoustical sealant to the top and bottom plates and both end studs before fastening. It may still be necessary to caulk after the timbers have stabilized.

Non-sound-deadening partitions can be made with 2x3s or 2x4s. Because standard electrical boxes are 3 in. or more in depth, 2x4s are more common.

When interior partitions don't align with timber posts, it is important that they be firmly attached to the exterior wall. If a built-up exterior insulation system is used, the problem can easily be solved by providing nailing for the stud that meets the exterior wall. But if the exterior wall is a stress-skin panel, some advance planning is necessary. Before the exterior siding goes on, screw the stud to the panel from the outside, using galvanized self-tapping screws that are long enough to penetrate the stud by at least 1 in. If this step is omitted, don't bother to tape the corner between the interior partition and the exterior wall, for it will inevitably crack.

Sound-deadening partition

2X3 STUDS 16" O.C.

DRYWALL

USE SPECIAL-ORDER, SHALLOW ELECTRICAL BOXES WHENEVER POSSIBLE.

SOUND-DEADENING BOARD

DRYWALL

DRYWALL

SOUND-DEADENING BOARD

Surface treatment

"There's no accounting for taste." "Beauty is in the eye of the beholder." And interior decoration has few rules. While the exterior of the house often must bend to its natural and architectural environment, the interior should be designed to satisfy the inhabitants. This is a personal and entirely subjective process. I have a friend who doesn't like things until they reach a state of nearly total decay. When plaster is cracked but still holding on, when paint is faded and beginning to peel, when floor boards are almost worn through from use, when moss is thick on the shingles, she is ecstatic; she thinks things are perfect the moment before disrepair. I know another person who requires that all things have the glitter of newness about them, that the colors be bright, that the brass and stainless steel be maintained with a showroom shine. To him, something used is old, and old things are ugly. We have designed homes to

have the look of a barn and some that were intended to have the elegance of a castle, and there's nothing wrong with either. What's important is that a timber-frame home is able to satisfy both requirements. When you hear the words "a timber-frame house," it should conjure an image of a method of construction, not a specific decorative style.

One of the important factors affecting interior style is the treatment of the interior surfaces. The timbers, walls and ceilings all should be planned carefully in advance to achieve the desired result. The exposed timber frame is an incredibly strong decorative element, and the species should be chosen mostly for its aesthetic value, since engineering should make the frame equally strong no matter what the wood. When deciding, consider that knotty wood of whatever species is more rustic than wood that is clear of knots, and straight-grained wood with tight growth rings

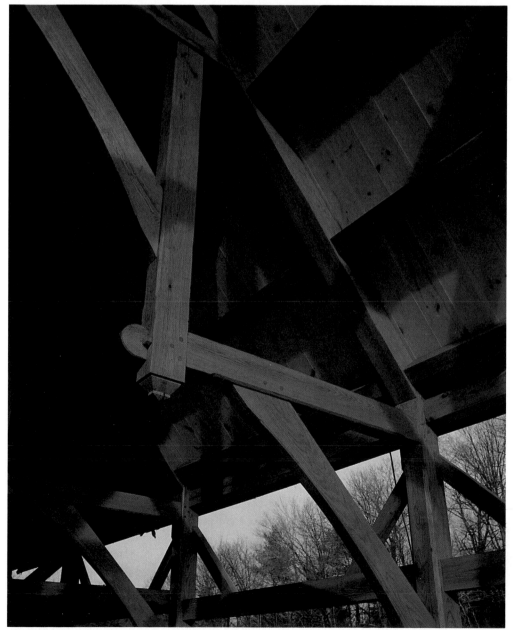

The timbers in the frame are usually planed and oiled, not only for appearance and ease of cleaning, but because planing the timbers to a common dimension makes joinery easier. A clear penetrating oil was used on these timbers.

is more subtle than highly figured wood with widely spaced rings. Oak and southern pine are generally coarser than pine and cedar. To make sure the wood of the frame will not clash with other design intentions, it is important to become familiar with all the options. Each person will bring to this decision personal prejudices and opinions. I once rented a basement apartment from a casket maker, where all the walls and the ceiling were paneled with reject pine from the casket business. The experience left me with very uncomfortable feelings about knotty pine. Another personal opinion I have developed is that the best timber frames are those that are the most subtle, that enhance instead of dictate.

There are two reasons why the timbers in a frame are usually planed and finished. First, it is easier to work timbers planed to specific dimensions rather than deal with varying thicknesses. Second, it is almost impossible to keep the timbers clean from the time cutting starts until the frame is raised. We usually finish-plane or sand the timbers and apply a finish to the interior surfaces just before the raising. The smooth surface also makes it easier to keep the timbers clean in the future. Although there are many possibilities, the most common surface finish is oil. If the timbers are green, it is important to apply a penetrating oil, which will allow the timbers to breathe as they dry.

Some timber framers use a mixture of linseed oil, gum turpentine and Japan drier with satisfactory results. For dry wood, a thin coat of shellac or polyurethane can be applied as a second or third coat to seal the surface and keep the mixture from bleeding. Tung oil can also be used as a base, and we have found it a little more durable while the frame is exposed to the weather. It also produces a harder finish without the addition of polyurethane or shellac. A number of commercial tung-oil finishes are available, of which our favorite for durability and appearance is Okene, made by the Pratt and Lambert Company. Your paint supplier can help you mix your own formula or choose among the different brands. One nice aspect of using an oil-based finish is that it is easy to repair marred surfaces, and new coats tend to blend in quite well. It is also possible to buy oil premixed with stain, but before applying any stain, try it on a sample of the same type of wood as the frame. "Medium walnut" (whatever that is), will look vastly different on fir than on pine, and stains are difficult to remove.

In my opinion, the first choice should be to find a wood that will naturally deliver a suitable color and texture with a clear oil finish. If that is not possible, then consider stain. A dark stain is helpful, for instance, if the frame is to blend with colonial decoration; unstained wood would probably

Old yellow-pine timbers were re-milled to make this frame. The patina of age can't be applied; it simply takes time.

always look too fresh. Still, the first choice might be a wood that would give an old appearance. On one of our projects, we used timbers resawn from wood salvaged from an old mill. The wood was old, and looked old.

On another of our projects, after the frame went up, one of the owners decided the timbers were too overpowering. She wanted the form and shape of the frame, but only as a background. Against my advice whitewash was applied to the timbers, allowing the grain and texture to show but masking the strong, dark wood. It was a radical solution, but the results are surprisingly good.

The wall and ceiling surfaces in a timber-frame home serve the function of a canvas backdrop, helping to highlight the artistic value of the timbers. For this reason, a successful treatment of the surfaces is very often simply a white or off-white paint, a deliberate development of the "negative space" enclosed by the "positive" surround. This is the traditional timber-frame interior style that has been used for centuries around the world. In older buildings, the walls and ceilings are usually plastered and the wood, having grown dark with age, helps to create the classic "black and white" appearance.

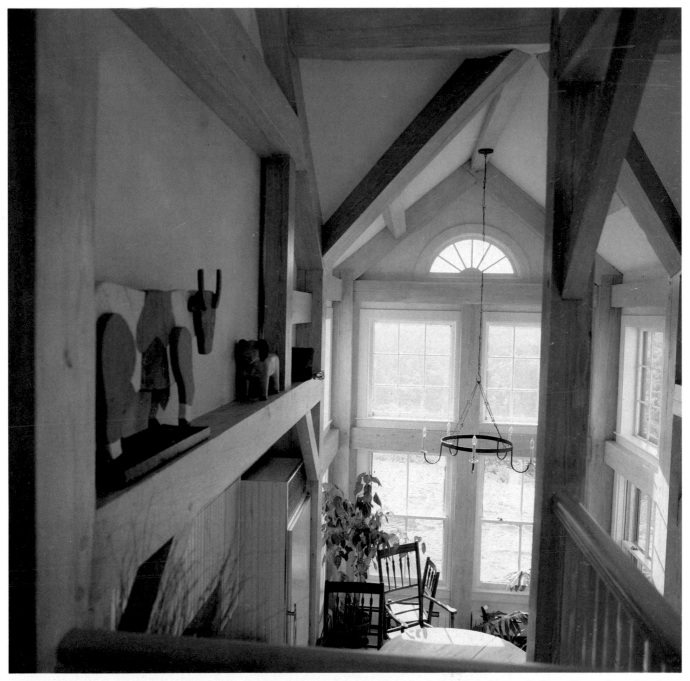

When a client decided the natural color of the timbers was too overpowering, she decided to whitewash them. The grain and texture of the wood still come through, but the dark color has been eliminated. (Design Associates, Architects; photo by Brian Smeltz.)

There are a couple of other specific uses for white (or very light) surfaces between timbers. They help to reflect light, making the spaces brighter and enhancing the volume. Small rooms and spaces with low ceilings therefore benefit the most from having light-colored walls and ceilings. For exactly the opposite reason, large spaces with cathedral ceilings can be made to feel more comfortable and cozy with wood ceilings to absorb the light and "bring the ceiling down." Another good reason for a white background between timbers is to create a place to hang art. In fact, it amused me to find fake timbers stuck to the wall in a large art gallery just to develop the feeling that comes naturally to a timber-frame home. The white backgrounds, framed by timbers, become individual focal areas for artwork, and the whole effect can have the atmosphere of a lively gallery. The introduction of artwork is also a great way to bring color into a house. On several occasions, clients have requested gallery space for specific paintings—a challenge we readily accept, because the timbers seem to function as an additional frame for the artwork, making it quite easy to achieve a satisfying display area.

Despite the arguments in favor of simple, light-colored surfaces between timbers, many people choose to use wallpaper with fine results. Simple print patterns seem to produce less clutter, although some of our creative clients have done striking things with rather extravagant wallpapers. As I have said, there are no rules.

All the exterior wall and ceiling surfaces are usually applied to the outside of the frame as a part of the enclosure system. In most cases, the interior surface is a drywall product. We use a plaster-base drywall, which can either receive a veneer coat of plaster or simply be taped and painted. Taping and painting the drywall is the least problematic because there is a distinct separation between the frame and the wall or ceiling surface. If the timbers shrink or twist, it isn't likely to cause any major problems. It might be necessary to touch up the paint edges as the timbers dry, but this is a much easier job than having to fill in gaps with spackling or caulking, which is almost certain to be necessary if plaster is applied to the drywall. As the timbers dry, there will be some eventual separation between the frame members and the plaster edges. Therefore, if green timbers are used for the frame, consider not using plaster at all or putting the task off until the timbers have stabilized. This same advice applies to wallpaper. It can be more than a little discouraging to fit paper precisely between the timbers only to find later that the timbers have pulled away from the edges. A better strategy is to paint the walls initially and then apply wallpaper after the frame has dried completely.

Off-white panels between timbers create a fine background for a display of art. In timber-frame design, it is usually helpful to know something about any artwork early in the process so that space will be left in the plan.

Ceilings, whether those of a timber floor or roof system, rarely justify plaster. The drywall is applied over the top, almost always in such a way that there are few, if any, seams. The ceiling surface easily can be finished just with paint. Because the timbers generally fall at the drywall edges, eliminating or reducing the need to tape seams, the drywall can even be painted before installation. Applying plaster on a ceiling is monumentally more difficult than paint because the timbers act as obstacles. There are also more timber edges to worry about while the frame stabi-

lizes. We often encourage clients who prefer plaster to use it on the walls but not on the ceilings. The surfaces are separate enough to have different textures, even if they are the same color. Wood ceilings are easily installed and reduce maintenance. The wood is usually oiled to bring out the grain and color. Future applications of oil will be greatly simplified if the same kind of oil is used on the ceiling boards that was used on the frame. Oil can then be applied to the entire ceiling without extra care being necessary at the edges.

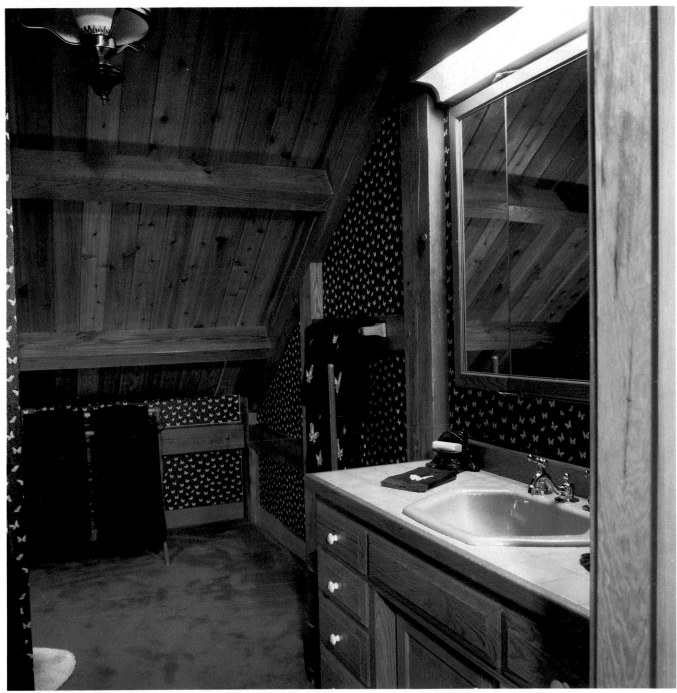

The bold print of this wallpaper contrasts with the simple lines in the frame. Because timbers shrink, it is best to apply wallpaper after the wood has dried.

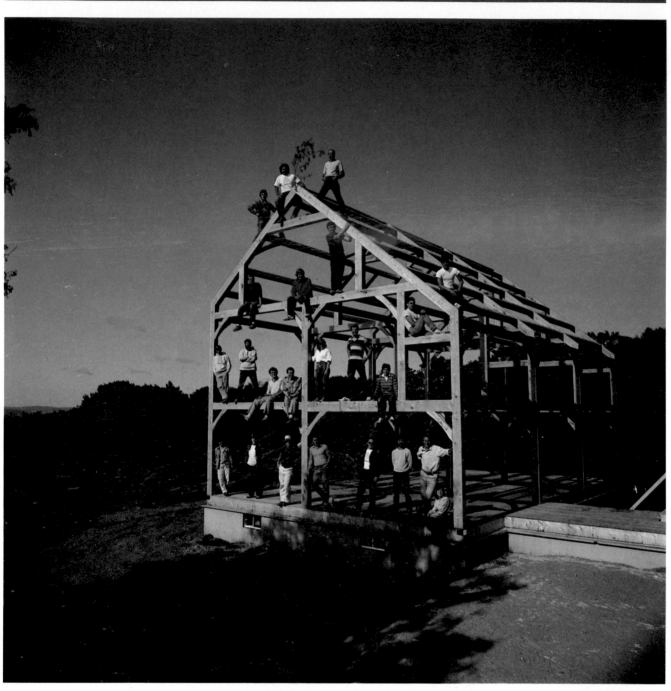

Photo: Emily Benson

Appendix **Stress-Skin Panel Suppliers**

Stress-skin panels are a complex and expensive product. Before making a choice, get as many facts as possible. It will be worth all the time it takes to search out the best possible supplier for the project at hand. Remember as you research that materials, methods of manufacture and recommended application techniques vary widely. Remember also that a good product is backed by a dedicated support staff. The stress-skin panel industry is relatively young. Experimentation continues, and the product constantly evolves.

Advance Energy Technologies, Inc.

Urethane foam; foamed in place

P.O. Box 387
Clifton Park, NY 12065
518-371-2140

Advance Foam Plastics, Inc.

EPS, urethane; laminated

5250 North Sherman St.
Denver, CO 80216
303-297-3844

Affordable Luxury Homes

EPS; laminated

Hwy. 224
P.O. Box 288
Markle, IN 46770
219-758-2141

Alchem Inc.

Polyurethane; foamed in place

3617 Strawberry Rd.
Anchorage, AK 99502
907-243-2177

Andrews Building Systems

Urethane foam; foamed in place

225 S. Price Rd.
Longmont, CO 80501
303-772-3516

Atlas Industries

Urethane, polystyrene; laminated

6 Willows Rd.
Ayer, MA 01432
Outside of Massachusetts
call 1-800-343-1437
Within Massachusetts call
1-800-332-1002

Big Sky Insulations, Inc.

EPS; laminated

P.O. Box 838
Belgrade, MT 59714
406-388-4146

Branch River Foam Plastics

Expanded polystyrene; laminated

15 Thurber Blvd.
Smithfield, RI 02917
401-232-0270

Century Insulation Mfg. Co.

EPS, polyisocyanurate; laminated

Industrial Park
P.O. Box 160
Union, MS 39365
601-774-8285

Cheney Building Systems, Inc.

Polyisocyanurate; polyurethane foam; foamed in place

2755 S. 160th St.
New Berlin, WI 53151
414-784-9634

Delta Industries

EPS; laminated

1951 Galaxie St.
Columbus, OH 43207
614-445-9634

Enercept, Inc.

EPS; laminated

3100 9th Ave. S.E.
Watertown, SD 57201
605-882-2222

EPS Molding, Inc.

EPS; laminated

2019 Brooks St.
Houston, TX 77026
713-237-9115

Foam Plastics of New England

EPS core manufacture only

P.O. Box 7075
Prospect, CT 06712
203-758-6651

Foam Products Corp.

EPS; laminated

2525 Adie Rd.
P.O. Box 2217
Maryland Heights, MO 63043
314-739-8100

Futurebilt, Inc.

EPS; laminated

A-104 Plaza Del Sol
Wimberley, TX 78676
512-847-5721

Homasote Co.

Polyisocyanurate; laminated

P.O. Box 7240
West Trenton, NJ 08628-0240
609-883-3300

Insulated Building Systems, Inc.

EPS; laminated

100 Powers Court
Sterling, VA 22170
703-450-4886

Insul-kor, Inc.

EPS; laminated

201 East Simonton
Elkhart, IN 46514
800-521-1402

J-Deck Building Systems, Inc.

EPS; laminated

2587 Harrison Rd.
Columbus, OH 43204
614-274-7755

Low-Temp Engineering, Inc.

EPS; laminated

308 East Main St.
Route 123
Norton, MA 02766
617-285-9788

Northern Energy Homes Inc.

EPS; laminated

Box 463
Norwich, VT 05055
802-649-1348

NRG Barriers, Inc.

Polyisocyanurate; foamed in place

61 Emery St.
Sanford, ME 04073
207-324-7745

Pacemaker Plastics Co., Inc.

EPS; laminated

126 New Pace Rd.
Newcomerstown, OH 43832
614-498-4181

Panel Building Systems Inc.

EPS; laminated

431 2nd St.
Reynolds Industrial Park
Greenville, PA 16125
412-646-2400

Pond Hill Homes Ltd.

Polyurethane; foamed in place

Westinghouse Rd.
RD4, Box 330-1
Blairsville, PA 15717
412-459-5404

Premier Building Systems

EPS; laminated

19041 80th Ave. South
Kent, WA 98032
206-242-9424

Riverbend Timber Framing Inc.

EPS; laminated

P.O. Box 26
Blissfield, MI 49228
517-486-4355

T.A.S. Building Systems

Resin-impregnated kraft-paper honeycomb; laminated

2540 Main St. Suite G
Chula Vista, CA 92011
619-429-7151

Thermal Foams, Inc.

EPS; laminated

2101 Kenmore Ave.
Buffalo, NY 14207
716-874-6474

Thermapan Industries

EPS; laminated

Box 479
Fonthill, Ontario
Canada L0S 1E0
412-892-2675

Therm-core Industries

EPS; laminated

5404 Columbus Pike
Delaware, OH 43015
614-548-7990

W. H. Porter, Inc.

EPS, polyisocyanurate; laminated

4240 North 136th Ave.
Holland, MI 49424
616-399-1963

Winter Panel Corp.

Urethane; foamed in place

RR5 Box 168B
Brattleboro, VT 05301
802-254-3435

Wisconsin EPS, Inc.

EPS; laminated

90 Trobridge Drive
P.O. Box 669
Fond du Lac, WI 54936-0669
414-923-4146

Bibliography

Alexander, Christopher, Sara Ishikawa and Murray Silverstein — *A Pattern Language.* New York: Oxford University Press, 1977.

The Timeless Way of Building. New York: Oxford University Press, 1979.

Anderson, Bruce and Malcolm Wells — *Passive Solar Energy.* Andover, Mass.: Brick House Publishing Co., 1981.

Audel's Carpenters and Builders Guides. 4 vols. New York: Theo Audel and Co., 1923, 1939, 1945, 1947.

Benson, Tedd and James Gruber — *Building the Timber Frame House.* New York: Charles Scribner's Sons, 1980.

Briggs, Martin S. — *A Short History of the Building Crafts.* Cambridge, England: Oxford University Press, 1925.

Brungraber, Robert (Ben) Lyman — *Traditional Timber Joinery: A Modern Analysis.* Thesis. Ann Arbor, Mich: University Microfilm Inc., 1985.

Brunskill, R.W. — *Timber Building in Britain.* London: Victor Gollancz, Ltd., 1985.

Cummings, Abbott Lowell — *The Framed Houses of Massachusetts Bay, 1625-1725.* Cambridge, Mass.: Belknap Press of Harvard University Press, 1979.

Downing, A.J. — *The Architecture of Country Houses.* New York: Dover Publications, Inc., 1969.

Fitchen, John — *The New World Dutch Barn.* Syracuse, N.Y.: Syracuse University Press, 1968.

Futagawa, Yukio — *Wooden Houses.* New York: Harry N. Abrams, Inc., 1979.

Traditional Japanese Houses. New York: Rizzoli International Publications, Inc., 1983.

Grosslight, Jane — *Light.* Englewood Cliffs, N.J.: Prentice-Hall, Inc., 1984.

Hansen, Hans Jurgen, ed. — *Architecture in Wood.* London: Faber and Faber, 1971.

Harris, Richard — *Discovering Timber Frame Buildings.* London: Shire Publications Ltd., 1978.

Hewett, Cecil A. — *English Historic Carpentry.* London and Chichester: Phillimore and Co., Ltd., 1980.

Isham, Norman M. and Albert F. Brown — *Early Connecticut Houses.* New York: Dover Publications, Inc., 1965

Kelly, J. Frederick — *Early Domestic Architecture of Connecticut.* New York: Dover Publications, Inc., 1952.

Kimball, Fiske — *Domestic Architecture of the American Colonies and of the Early Republic.* New York: Dover Publications, 1966.

Langdon, Philip — *American Houses.* New York: Stewart, Tabori & Chang, Inc., 1987.

Langdon, William Chauncy — *Everyday Things in American Life, 1607-1776.* New York: Charles Scribner's Sons, 1943.

Makinson, Randell L.   *Greene and Greene, Architecture as a Fine Art.* Salt Lake City, Utah: Peregrine Smith, Inc., 1977.

Mazria, Edward   *The Passive Solar Energy Book.* Emmaus, Pa.: Rodale Press, 1979.

Mullin, Ray C.   *Electrical Wiring Residential.* New York: Van Nostrand Reinhold Co., 1981.

Mullins, Lisa C., series ed.   *Architectural Treasures of Early America.* 10 vols. Harrisburg, Pa.: Historical Times Inc., 1987.

Mumford, Lewis   *Roots of Contemporary American Architecture.* New York: Dover Publications, Inc., 1972.

Packard, Robert T., A.I.A., ed.   *Architectural Graphic Standards.* New York: John Wiley and Sons, 1981.

Poor, Alfred Easton   *Colonial Architecture of Cape Cod, Nantucket and Martha's Vineyard.* New York: Dover Publications, Inc., 1932.

Price, Lorna   *The Plan of St. Gall in Brief.* Berkeley and Los Angeles, Calif.: University of California Press, 1982.

Rempel, John I.   *Building With Wood.* Toronto: University of Toronto Press, 1967.

Rybczynski, Witold   *Home: A Short History of an Idea.* New York and Canada: Viking Penguin Inc., 1986.

Schwolsky, Rick and James I. Williams   *The Builder's Guide to Solar Construction.* New York: McGraw-Hill, Inc., 1982.

Sobon, Jack and Roger Schroeder   *Timber Frame Construction.* Pownal, Vt.: Garden Way Publishing, 1984.

Stickley, Gustav   *Craftsman Homes.* New York: Dover Publications, Inc., 1979.

Tarule, Rob   "The Landscapes of England and New England in the Early Seventeeth Century." Illustrated lecture delivered at First Annual Conference of Timber Framers Guild of North America, Hancock, Mass., 1985.

West, Trudy   *The Timber Frame House in England.* New York: Architectural Book Publishing Co., 1971.

Williams, Lionel Henry and Ottalie K. Williams   *Old American Houses, 1700-1850.* New York: Crown Publishers, Inc., 1962.

   Wood Handbook: Wood as an Engineering Material. Washington, D. C.: Superintendent of Documents, U.S. Government Printing Office, 1974.

Wood, Margaret   *The English Mediaeval House.* New York: Harper and Row, 1965.

Woodforde, John   *The Truth about Cottages.* London: The Country Book Club, 1970.

Wright, Frank Lloyd   *The Natural House.* New York: The Horizon Press, 1954.

Yoshida, Tetsuro   *The Japanese House and Garden.* New York: Fredrick A. Praeger, 1954.

Index

Managing Editor	Deborah Cannarella
Editor	Laura Tringali
Design Director	Roger Barnes
Art Director	Ben Kann
Layout Artist	Marianne Markey
Illustration Assistant	Deb Rives-Skiles
Copy/Production Editors	Victoria Monks, Ruth Dobsevage
Director of Manufacturing	Kathleen Davis
Production Manager	Peggy Dutton
Pre-Press Manager	Austin E. Starbird
Production Coordinator	Ellen Olmstead
System Operators	Dinah George, Nancy-Lou Knapp
Production Assistants	Lisa Carlson, Mark Coleman, Deborah Cooper
Pasteup	Marty Higham, Cynthia Lee Nyitray
Indexer	Harriet Hodges

Typeface	ITC Cheltenham Book, 9 point
Paper	Warrenflo, 70 lb., neutral pH
Printer and Binder	Arcata Graphics/Kingsport, Kingsport, TN